W9-BYB-819

M-GOV-
MR927

RETURN MIGRATION:
Journey of Hope or Despair?

Edited by

Bimal Ghosh

United Nations

IOM • OIM

b2 5484/75

IOM is committed to the principle that humane and orderly migration benefits migrants and society. As an intergovernmental body, IOM acts with its partners in the international community to: assist in meeting the operational challenges of migration; advance understanding of migration issues; encourage social and economic development through migration; and work towards effective respect of the human dignity and well-being of migrants.

International Organization for Migration
17 route des Morillons
1211 Geneva 19
Switzerland
Tel: +41.22.717 91 11
Fax: +41.22.798 61 50
E-mail: hq@iom.int
Internet: http://www.iom.int

The study is prepared with the support of the International Organization for Migration and the financial assistance of the Ministry of Foreign Affairs of the Netherlands Government. The opinions expressed herein are those of the authors and do not necessarily reflect the views of IOM or the United Nations.

All rights reserved. No part of this publication may be reproduced, stored in a retrieval system, or transmitted in any form or by any means, electronic, mechanical, photocopying, recording, or otherwise, without the prior written permission of the publishers.

Copublished by the International Organization for Migration and the United Nations.
© International Organization for Migration and the United Nations, 2000

ISBN 92-9068-096-2 (International Organization for Migration)

United Nations Publication
Sales Number: E.00.III.S.1

UN2

DPI/SALES/2000/19

TABLE OF CONTENTS

ACKNOWLEDGEMENTS

The editor of this volume and director of the project New International Regime for Orderly Movements of People (NIROMP) is deeply grateful to the Netherlands Government for its financial contribution which made it possible to bring out the publication. The Netherlands Government also provided financial support to organize, within the NIROMP framework, an interregional meeting on return and readmission (Geneva, December 1998). As indicated in the Introduction, the documents prepared for the meeting and the discussion thereon served as a main basis for the book.

Acknowledgements are also due to the United Nations Population Fund (UNFPA) and the Swedish Government for their generous contributions to the NIROMP project as well as to the International Organization for Migration (IOM) which served as the executing agency of the project. Several IOM officials, notably Peter Schatzer and Reinhard Lohrmann, took an active interest in the whole endeavour and provided valuable assistance at different stages.

A special word of thanks to all the contributors for complying with the requests of the editor and showing patience and understanding during the whole process.

Sincere thanks are also due Sarita Seghal and Niusca Magalhães who so efficiently and cheerfully carried the main burden of organizing the 1998 meeting and helped the editor in many different ways.

NOTES ON CONTRIBUTORS

BIMAL GHOSH has a long record of activities running concurrently between international organizations and academia. A former senior director in the United Nations system, he is the director of the global project on migration management: New International Regime for Orderly Movements of People (NIROMP) and Emeritus Professor at the Colombian School of Public Administration. Ghosh has led various UN (inter-agency) and UNDP/World Bank missions on migration, refugees and development related issues in different regions, and has been writing and lecturing extensively on these and other international subjects. Recent publications include: *Managing Migration: Time for a New International Regime?* (editor and co-author, Oxford University Press, 2000), *Huddled Masses and Uncertain Shores: Insights into Irregular Migration* (Kluwer Law International, 1998); and *Gains from Global Linkages: Trade in Services and Movements of Persons* (Macmillan, 1997).

RUSSELL KING is Professor of Geography and Dean of the School of European Studies at the University of Sussex, where he also co-directs the Sussex Centre for Migration Research. Before moving to Sussex in 1993 he was Lecturer in Geography at the University of Leicester and Professor of Geography at Trinity College, Dublin. He has also taught at the University of Malta, Ben Gurion University of the Negev and the University of Trieste. He is the author or editor of several books on various aspects of migration and has carried out empirical research on return migration in Malta, southern Italy and the west of Ireland.

KHALID KOSER is Lecturer in Human Geography and a member of the Migration Research Unit at University College, London. He has been writing on issues related to return and reintegration of refugees, asylum seekers and other categories of migrants. His current research focuses on the mobilization and participation of transnational exile communities in post-conflict reconstruction, comparing the cases of Bosnia and Eritrea. Recent publications include: *The End of the Refugee Cycle?* (Berghahn, 1999, co-edited with Richard Black) and *The New Migration in Europe* (Macmillan, 1998, co-edited with Helma Lutz).

FRANK LACZKO is Head of the Research Unit at the International Organization for Migration, Geneva. Previously, he was Head of Research at the IOM Technical Cooperation Centre for Europe and Central Asia in Vienna. He has recently edited a book on *Migrant Trafficking and Human Smuggling in Europe: A Review of the Evidence*, (IOM, October 2000) and contributed to the chapter on "Migration in Central and Eastern Europe and the Commonwealth of Independent States", in the IOM *World Migration Report 2000*.

GREGOR NOLL teaches international law at the Faculty of Law, University of Lund, Sweden. He has been lecturing extensively on refugee and migration issues focusing on flight, asylum and return, and has written articles on burden-sharing, gender and persecution , the return of rejected asylum seekers as well as the democratic legitimacy of refugee law. He is currently working on the legality of the asylum *acquis* in the European Union, which will lead to a book foreseen to be published by Kluwer Law International this year (2000).

LIST OF FIGURES

LIST OF TABLES

Introduction

Return Migration:
Journey of Hope or Despair?

Bimal Ghosh

Although an integral part of the migration process, return move-ment, including its social and economic implications, has so far re-mained inadequately unravelled in the migration debate. One of the most neglected areas of migration research, it also has failed to re-ceive adequate and systematic attention from policy-makers. Even when return has been a specific subject of public policy considera-tion, the tendency has generally been to look at the returnees on a non-differentiated or aggregate basis, without giving much attention to selectivity in terms of their personal characteristics, duration of stay in the receiving country, and the motivations underlying differ-ent types of return.[1] Realistic policy formulation has thus been constrained.

This is not to suggest that return movements have been com-pletely ignored in the migration literature. Occasionally, analysts have indeed given some particular attention to return as they did, for example, in the 1970s – following the dismantling of Western Europe's "guest workers programme", and in the context of the re-turn of migrant workers from the Gulf States. But these analyses have generally been handicapped by the absence of adequate longitudinal

---

[1] See, for example, Odded Stark, "On the Microeconomics of Return Migration", Department of Economics ,University of Oslo, Norway, January 1996 (mimeo). The paper suggests some interesting new models with implications for research and policy formulation related to return.

data; and most studies have in fact tended to rely heavily on isolated empirical or anecdotal evidence, often lacking a robust theoretical base or a coherent policy-oriented framework.

The situation is however changing. As mobility of people, especially trade- and investment-related, short-term movements, gather pace alongside increasing economic globalizaton, issues related to return movements are bound to receive wider attention. Meanwhile, a sharp rise in the numbers of irregular migrants and rejected asylum seekers, and sudden waves of temporary refugees resulting from a series of ethno-political crises such as those in the former Yugoslavia have already pushed return migration up on the political agenda, notably in the receiving states of Western Europe.

Against this background, it was considered important to include return as a specific issue within the scope of a new global project – entitled New International Regime for Orderly Movements of People (NIROMP) – which was launched in 1997, aiming at making movements of people more orderly and predictable and thus more easily manageable, on the basis of a set of internationally harmonized principles.[2] Promotion of conditions for orderly return, with due regard to the interests and concerns of all the parties involved, is certainly an integral part, and an essential condition of better management of all migratory movements – which is precisely the objective of the NIROMP project.

There was a further important consideration. If return has shot up on the political agenda, it has also proved to be a politically sensitive and, in many ways, highly controversial issue. The current debate is generally marked by sharp differences between sending and receiving states, with transit states and the migrants themselves frequently playing a part in the controversy. The main reason for this is that return is perceived to be an area where their respective interests diverge and often clash. This is particularly so in the case of irregular migrants, rejected asylum seekers, and temporary refugees.

For these groups, for example, the protection of basic rights both in the pre- and post return periods often becomes a bone of contention among the parties involved. The returning states tend to consider such protection as an impediment to a speedy return of

---

[2] For additional information concerning NIROMP, see Bimal Ghosh (Ed.) *Managing Migration: Time for a New International Regime?* Oxford University Press, Oxford, England, August, 2000; also "Background, Objectives and Methodology" and the "Meeting Report", Informal Meeting on NIROMP, 26-27 September 1997, IOM, Geneva.

unauthorized persons or temporary refugees from their territory. The migrants fight hard to preserve their human rights and their dignity as well as their economic entitlements such as earned wages. The states of origin are likely to resent gross mistreatment of their nationals in a foreign country, and at the same time may not be too anxious to accept large inflows of returnees when the economy is facing recession and unemployment or is otherwise under strain. They may be unwilling or unable to guarantee safe conditions to returning refugees and rejected asylum seekers or may wish to avoid loss of foreign exchange flows in the form of migrants' remittances. The transit states, for their part, may be reluctant to see third country nationals returned to their territory, with the costs of return shifted to them; more so when they lack financial and other resources needed for the operation. Seen in this light, return tends to become a source of tension and conflict between and among the parties concerned.

However, in the context of the NIROMP project it was felt that return need not necessarily be seen by the parties involved from an adversarial perspective. It may well be turned into a common ground where the interests of the parties concerned largely converge. But such commonalty of interests is achievable only on the basis of joint recognition of a set of inter-related principles.

First, return must be regarded as an important interlocking element of an open policy of orderly migration; it is not just an isolated event or the final part of a closed system, buttressed by a "fortress" approach to migration. Second, control over immigration, including the right to repatriate irregular immigrants, is both a prerogative of a sovereign state and an essential requirement for the smooth functioning of an open system of migration. Third, states must abide by the right to return of their citizens and other persons who are in an analogous situation. Fourth, return should in all cases, including those involving irregular migrants, take place in conditions of freedom and dignity, with full protection of basic human rights of migrants. Finally, for any type of *forced* migration return is sustainable only when the conditions or circumstances – whether political, economic or environmental – which led to the flight in the first instance are changed, and new opportunities opened up for returnees to have a fresh start in life.

But are these principles acceptable to all the parties concerned? Could they provide the essential elements of an agreed framework for return?

To explore the possibility of finding a multilaterally harmonized approach to return along the lines indicated above, an inter-regional meeting was held in Geneva on 7-8 December 1998.[3] Organized within the framework of the NIROMP project, executed by IOM, the meeting brought together representatives of origin, receiving and transit countries, inter-governmental organizations as well as NGOs. The discussion at the meeting was both stimulating and constructive. It led to a consensus on a set of general principles, and thus constituted a significant initial step towards an agreed framework for return as part of an open and forward-looking migration system. The meeting firmly believed that securing close and genuine cooperation between origin, receiving and transit states was an essential element in the success of return programmes. And the fact that the three groups of states were often located in different regions lent special importance to the establishment of a common multilateral framework for successful return.

At the same time, the meeting recognized that, consistent with the basic concept and approach of NIROMP itself, formulation of multilateral principles should not be seen as a rigid, supra-national construct to be imposed on nation states.[4] Rather, these were to constitute a common frame of reference and serve as useful guidelines to stimulate and facilitate regional, subregional and bilateral negotiations and arrangements, while ensuring adequate coherence in all such actions. Thus, not surprisingly, the participants also recommended a wide dissemination of the information contained in the documents prepared for the December 1998 meeting and its conclusions in order to help and encourage follow up action, including operational programmes, in different regions.[5]

The present volume is largely a response to this request. Aside from drawing heavily on the documents presented to the meeting

---

[3] Managing Migration: New International Regime for Orderly Movements of People. Inter-regional Meeting on Return and Readmission of Migrants, 7-8 December 1998, IOM headquarters, Geneva.

[4] See, in this connection, Bimal Ghosh, "New international regime for orderly movements of people: How will it look like?" in *Managing Migration: Time for a New International Regime?* op.cit. chapter 9.

[5] Largely as a follow up to the Geneva meeting, the Senegalese Government was planning, with the active involvement of the International Organization for Migration (IOM), an inter-regional meeting in Dakar in the summer of 2000. The meeting, which at the time of writing was still in a preparatory stage, was expected to cover countries in west and north Africa and the corresponding receiving countries in west Europe as well as the USA.

and its conclusions, it includes some additional contributions and further reflections on the various issues involved. These additions, it is hoped, will enhance the intrinsic value of the book and enhance its practical relevance.

The book is divided into six chapters. As a whole, it covers all major categories of returnees, although the focus varies from one chapter to another. The main emphasis, however, is on the problematic return of irregular migrants, rejected asylum-seekers and refugees, including in particular temporary refugees. The first chapter provides an historical retrospect of voluntary return migration, with a focus on two major return movements and posits a set of generalizations based on empirical evidence; the second gives an analytical overview of current policy frameworks and operational programmes related to return. The third chapter examines issues concerning protection of dignity and human rights of different categories of irregular migrants as returnees, and underscores the argument that safeguarding rights can help voluntary return. The fourth chapter has a specific regional focus. It examines some of the major policy issues and operational challenges facing countries in Central and Eastern Europe as they deal with the return of irregular migrants. The analysis assumes special relevance as the European Union presses ahead with its eastward enlargement in the coming years.

Widening the background of the discussion to cover all major categories of returnees, the fifth chapter of the book shows how return can be made more attractive and sustainable by forging links between return, reintegration and the development of the country of origin. It also addresses a number of key issues, and possible lines of action, related to the sustainable return of refugees. The book ends (chapter 6) with a set of conclusions, incorporating, with necessary adaptation, those which emerged from the December 1998 NIROMP meeting on return and readmission. The focus once more is on irregular migrants, rejected asylum-seekers and refugees in a wide sense of the term.

The contributors, including the editor, sincerely hope that the book will be of interest to policy makers, academics, professionals and the general public alike. They will consider their endeavour amply rewarded if it can contribute to the development of a consensual approach to return as part of a fair, predictable and open migration system.

Chapter 1

Generalizations from the History of Return Migration

Russell King[1]

INTRODUCTION

Return migration is the great unwritten chapter in the history of migration. The historiography of migration studies has nearly always tended to imply that migration was a one-way process, with no return. Studies have focused on departure, the migration journey, arrival, settlement and "integration"; rarely on return. Often one finds, perhaps hidden in a footnote, the lament that "little is known of those who returned".

A brief review of some major recent texts on migration reveals the truth about this generalization. Robin Cohen's monumental *Cambridge Survey of World Migration* (1995) contains, in its half a million words and 95 chapters, no specific entry on return migration. Aaron Segal's *Atlas of International Migration* (1993) contrives to completely ignore return movements. And other important recent texts (Castles and Miller, 1998; Gorter et al., 1998; Hammar et al., 1997; Lucassen and Lucassen, 1997) mention return migration, if at all, only in passing. There remains, to this day, just one book which attempts a global overview of the theme of return migration (King, 1986).

[1] I gratefully acknowledge the research assistance of Louise Madden in locating some of the literature referred to in this chapter.

On the other hand, a scattered empirical literature on return migration has been steadily accumulating: case studies of countries, regions and villages, and covering a range of historical periods. Most of this literature has been produced over the last thirty years. It is not the intention of this chapter to make a complete review of this literature; several bibliographic syntheses exist, although none very recent (Böhning, 1986; Bovenkerk, 1974; Gaillard, 1993; Gmelch and Rhoades, 1979; King and Strachan, 1983; King et al., 1983; Tassello, 1983). Instead, our coverage in this chapter will be selective and thematic: we will be mainly concerned with *international* return migration and with *voluntary* return, not with refugee movements or forced repatriation, nor with intra-national return migration.

There are three potential ways of organizing a survey of return migration: historically, geographically, or in terms of a series of conceptual or thematic frameworks. A fully-developed chronological or regional account would lead to an overblown, repetitive narrative. Hence, what this chapter tries to do is to draw generalizations on the basis of historical evidence from different migration settings in different parts of the world. To avoid too abstract generalizations, two contrasting case studies will be included: return from the United States in the nineteenth and early twentieth centuries, and return to the Caribbean during the post-war period.

DEFINING AND MEASURING
RETURN MIGRATION

Return migration may be defined as the process whereby people return to their country or place of origin after a significant period in another country or region. The term *repatriation* may be used when the return is involuntary and forced on the migrant by political authority or by some natural or personal disaster. Clearly return migration must be related to the emigration which preceded it; furthermore, return may be the prelude to further episodes of spatial mobility. Return may be embedded in a cyclical process of repeat migrations, for which a variety of terms is used such as circular migration, shuttle migration, commuter migration and so on. Seasonal labour migration is an obvious example of this. Already, the variety of words used to describe different (and the same) types of migration is becoming clear. Scanning the literature, return migration has also been referred to by terms such as counterstream migration,

8

reflex migration, retro-migration, back-migration, U-turn migration and many more.[2]

To the extent that return migration statistics exist, they are usually published as national aggregate flows with no indication of precise destination. Hence the proportion of returning emigrants who go back to their specific community of origin (a village or an urban district, for example), as opposed to those who resettle elsewhere within their country, is unknown. In fact the statistical basis for studying return migration is almost invariably weak, a situation which can be seen as both a cause and a consequence of the fact that return migration has been a neglected aspect of population studies (King, 1978). Many countries fail even to record returning migrants, let alone monitor their characteristics. Confusion also exists as to what constitutes a returning migrant. During the 1960s and 1970s the statistical bureau in Greece – a country much affected by emigration and return at that time – defined a returning migrant as one who had lived abroad for at least one year and who was intending to stay in Greece for one year or more. Other countries adopted different criteria, making inter-country comparison almost impossible. Even where the same flow was being measured, the data seldom matched – as with the Italian return flow from West Germany during the 1960s, three times larger, according to the German statistics on exits, than the entry data for Italy.

TYPOLOGIES OF RETURN

A first typology concerns the levels of development of the countries linked by migration and return. Three situations may be envisaged:

- the return (or repatriation) of migrants from less-developed countries, often colonies or ex-colonies, to highly-developed countries, often colonial metropoles; examples are the return of the British

---

[2] Some of these terms are highly ambiguous. Counterstream migration, for instance, has been used to describe returning migrants, a flow of migrants (not returnees) moving in the opposite direction to a dominant flow, or a combination of both. Even more confusing is the term "remigration" which Unger (1981), for instance, uses to denote return migration and Philpott (1977) uses in the sense of re-emigration (the subsequent emigration of a returnee) – two very different migration processes! For further comments on definitions see Bovenkerk (1974: 4-6); King et al. (1983: 5-8).

from India and East Africa, the French from Algeria, or Portuguese from Angola and Mozambique;

- the return migration of labour migrants from the developed industrial countries to their less-developed home countries; examples include Caribbean migrants returning from Britain and North America, Turks returning from West Germany or Portuguese from France;

- return movements between countries of broadly equal economic status, such as the British returning from Australia, Canadians from the United States, and interchanges and returns amongst West European countries such as Germany and the Netherlands.

These three types by no means exhaust the cases of return migration as defined by the economic character of the countries, and migrants, involved. The oil-rich economies, particularly those of the Gulf, have played a key role in the evolution of the global economy in recent decades, and this development has been strongly linked to the massive recruitment of migrant labour – low-skilled manual workers – from developing countries such as India, Pakistan, Sri Lanka and the Philippines, and high-skilled contract personnel from countries like the United Kingdom and the United States. Permanent settlement of migrants has been discouraged, and returns have been frequent, swollen at times of crisis such as the Gulf War (Gunatilleke, 1991). "Brain drain" and "brain return" are migrant flows which have often developed along colonial lines and, more recently, across the former Iron Curtain. Other return flows, prompted by religious, political or ideological reasons, such as the "return" of the Jews to Israel or the *Aussiedler* (ethnic Germans) to Germany, may be between countries at varying levels of development, and some of these moves may be a kind of "ancestral" return rather than the return of people who had themselves emigrated (King et al., 1983: 8-12).

A second simple typology is based on the length of time spent back in the home country. There is a symbiotic relationship between these return periods and the types of migration that lead up to, or are coinvolved with, the return moves. Four types can be recognized in this typology:

- *Occasional returns* are short-term, perhaps periodic (e.g. every month), and consist of visits to see relatives, to stay for a holiday, or to participate in a family event such as a marriage or funeral. Usually the migrant returns for a brief period of relaxation, or perhaps to attend to some business such as the purchase of property.

- *Seasonal returns* are dictated by the nature of the work activities followed, for instance the integration of construction or hotel work abroad with agricultural labour in the home country.
- *Temporary returns* take place when the migrant returns, remains in the home country for a significant period, perhaps finding a job there, but retains the intention to re-emigrate abroad.
- *Permanent returnees* are those who resettle in their home countries for good.

Whilst the above temporal types of return can be based on observed behaviours, a distinction can also be drawn between intended behaviour and the eventual migration outcome. This leads to a third typology, which has been proposed by Bovenkerk (1974: 10-18) and commented on and elaborated by Gmelch (1980: 137-138) and King et al. (1983: 18-21). Under this typology, four types can again be recognized:

- Migrants who emigrate with the *intention of returning and who do in fact return*. "Target migrants" who move abroad with a specific aim in mind – to accumulate a certain sum of money or to obtain an educational qualification – are part of this group; their plans are fixed and their return predetermined by the attainment of their migration target. Others may emigrate with return in mind but be rather vague about when it might take place. Often return is postponed and occurs later than originally intended.
- *Intended temporary migration without return*: the case when the act of return is continuously postponed until it never happens. This outcome occurs amongst students who go abroad to study, and who stay on after finishing their courses – the typical brain-drain phenomenon – or amongst labour migrants who decide to stay and settle in the destination country rather than return.
- *Intended permanent migration followed by return* is produced either by external factors forcing migrants to return, or by a change of heart on the part of the migrant due to homesickness or some other personal factor. Alternatively, return takes place because of an improvement in the economic, social or political conditions in the home country, which has the effect of changing migrants' outlook and pulling them back.
- Finally there is *intended permanent migration without return*.

Once again, these types provide a springboard for discussion of more subtle issues and outcomes. According to Gmelch (1980: 138), most migrants "do not have definitive plans ... they go on a trial basis, letting their decision ... be guided by the opportunities they find in the new society". The interactions between intention, observed migration behaviour, and feelings about identity lead on to a complex debate about the *myth of return* (Anwar, 1979) and about what other authors have termed the *return illusion* or the *ideology of return* (Brettell, 1979; Rubenstein, 1979). In brief, the myth of return expresses a contrasting set of beliefs and actions whereby, no matter how settled, migrants talk and behave as if one day they will return. However, this orientation to an eventual return is at variance with the objective realities of migrants' lives in the destination country, where factors such as regular and well-paid work, family settlement and children's education make it increasingly unlikely that they will ever return. At the same time, the myth of return often functions as a defence mechanism against migrants' unwillingness or inability to assimilate to the host society. Much has been written on the myth of return amongst Asian migrant communities in Britain where "the myth of return is used to legitimize continued adherence to the values of their homeland" in the face of unease about British cultural characteristics and racism (Ballard and Ballard, 1977: 40).

The fourth and final typology presented here is that developed by Cerase (1970; 1974) based on his research on return migration from the United States to Italy. This typology can claim to be a more integrated conceptualization of return as it is built around the historical evolution of the migration process and reflects the dialectical relationship between return, on the one hand, and the acculturation of Italian migrants to American society on the other. Once again, this is a model consisting of four types:

- The *return of failure* takes place when migrants fail to adapt to the host society and return quickly to their homeland. As the process of integration into American society never really started, the returnees are reabsorbed easily into their home society.
- For migrants who remain longer in the country of destination, perhaps as target migrants, the return, once it takes place, perhaps after a few years, is a *return of conservatism*. Throughout the stay abroad, acculturation has been fairly minimal: the orientation has always been to the country of origin, with remittances and savings

channelled to the home community. Post-return behaviour reinforces the values and social system of the society of origin.

- Migrants who remain in the destination beyond the "target return" see themselves increasingly with reference to the host country's system of stratification and cultural values. At a later stage, however, realizing that their acculturation can never be complete, a return takes place – a *return of innovation* – by which migrants take new ideas, values and ambitions back to their home countries.
- A fourth returning point is reached by migrants at the end of their working lives – the *return of retirement*.

From the point of view of change and development in the country of origin, the crucial type is the return of innovation. Unfortunately this type of return does not seem to be very common, on the basis of historical evidence (Böhning, 1975). The migrants with the most drive and ambition, who succeed in the destination country, are those who are least likely to return. But this is a generalization which has many exceptions. In some cases "failures" dare not return, fearful of the shame in not having succeeded. And for some long-distance migrations, particularly in the past, only the successful could afford to go back – this is mentioned for Irish migrants in the USA (Bovenkerk, 1973) and early Jamaican migration to Britain (Davison, 1968).

WHY DO MIGRANTS RETURN?

Figure 1.1 provides a diagrammatic summary of this and the next two sections of the chapter. Here we look at reasons for return; the next section examines reintegration problems and the influence of return migration on social change; and the one after that evaluates the contribution of return migration to the development of the areas of origin. The diagram portrays return migration as a *process* initiated by various *causal factors* and leading to a variety of *effects*. The ensuing discussion focuses mainly on the history of return migration from rich to poor countries.

FIGURE 1.1

CAUSES AND EFFECTS OF RETURN MIGRATION

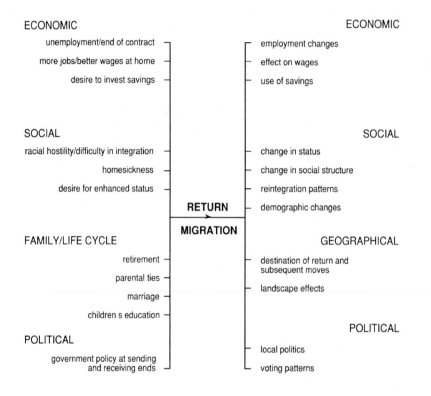

Reasons for return vary from macro-scale economic or political events to individual migrant perspectives. In reality, the causes of return migration are many and varied, and a migrant may decide to return home for a complex of reasons rather than just one. Figure 1.1 attempts to set out the main influences, based on a survey of the literature. As indicated earlier, this literature is now too extensive to be cited in full, but there are useful attempts to synthesize the material on motives for return by Bovenkerk (1974: 20-25), Gmelch (1980: 138-141), King et al. (1983: 25-31) and Rogers (1984: 288-292).

Economic stimuli may involve "pull" factors from the area of origin such as higher wages and economic development, as well as "push" factors such as redundancy or an economic downturn in the country to which migrants had emigrated. Alternatively "target migrants" may be returning to realize a specific objective, such as investment of their savings in land or a business.

Social motives for return also involve push and pull mechanisms. Push factors include racism and other difficulties of integration. These are naturally accompanied by a corresponding pull factor of nostalgia. A more positive social motive for returning is the desire to enjoy an improved status upon return, perhaps through business ventures, donations to community projects, or simply the building of a luxurious new house.

Next come causal factors of a life-cycle or family nature, most of which involve links to the home area pulling the migrant back by kinship and social ties. Four life-stage examples may be given: single emigrants may return to find a spouse; migrants who emigrated with young children or who had children whilst abroad may return for their offspring to be educated in the "home" country and its language; adult migrants might feel obliged to return to look after elderly or sick parents; and migrants may return when they reach retirement.

Finally there are political causes. These range from forced expulsion to incentives for voluntary return. Other "policies" may be less direct, such as restrictions or subsequent curtailment of migrants' rights to change jobs, bring in families, or enjoy other citizenship benefits. All these measures operate from the immigration country. Some emigration countries have promulgated policies to encourage and facilitate return such as tax benefits, social assistance and housing grants.

If we leave aside, for the time being, forced repatriation and the repeat returns which are part of cyclical migration, the main groups of reasons for return are economic, social and family-related. A further basic division exists between push and pull factors. What is the relative importance of these sets of motives for return?

Two preliminary generalizations can be made on the basis of historical evidence: that pull factors reflecting the positive attractions of the home societies have more influence in return migration decisions than push factors from the host countries; and that non-economic factors generally weigh more heavily in the return decision than do economic factors, certainly in comparison to their role in the original decision to emigrate, which was often strongly determined by economic motives.

Nevertheless, several studies point to unfavourable economic conditions in the immigration country as the key to episodes of mass return – flouting both of the above generalizations. A recession leads to lay-offs in certain industries and employment sectors, and it is often the migrant workers who are made redundant because of their marginal, unprotected status in the labour market. Thus Saloutos (1956) writes of the streams of Greek migrants returning from the USA during the depression years of the 1890s, and Levi (1948: 120-130) describes the return of the *americani*, Italian emigrants to the United States, as a result of the Wall Street crash of 1929. Moving to post-war intra-European labour migration, one of the most thorough studies of cyclically-determined return is Kayser's (1972) analysis of the West German recession of 1967. Kayser documented very considerable return flows to southern European countries such as Italy, Greece and Yugoslavia, but also substantial re-emigration when the German economy recovered strongly in the late 1960s. A few years later, other studies described the large-scale return migrations of the mid-1970s, occasioned by the first oil crisis and the concomitant economic recession. Böhning (1979) estimated that 1.5 million migrant workers returned home during those years. He pointed out how the oil crisis starkly revealed the inequities of the European migration system: by laying off vulnerable migrant workers the rich and powerful countries shifted the burden of unemployment onto the poorer and weaker economies of the Mediterranean Basin (Böhning, 1979: 404).

Whilst at the aggregate level it can be demonstrated that a link exists between economic crisis in the host country and return migration, most studies which look at individual-scale aspects of the return decision find that economic arguments are contextual rather than paramount. Part of this context is the existence of improved economic conditions in the country of origin – a "pull factor" which helps to make a positive decision to return. In a detailed study of return migration from the United States to Puerto Rico, Hernández Alvarez (1967) showed how the large-scale returns of the 1960s were stimulated by increased job opportunities in the island. Return migration to southern Europe during the second half of the 1970s was much higher to those countries like Italy and Greece, whose economies were rapidly developing, than it was to Turkey, whose economy remained in a more backward state. The Irish case provides further corroborative evidence. After more than a century of continuous emigration, returns dominated during the 1970s when the Irish economy boomed as a result of EEC accession and inward investment. Net emigration resumed throughout the 1980s, but then new return flows, complemented by inflows of highly-skilled immigrants, occurred during the 1990s in response to the rapid economic growth of the "Celtic Tiger" (Barrett and Trace, 1998).

When migrants are asked to indicate their reasons for return in questionnaire and interview surveys, most studies report the predominance of non-economic factors. The most frequently mentioned motives are family ties and the desire to rejoin kin and old friends.[3] Although there are occasionally some important push influences, such as racial harassment or even the difficulty of adapting to a different (usually colder) climate, in general the positive attractions of the home society are dominant in the migration decision. This proposition has been tested by Toren (1976) in one of the more methodologically sophisticated pieces of research on returning migrants. Instead of asking returnees (in this case from the United States to Israel) to articulate the reasons for their return, Toren presented them with an array of 18 reasons, and asked respondents to score the importance of each reason on a five-point scale. The 18 reasons were divided into three groups – economic/occupational, social/patriotic and personal/familial – each containing three push factors, representing negative forces associated with the host country, and three pull factors, representing pull forces operating from the home country. Social/patriotic and personal/familial motives dominated over economic/occupational factors, and pull factors were much more important than push factors. That feelings of patriotism should rank high in the case of returning Israelis is not altogether surprising given the relatively recent birth of the state of Israel, its political situation and the nature of Zionist ideology. But nationalistic sentiments have also been found to be paramount in other studies such as those on brain drain and return in developing countries (Glaser, 1978) and in even those on return migration to advanced countries, such as the return of British migrants from Australia and Canada which also appears to be characterized by homesickness and the desire to rejoin the national culture (Appleyard, 1962; Richmond, 1968).

In a society where kinship obligations are strong, elderly or ailing parents may impose care responsibilities which are impossible to ignore. Such semi-forced returns generally take place to the community of origin. They interrupt the migrants' plans for a longer stay abroad

---

[3] For a selection of case studies based on extensive historical evidence or social surveys see Caroli (1970), King (1980), King et al. (1986), Paine 1974), Unger (1981).

and often involve considerable economic hardship for all concerned, owing to the difficulty of finding remunerative employment in the place of origin, which may be a remote village. Gmelch (1980: 139) believes that the importance of family ties in return migration is reflected in the large numbers of migrants who return to their native communities instead of returning to a town or region where economic opportunities would be better.

One of the largest surveys of return motives was carried out in 1969 by the Italian government statistics bureau ISTAT. The results of this massive questionnaire survey (80,000 respondents) are summarized by Livi-Bacci (1972: 109-113), and demonstrate once again the greater importance of factors not connected with employment. For the whole sample, 27.4 per cent gave "expiry of contract" as their main motive for return, compared to 14.9 per cent who had a job in Italy, 32.6 per cent who returned for family reasons, 21.8 per cent who returned for personal reasons such as illness or homesickness, leaving 3.3 per cent who returned for "other" motives.

It must be said, however, that the value of such large and impersonal questionnaire surveys in teasing out the real reasons for migrants' return is somewhat limited. Migrants' motives are undoubtedly more complex than can be expressed by declaring one main reason in a survey. Some returnees may not want to divulge the real reasons, or they may not be able to articulate them in the way demanded by the investigator. The return may have been an impulse not easily explained or rationalized, whilst for returns which took place several years earlier, the memory might have played tricks. The implication of many of these points is that a *qualitative* approach, which sacrifices statistical coverage for depth of analysis, may be more appropriate to uncover the complex and multi-layered nature of return migration processes and decisions. Some examples of qualitative methodologies will be given in the case studies made in the second half of the chapter.

REINTEGRATION AND SOCIAL CHANGE

Returning to Figure 1.1 and looking this time at the "effects" side of the diagram, what are the social effects of return? Let us first analyse these with reference to the standard model of return migration whereby migrants originating from a rural, less-developed milieu return home after a period in a more advanced, urbanized and industrialized setting. Other chapters in this volume will concentrate more on the reintegration of refugees and displaced persons.

Following Cerase (1974) and del Campo and Garmendia (1974), the issue of return and reintegration can be formulated as a dual hypothesis. The first hypothesis states that the more urban and industrial the value structure of the returning migrant, the greater will be the conflict in readaptation, and the greater will be the probability of the returnee inducing social change. The alternative hypothesis states the converse: the more traditional and rural the value orientation of the migrant, the greater will be the probability of an easy readaptation *sui generis* and the less the likelihood of innovation or social change.

The broad pattern of evidence seems to support this dual hypothesis. For instance, students of migrant labour in Africa south of the Sahara frequently remark on how easily migrants returning from the city or the mines fit back into village and tribal life. Initially there may be a brief spell of idleness and display of new clothes and other acquisitions, but soon the returnees settle down and revert to their normal routine almost as if nothing had happened (Bovenkerk, 1974: 27). The modernizing role of urban-rural returnees in developing countries in Africa and elsewhere should not, however, be overlooked. Urban-rural returnee links act as effective channels for cultural diffusion, and economic improvements are sustained by a regular flow of remittances from the cities and from abroad (Adepoju, 1974; 1981).

From other studies, chiefly of international return migration, there is considerable evidence of reintegration difficulties for returnees. These difficulties can be examined under two perspectives: etic and emic (Gmelch, 1980: 142). The first examines the *objective* criteria of reintegration: the extent to which returnees have found jobs and satisfactory accommodation, developed personal relationships, participated in community organizations, and so forth. The emic perspective focuses on migrants' *own perceptions* of their adjustment and the extent to which they feel the homeland satisfies self-defined needs. Much of the literature on the second approach tends to deal with questions of unhappiness and dissatisfaction, which are often reflected in a desire to re-emigrate. To quote the titles of two relevant studies, returnees experience a kind of "reverse culture shock" (Eikaas, 1979) and find there is "no place back home" (Davison, 1968).

In reality the migrants' return is often accompanied by considerable ambivalence. Many studies hint at this but few analyse it explicitly. On the one hand, returned migrants are comforted by being back in their own culture: they need not worry about communicating in a foreign language or being treated as inferiors, they are happy to see old friends and they re-identify with the local way of life. Yet they also begin to realize that, as people who have "been away", they are viewed differently. Certain things are expected of them. There can be no return to the *status quo ante.*

This ambiguity is best captured by those sociologists and social anthropologists who have observed returnee behaviour and the dynamics of interactions and expectations between returned migrants and non-migrants, usually in a village setting. Once home, migrants are expected, and indeed are under some pressure, to behave as "migrants" and not to revert to their former roles. They must display their "success", and are virtually forced to do so. Local institutions and customs are built up around return migration. Dahya (1973) has described how returnees to Pakistan are obliged to distribute plates of sweetmeats to the poorer villages and to pay troupes of singers and dancers to perform to celebrate their return. Chinese restaurant workers returning to their Hong Kong villages are expected to make generous donations to community projects and to throw lavish "re-entry banquets" (Watson, 1977). In the Philippines, too, returnees are expected to give large parties, and they are instrumental in financing the local fiestas (Griffiths, 1979; McArthur, 1979). Such extravagant behaviour may appear to be economically irrational, but it has the vital effect of legitimizing the individual returnee's new social position.

To a certain extent the returnees themselves contribute to this model of "expected" behaviour by their own attitudes and actions. Having "seen the world", they exhibit an arrogant and superior attitude. In a passage not without ironic humour, Dahya (1973) describes how returning Pakistani factory workers from Britain, on their arrival in their home villages, wear foreign suits, display expensive wristwatches and fountain-pens and carry briefcases – all are affectations which are largely meaningless in a hot climate, in a society where time is not rigorously measured and where literacy is not widespread. The meaning, rather, is *symbolic*, for the returnees are trying to present themselves as part of the new Pakistani middle class.

The most outwardly visible signs of returnee status are the new houses built in many villages deeply affected by emigration. In Pakistan these *pakka* houses, two or three storeys, stand out boldly against the low mud dwellings of the non-migrants (Dahya, 1973). Similar houses built in Hong Kong by migrants in Britain are called "sterling houses" (Watson, 1977). In Malta many houses have name-plates which blatantly indicate their occupants' migrant experiences – "Manhattan", "New York House" and even "God Bless America" (King, 1980).

Returnees' readjustment problems may also be a function of unrealistic expectations (Gmelch, 1980). Migrants' memories of their home society are out-of-date, idealized and nostalgic. The positive elements are stressed and the negative aspects recede from memory. Vacation return trips may reinforce the idealization of "home", for such visits take place in a holiday mood when the weather is good and a festive atmosphere prevails. In the hope of persuading their kinfolk to return, relatives may exaggerate the good points of life back home, glossing over economic problems like unemployment, low wages and inflation. Together these factors raise returnees' expectations higher than can be actually satisfied by the reality of the economic situation to which they return. The result is that, after a while back home, returnees see themselves as suffering from a sense of "relative deprivation" by which they compare their lives not with what they were like in the past but with what they think they should be like now and in the future (Taylor, 1976). Such disillusionment often leads to re-emigration.

Readjustment problems can also be differentiated by life-cycle and gender. Migrants who return to retire after several decades abroad are often no longer in touch with the society they left behind which, in the meantime, has itself changed. Some studies portray "retirees" as a marginal group who find little in the local society to relate to and who withdraw from it by spending their time with other elderly returnees reminiscing about their lives abroad (Cerase, 1970). Women face particular problems with return. In many cases they enjoyed a more independent life-style abroad, partly because of their experience of paid work in a more open and egalitarian society. Upon return, however, they have to face barriers to employment and emancipation.[4] Even more problematic, and less understood, are the problems of "returnee" children, particularly those who were born and who started their education abroad. Depending on their age and other factors, they may have great difficulty, at least for a time, in

---

[4] The question as to whether emigration is a liberating experience for women is a wide issue which was touched on briefly in the literature of the 1970s (see, for instance, Abadan-Unat 1977; Kosack 1976) and has been re-opened in more depth in the 1980s and 1990s (for example Phizacklea 1983; Buijs 1993).

adapting to life in the home country of their parents: different customs, different types of play and a different language in school are just some of the difficulties returning children (who usually play no part themselves in the return decision) have to deal with. Almost no research has been done on the problems of the children involved in return migration.

What, then, of returning migrants' social position? Here again a variety of evidence exists. Insofar as it is possible to generalize, it can be argued that migration abroad, or to an urban area where higher wages are paid, does enable some upward mobility and fluidity in social structures where status, both economic and social, can be bought. Such was the conclusion reached by Form and Rivera (1958) in an early study of a small Mexican border town, where returning wage-labourers from the United States enjoyed upward mobility into a widening middle class. Lopreato's (1967) study of rural social change in a south Italian village identified returning emigrants from the USA as the key element in the community's new social structure. Emigrants left from the poorer peasant and labouring classes, but with their accumulated wealth they were able to return as a new bourgeoisie, joining the shopkeepers, artisans and small landowners. Crucially for the future, they were able to invest in the education of younger family members, thus ensuring upward mobility for the generations to come. Hardly ever, however, are returning labour migrants, no matter how wealthy, admitted into the ranks of the traditional upper class which, in most emigrant societies, remains the prerogative of inherited wealth and established dynasties. In South Asia caste boundaries impose further limits on returnees' upward mobility.

Part of the debate over the changing social class position of returned migrants can be cast in terms of occupations. In the large ISTAT survey mentioned earlier no less than 65 per cent of migrants did the same job on return as they did prior to emigrating (Livi-Bacci, 1972: 102). This high percentage supports the contrary hypothesis to the one stated above and suggests that return migration contributes only to a small degree to changing the class structure of the emigration region. Similar evidence comes from Turkey: Krane's (1973) processing of 1,433 migrant dossiers found that 61 per cent of returnees remained essentially immobile socially, and only 16 per cent experienced a clear upward shift in status when compared with pre-migration employment. Abadan-Unat (1974) has claimed that there is a great aversion amongst Turkish returnees to blue-collar work: a returning migrant is not expected to rejoin the working class – indeed the very *raison d'être* of the emigration was to escape the drudgery and low status of the peasant or labouring classes. Likewise in Jamaica Taylor (1976) found that returnees were unwilling to take up their pre-migration jobs because they would lose prestige in the eyes of their relatives and neighbours who expect them to be upwardly mobile. This upward mobility may also involve the expectation in the community that returnees will become active in politics or as their leaders, although there may be concern in this regard if returning migrants import alien political ideologies learnt abroad. In Mediterranean societies, on the other hand, migrants (by their absence abroad) have detached themselves from the networks of political influence, and lack the patronage for careers in local politics (King, 1988: 134).

RETURN MIGRATION
AND ECONOMIC DEVELOPMENT

In his 1974 review essay on the sociology of return migration, Bovenkerk was struck by the lack of attention paid to the economic aspects of return (Bovenkerk, 1974: 31). Twenty-five years later, it is clear from a growing volume of literature that the consequences of return migration for the economic development of lagging regions and underdeveloped countries have been the object of considerable debate. Yet there is little agreement on the balance of positive and negative effects of return. On the one side are authors who argue from a broadly neoclassical economic viewpoint, stressing the positive economic contribution that return can make (Griffin, 1976; Miracle and Berry, 1970). On the other side there is a large body of evidence, some of it from micro-scale field studies carried out by social anthropologists and human geographers, which points to a minimal, or even negative, economic impact of return (see for example Castles and Kosack, 1973: 408-420; King, 1986; Piore, 1979; Reyneri, 1980; Swanson, 1979).

Figure 1.1 details the main economic effects associated with return migration: on wages, employment, and savings and investment. Some comments on employment changes associated with return migration were already made above, and Chapter 5 in this book provides a more detailed analysis of the interlinkages between return migration and development. As Ghosh points out, a useful distinction can be made between the economic welfare of the individual returning migrant or family, and the aggregate contribution that return migration makes to the country, region or community of origin.

Bovenkerk (1974: 45-49) lists a number of factors which may control the potential of return migration to be a developmental force. The first is the *number of returnees*. A large number may provide the critical mass to effect change, whereas smaller numbers will have little impact. On the other hand, a massive repatriation, concentrated in a short period of time, may overstrain the absorption capacity of the country of origin and arouse hostility amongst the indigenous population. Another relevant variable, as we saw from Cerase's (1974) typology, is the *duration of absence*. If this is very short, the returning migrant may have little power to be a modernizing or developmental influence on the home region: Cerase's return of failure. If too long, returnees may be so old, or so alienated from their "home society", that again the influence they can exert will be small – Cerase's return of retirement. Somewhere in between, the potential exists for Cerase's return of innovation, whereby migrants have the right combination of accumulated skills, attitudes and energies to bring about real change in the places to which they return. A third variable is the *destination of the return*: whether migrants return to the community of origin or to another part of their home country where, perhaps, the possibilities for an economically successful return are greater; and, linked to this, whether returnees are geographically mobile within their home countries after return (Figure 1.1). Fourthly, *social class* may have a strong differentiating effect, linked in turn to the *nature of the training* received abroad: returning professionals or graduate students are likely to have more of an economic and cultural effect than returning manual labourers. Finally, much may depend on *how the return is organized*. If it is spontaneous and uncoordinated, little effect may result; on the other hand, if it is well organized and related to other aspects of national and regional economic policy, then potential benefits are likely to be greater.

Returning to the economic influences posited in Figure 1.1, a large-scale return of working-age migrants could act to depress wages in the home region because they contribute to an over-supply of labour. However, the effect is to some extent mediated by the types of employment sought – and we have already noted that much of the historical evidence shows that returnees do not want to go back to their old, low-paid, low-status jobs. The two key economic variables associated with return are the human capital accumulated abroad through education, training and the acquisition of on-the-job skills; and the financial capital channelled to the home region through remittances and savings.

The theory of human capital gain through migration and return rests on the belief that countries of emigration can acquire a skilled or innovative labour force through the mechanism of migration and training abroad. Where the training is the specific objective of the migration – for instance to study for a degree abroad which is explicitly related to the developmental needs of the home country (for instance in agricultural science or civil engineering) – this investment in human capital through migration for education is a clearly rational strategy – as long as the migrants return. With labour migration the benefits are far less evident, since such migration takes place according to the dictates of the labour market and development needs of the destination country, not the country of origin. Indeed, some evidence of deskilling exists, where migrants are asked to do jobs abroad which are menial and unskilled, and unrelated to the skills (as farmers, craft workers, mechanics etc.) they may have had in their home countries. Taking the Turkish example for a moment, Paine (1974) estimated that less than 10 per cent of Turks returning from Germany had received any kind of useful training whilst working abroad. Even those who had experience of factory work involving skilled operations were of limited use. Factories in Turkey were not short of labour, and there is the question of returning migrants' social aspirations noted in the previous section. After years of sacrifice abroad it is not the intention of the returnees to opt for tough factory or farm work when savings can buy independence and prestige. Going to Germany thus seems to convert peasants and rural labourers into petty bourgeois whose new economic roles as shopkeepers or taxi-drivers are often highly marginal from an economic point of view (Abadan-Unat, 1974; 1976). On the other hand, where returnee small businesses are linked to an ongoing process of economic transformation, such as tourism in the Mediterranean region, a more positive input by returnees into the development process can be achieved. This is borne out by studies of returnees in tourist areas such as Dalmatia (Bennett, 1979) and the Greek islands of Corfu and Rhodes (Manganara, 1977).

Different again is the experience of return migration to the rural areas of the poorer countries of the world. In contrast to the situation in semi-peripheral regions such as Turkey and the Mediterranean, where returnees tend to shun farming, in the less-developed world research shows that returnees often make a positive contribution to agricultural development. For example, McArthur (1979) found that migrants returning from Hawaii to the Philippines were agriculturally innovative, buying paddy land, planting new rice varieties and applying fertilizer. In the Punjab, Oberai and Singh (1982) found that many of the early innovators of the Green Revolution were returned migrants with the capital and enterprise necessary to invest in new farming technologies. And in New Guinea returnees were amongst the first to expand coffee plantations in highland areas (Mayano, 1973). These examples show that returnees with capital and energy are able to stimulate local and regional development. They contribute to a renovation of the landscape, including intensification of farming, irrigation, mechanization as well as an improvement in the material conditions of living, especially housing and children's education, which it would be difficult to imagine without the driving force of migration behind it.

The economic impact of migrant remittances and savings has been reviewed by many authors (e.g. Asch, 1994; Connell et al., 1976; Díaz-Briquets and Weintraub, 1991; Ghosh, 1996). Although remittances are not directly linked to return (obviously, they can only take place so long as the migrant does *not* return), in many cases they are used, together with accumulated migrant savings, to realize the same objective, which is the support of the family in the area of origin and some kind of investment (land, a house, a business) which is built up to await the migrant's return.

Migrants returning after many years of hard work and scrimping and saving may bring back sums of capital which are very considerable by local standards. But the key question is how this capital is deployed. Although, as we have noted, there is plenty of evidence documenting the productive investment of savings accumulated by returnees in sectors such as agriculture, tourism and small businesses, there is also a consistent picture of an almost obsessive spending on housing. The new or enlarged house, a near-universal symbol of status, is the personal monument to the migrant's success and establishes, in the eyes of the local community, the fact that, at least materially, the migrant is on a par with the local elite. As was noted earlier, the *pakka* and "sterling" houses (respectively in Pakistan and Hong Kong) "vindicate to one and all the migrant and his family's achieved status" (Dahya, 1973). Rhoades (1979) has similar passages which describe the conspicuous consumption of housing and domestic durables amongst Spanish returnees in Andalusia: migration enables the move "from caves to main street". Ironically, however, the new house is often abandoned after a few years when the returnee, faced with little work available locally, "is forced to re-join the industrial proletariat of a foreign country which neither knows nor cares about his symbol of success back home" (Swanson, 1979: 49).

In sum, it seems that the economic benefits of return migration and savings are chimeric. Personal prosperity may be achieved by some, but this makes the distribution of income in the sending society more unequal (Lipton, 1980). It is true, nevertheless, that in theory migration *can* be a real stimulus to home-country development. Migrants *can* be given relevant training by the receiving country; they *can* be given incentives to invest and reintegrate upon return for the general good of the home societies; and industries and other sustainable economic activities *can* be encouraged to locate in areas where returnees' skills can be maximized. But these policies need careful planning and can only happen if there is greater cooperation between sending and receiving countries (see also Chapter 5).

THE LITERATURE ON RETURN MIGRATION: AN INTRODUCTORY HISTORICAL OVERVIEW

Until the 1960s, studies of migration made little or no reference to return. It is true that Ravenstein, father-figure of migration studies, mentioned "counterstreams" in both of his seminal papers on the "laws of migration", but he failed to clarify whether these counter-flows were mainly returnees or were made up of other migrants moving in the opposite direction to the dominant flow (Ravenstein 1885: 187; 1889: 387).

Two important studies of return migration were published before 1960: Saloutos' (1956) pioneering portrait of Greeks returning from the United States during the early decades of the twentieth century, and a lesser-known account by Useem and Useem (1955) of the return of the "Western-educated man" to India. Historical studies of return migration (in the sense of documenting the phenomenon of return in the period before the Second World War) are also fairly rare. Mostly they comprise studies of return migration from the United States in the nineteenth century (Axelrod, 1972; Gould, 1980; Wyman, 1993), including some specific nationality studies on the

English (Shepperson, 1965), Finns (Virtanen, 1979), Germans (Molt-mann, 1980), Italians (Caroli, 1970) and Croatians (Kraljic, 1978).

Since 1960, the development of return migration literature has followed the evolution of the return currents themselves. During the 1960s, three groups of studies can be recognized. The first of these comprised further analyses in the context of return from the United States to Italy (Gilkey, 1967; Lopreato, 1967) and to other labour suppliers such as Puerto Rico (Hernández Alvarez, 1967; Myers and Masnick, 1968) and Mexico (Hernández Alvarez, 1966). The second group were studies of British return migration from Australia (Appleyard, 1962; Richardson, 1968) and Canada (Richmond, 1966; 1968). The third were studies of return migration from Britain to the Caribbean (Davison, 1968; Patterson, 1968).

Return migration literature expanded significantly in the 1970s, especially in association with the growth of return flows provoked by the economic slump in Europe, which unleashed both economic and political pressures for migrants to return to their home countries, mainly in Mediterranean Europe and the Maghreb (for reviews of the return literature of this period see Entzinger, 1978; King, 1979; Papademetriou, 1985). This literature on return from the main groupings of advanced capitalist countries – chiefly North America and Western Europe – continued a steady output during the 1980s and 1990s (for some examples see Ahlburg, 1994; Gmelch, 1987; King et al., 1984; Lever-Tracy, 1989; Lindstrom, 1996; Muschkin, 1993; Ramos, 1992; Thomas-Hope, 1999), and was also joined by studies of return migration within other migrant labour systems such as those based in the Gulf and Asia (Arif and Irfan 1997; Athukorala, 1990; Gopinathan Nair, 1999; Gunatilleke, 1991; Lawless et al., 1982).

The above examples constitute only a small selection of the total published research, which is now extensive. Rather than attempt to chronicle all this literature – an impossible task within the confines of a single chapter – we now examine two case studies from different historical and geographical contexts.

RETURN MIGRATION FROM THE UNITED STATES: THE MYTH OF NON-RETURN

Transatlantic emigration was one of the great human processes of the nineteenth century; according to Baines (1991: 7-9) around 35 million Europeans emigrated to North America between 1850 and

1914. Fleeing overcrowding and poverty fuelled by centuries of rapid population growth, mass emigration to North America (and to other transoceanic destinations such as South America, South Africa, Australia and New Zealand) was a safety-valve to keep Europe's overpopulation in check (King, 1996: 35).

The nineteenth-century view of transatlantic emigration was that it was a one-way, once-and-for-all phenomenon. And yet between one quarter and one-third went back: returnees who have been "barely noticed by social scientists" (Gmelch, 1980: 135). Two questions arise: why did so many supposedly "permanent emigrants" return? What were their experiences after returning home? Before we answer these questions it is worth considering why return migration from the United States has been so little studied. Much has to do with ideology – both of migration and of American history. With very few exceptions, American historians have tended to imply that immigration to the USA necessarily meant permanence. Such historians have defined their subject in such a way as to exclude consideration of return migrants. Migrants are subordinated to the wider context of American society and history, so that people who returned to their countries of origin were seen as somehow deviant or behaving illogically. The symbolism of the Statue of Liberty welcoming the "huddled masses yearning to breathe free" as they arrived on migrant ships entering New York Harbour made it impossible to visualize departing ships carrying millions of migrants back to their homelands. Yet 10 million returned between 1870 and 1940. The "myth of no return" (Sarna, 1981) was compounded by a lack of statistical information about returning migrants. "Departing aliens" were not officially recorded by the US authorities until 1908 (Caroli, 1970: 5), and many records were subsequently destroyed. Literary evidence is likewise scarce: in contrast to the wealth of "ethnic literature" on immigrant groups in the United States, returnees left little by way of documentary evidence. Some compensation is offered by a more unorthodox source: migrant novels and autobiographies display an awareness of return which is often highly insightful. As Shumsky (1995) points out, migrant novelists have captured with great sensitivity the *mentalité* of migrants in the US and their thoughts, plans and experiences of return.

To the question of why so many migrants returned, three possible answers can be given (aside from a myriad of individual personal factors): that migrants found conditions on arrival in America to be much less advantageous than they had hoped or been led to believe; that conditions in America changed for the worse during their stay, precipitating their return; or that a substantial portion of the migrants never intended to stay permanently and had always projected an eventual return. Evidence exists for all these explanations.

Cerase's (1974) "return of failure" has already been noted as one of the types of return, occurring when a migrant fails to adapt or quickly becomes disillusioned. According to Wyman (1993: 5) some migrants became disillusioned so soon after their arrival in the United States that they went back on the same ship that had brought them out a few weeks earlier. Others stayed on longer but then returned to escape the harsh realities of life in America – irregular work, inhuman conditions in factories, mines and dockyards, and overcrowded, unsanitary housing. Many returned because of ill-health or injury at work – circumstances amply documented by Wyman. Yet others returned after a few years, as soon as they had saved enough to realize their "target" – a piece of land, money for a dowry or a "dream house" back in their home village.

Returns were also triggered by deteriorating conditions in the United States. The onset of World War One generated a sharp increase in the rate of return to Europe, the combined product of patriotism for the "home country", a concern for family members who had remained behind, and of the misgivings of some non-naturalized "aliens" as regards their status and treatment should the USA become involved in the war. Then the Great Depression provided the *coup de grâce* for transatlantic emigration, for, as Gould (1979: 621) pointed out: "there was little point in fleeing unemployment in Naples merely to suffer unemployment in New York". Indeed the Depression caused a net movement back to Europe.

It is also true that many emigrants never intended to stay in the USA permanently, and that transatlantic emigration was seen more and more as a temporary project, especially after 1900. Italian and US data exemplify these trends, demonstrating how a more-or-less permanent emigration of nuclear families came to be replaced by an emigration of single males and married men without their families, followed by a return after an average of three or four years. According to US sources, the rate of repatriation from the United States to Italy rose from 43 per cent during 1880-90 to 48 per cent during 1890-1900, and then to 53 per cent in 1900-10 and 63 per cent during 1910-20 (Gould, 1980: 86).

At an aggregate level, for the USA as a whole, the increasing trend to higher rates of return after 1900 is partly correlated with a progressive switch in emigration from the so-called "old" countries of emigration (Britain, Ireland, Germany, Scandinavia) where permanent settlement was the rule, to the "new" emigration countries in southern and eastern Europe (Italy, Greece, Bulgaria etc.). Gould (1980) presents many comparative statistics on these trends. In one set, he shows the contrast between countries with high "repatriation ratios" – Bulgaria, Serbia, Montenegro (69%), Greece (63%), Italy (58%) – and those with much lower ratios (Germany 22%, Russia 16%, England 12%, Ireland 6%[5]). Part of this difference can be related to the kinds of places and jobs occupied by migrant nationalities in the United States: Northern European migrants tended to settle in farming areas and not to return, whereas South Europeans migrated to urban areas and took more insecure forms of employment. Southern Europeans' integration to American culture tended to be weaker because of their lack of education and poor language preparation.

The origin-country impacts of return migration from the US during the late nineteenth and early twentieth centuries were obviously many and varied. An overall survey is given by Wyman (1993), and there are country-specific studies of Ireland ('t Hart, 1985), Greece (Saloutos, 1956) and especially Italy (Caroli, 1970; Cerase, 1970; 1974; Cinel, 1991; Gilkey, 1967; King, 1988: 15-34). The main theme echoing through this literature is the migrant ideology of leaving poor and returning rich. Returning migrants – "Yanks" as they were known in Ireland, or *americani* in Italy – paraded their experience and built new houses, often known as "American houses", in their villages. The psychological impact of the first returnees was dramatic: "European peasant villages that once seemed impenetrable in their backwardness, their isolation, now boasted residents who could describe the wonders of the New World – skyscrapers, elevated trains, deep tunnels. Men and women who formerly quailed at a visit from the landlord now proudly described how they had seen the president of the United States in person" (Wyman, 1993: 6).

In the west of Ireland in the nineteenth century, some returnees from the United States came back because they inherited a farm. Others returned to retire, often in poor health. For younger returnees a common aim was to buy a pub or a shop; indeed 't Hart (1985) comments that it was easier for returned migrants to buy a pub than farmland and that in some parts of rural Ireland most of the publicans were "returned Yanks". The same author notes a higher than

---

[5] It should be pointed out that the Irish who emigrated to the United States tended to be largely made up of permanent settlers since, for those who were looking to emigrate temporarily, Britain was close by.

average propensity for fishermen to return: "a lot of fishermen came back and went fishing again", preferring the free life to the regime of "bosses and clocks" ('t Hart, 1985: 225). The notebooks of the Irish Folklore Commission, which refer mainly to the early twentieth century, contain many accounts of "returned Yanks" building new houses in rural Ireland. Historical continuity is evident when the above findings are compared with those from two studies carried out on return migration to the west of Ireland in the 1970s (Foeken, 1980; Gmelch, 1986). A propensity to build new houses – often ranch-style bungalows – is clearly evident, along with returning to inherit a farm or set up a small business such as a pub or shop. Such businesses often reflect the transatlantic influence: American-style small supermarkets were introduced into rural towns, and pubs carried names like "The Chicago Bar" or "The American Lounge".

Similar economic innovations are noted by researchers studying return migration from the United States to other source countries. For instance, Saloutos (1956) describes the introduction of industrialized milk production into Greece by returnees from America, and Lopreato (1962) reports the setting-up of an olive oil press run as a cooperative by returnees in a southern Italian village. Wyman (1993: 127-209) presents a wealth of evidence on return migration to southern Italy, Ireland, Poland, Hungary, Norway, Sweden and other parts of Europe during the early nineteenth and twentieth centuries. New houses, improved standards of living, enlarged farm holdings and new businesses are all recurrent themes across destinations ranging from north Norway to Sicily. "American houses" were going up "all across Europe as the nineteenth century closed – houses with tile or slate roofs instead of thatch, a large window with a view to the road, walls of brick or plastered white, doorways sprouting brass knobs and shiny varnish" (Wyman, 1993: 127). Houses were important and, above all, visible; but land was the prime concern for returnees of peasant origin. New dwellings were generally second in importance, followed by shops and other businesses, and then personal interests such as education, a dowry, medical care and paying off debts. Land conferred prestige on returnees, boosting their income, and the marriage prospects of their offspring. But land prices inflated, to the disadvantage of local peasants who had not been abroad and who wanted to set up and enlarge farms. Especially in Germany and Scandinavia, whose emigrants had often worked on farms in the USA, returnees brought back agricultural innovations: new seeds, farming techniques, tools and machinery. Agricultural innovation was less in southern Europe where Cerase's (1974) "return of conservatism" prevailed, "reproducing an agrarian structure which had already proved itself unviable".

Apart from material goods and new technological inputs, returnees also brought back new ideas and customs, a new "flexibility of mind" (Wyman, 1993: 196). These comprised a wide range of values including democratic ideals, notions of freedom and the rights of the individual, new standards of hygiene, respect for work and the discipline of the workplace, trade union practices, and new religious (and secular) beliefs. Again Wyman (1993) provides many examples: social democrats, labour activists and socialist radicals who learnt their new ideologies in the United States and then returned to become active in local or even national politics; and converts, usually from Catholicism, to "new" evangelistic religions (Pentecostalists, Mormons, Baptists etc.), who spread their new beliefs in their home communities. Elsewhere, returnees were secularizing influences on established Catholic or Protestant societies, and the power of local clergy was challenged by returnees who refused to adopt traditional deferential attitudes to the twin pillars of local rural society, the landlord and the priest. Behavioural changes included new modes of dress (the ubiquitous gold watch and chain, shiny shoes and hard hats), Americanisms in speech, new dances, and foodstuffs like apple pie and ice cream. Small wonder that throughout the European regions of return, returnees were known as "Americans", for they stood in both the Old World and the New (Wyman, 1993: 203).

HOME IS WHERE YOU LEAVE IT:[6]
RETURN MIGRATION TO THE CARIBBEAN

Few areas of the world have been so deeply affected by migration as the Caribbean islands. Although the largest-scale migrations were those of the 1950s and 1960s, the essence of Caribbean life has always been geographical movement (Pessar, 1997), often culminating in one or multiple returns. This "return ideology" has powerful effects on the behaviour of both the migrant abroad and those remaining behind in the island society (Rubenstein, 1979). Indeed such has been the scale and impact of migration on many Caribbean islands, particularly the small ones such as Montserrat, St. Kitts and Nevis, that

---

[6] I take the phrase "home is where you leave it" from Olwig (1993: 137).

migration has become institutionalized as the central part of local culture, livelihood and way of thinking. In Kingston, Jamaica, there is a local saying that the shortest route from the shanty-town to the hills (where the high-class residences are) is through London or New York (Phillips, 1980: 66).

Ever since colonial times, the history of the Caribbean has been one of mobility: the forced transfer of slave labour from Africa and of indentured workers from India and China; the movement of emancipated slaves around the region according to the labour needs of colonial capital and business interests; and further, longer-distance emigrations dictated by the collapse of the colonial economies based on plantation crops. According to Olwig (1993: 177), the plantation system was "characterized by a capitalist reason and praxis which was ultimately destructive of the Afro-Caribbean population's conditions of objective existence". Monocrop agriculture is unsound over the long term, both ecologically (leading to soil exhaustion) and economically (over-dependency on world market prices for the product); this vulnerability is exaggerated within the small island context because of shortage of land, isolation and lack of alternatives when a society and an economy built up on a narrow base collapse (Connell and King, 1999). Sugar, coffee and cotton all boomed and then went bust. Currently the cultivation of bananas, the mainstay of several small island economies such as St. Lucia and Grenada, is under threat because of global trade and price wars in which Caribbean smallholders are pitched against American multinationals running huge plantations with higher productivity in Central and South America.

Between Emancipation and the Second World War several migrations of population, often followed by returns, occurred within the wider Caribbean region (Byron, 1994: 23-45); Richardson, 1983: 3-31). Immediately following Emancipation in 1834, migrations of freed labourers took place, especially from small, overcrowded islands where ex-slaves had difficulty finding work or land, to bigger islands and adjacent mainland territories where land was available as well as work on newer, bigger plantations. For example, ex-slaves from St. Kitts and Nevis migrated in their thousands to the southern Caribbean colonies of Trinidad and Guiana in the 1840s. This migration was rarely permanent: migrants "usually returned home, once more braving the hazards of the interisland passage", which often involved a voyage of several days and nights on light wooden sailing boats (Richardson, 1983: 18, 90). Such returnees were viewed with esteem and respect; they constituted a "labouring elite" who had "beaten the system" (Richardson, 1983: 19).

Later the Dominican Republic, Cuba and Costa Rica were temporary destinations for intra-Caribbean labour migration, much of which was seasonal. The migration to Dominica lasted several decades, until the Depression of the 1930s; again cycles of emigration and return were built into the migration biographies of many Caribbean islanders (see the life-histories presented by Byron, 1994: 40-42). Other sources of work for temporary migration within the region were Panama, for canal construction; Bermuda, where the naval dockyards were being constructed; and the Netherlands Antilles, where good wages were available in activities linked to the oil industry. Returnees from the Dutch Antilles – Aruba and Curaçao – often opened shops or used their savings to finance the education (and hence, often, the further emigration) of younger family members.

By the 1950s, when emigration reached its most intense proportions, migration had already been conceptualized as a survival strategy of Caribbean populations, especially by the lower-class blacks. Although some of the earlier migrations were permanent (leading to widespread settlement of Caribbean islanders on the east coasts of Honduras, Nicaragua and Costa Rica, for example), the return element of the migration cycle was clearly embedded in the ideology of Caribbean migration – both temporary returns between individual emigration events, and a more definitive return as the culmination of the migrants' working lives.

Post-war Caribbean migration to Britain was shaped by many factors. At a structural level it was seen by authors such as Castles and Kosack (1973) and Cohen (1987) as part of the exploitation of the dependent periphery by the capitalist core of the global economic system. Britain's colonization of much of the Caribbean Basin created an obvious historical linkage which functioned at several levels: the granting of citizenship rights (until 1962) to Commonwealth Caribbean migrants who came to Britain; an educational curriculum which virtually brainwashed Caribbean children into thinking of Britain as the mother country where they would be welcomed and which would value their "British" education and loyalty to the Crown; and a general orientation to the British way of life and culture (including a love of cricket!).

The migration was triggered by the movement of several thousand volunteer workers who served in the armed forces and in the munitions factories during the war. Disillusioned by their return to the economically depressed Caribbean, many re-emigrated to civilian employment, having already gained a knowledge of Britain and job opportunities there. Formal recruitment by British Rail, London Transport and the National Health Service, occurred in Barbados in the 1950s. Aside from these channels, much of the movement was more spontaneous, shaped by chain migration and personal and kinship networks (Byron, 1994). The peak years were 1955-61, during which more than 220,000 migrants from the Commonwealth Caribbean territories entered Britain. The largest groups were from Jamaica (143,000) and Barbados (18,700) but, in terms of the intensity of departure, it was the smaller islands which were most affected, such as Montserrat, which lost around 4,000 people, a third of its population, during the years between 1955 and 1961 (Philpott, 1977).

What of the patterns of return to the Caribbean? Studies on return migration to the Anglophone part of this region from Britain span more than thirty years and refer to a range of islands: Jamaica (Davison, 1968; Nutter, 1986; Patterson, 1968; Taylor, 1976; Thomas-Hope, 1999); Barbados (Gmelch, 1987, 1992; Western, 1992); St. Vincent (Rubenstein, 1979); Montserrat (Philpott, 1968; 1977); and Nevis (Byron, 1994; Olwig, 1993). The Puerto Rican case is somewhat different since it is, in effect, intra-national return migration from the US mainland (Hernández-Alvarez, 1967; Myers and Masnick, 1968; Ramos, 1992). Much the same could be said of return from the French metropole to Martinique and Guadeloupe, *départements d'outre-mer* (Condon and Ogden, 1996).

The rest of this review of post-war return to the Caribbean will focus mainly on return to the (former) British Commonwealth islands. Here a distinction can be made between the large and the small islands. In the larger islands there is a more complex economic context to return to, with a more structured labour market consisting, for example, of work in agriculture, industry, tourism, the private and public service sectors, including some possibilities for return migrants to create for themselves an entrepreneurial future. In the small islands, on the other hand, the labour market opportunities may be very restricted, as the following examples will show.

In islands like Montserrat and Nevis where, already by the 1960s, emigration to Britain had taken the majority of working-age males as well as significant numbers of females out of the island population, the insular economy had become almost entirely dependent on remittances. An "emigration culture" had developed where emigration was practically the only option available for young adults. Agriculture had virtually collapsed, and this collapse, which pre-dated migration, was hastened by the exodus both because of the withdrawal of labour and because of the low social status associated with working the land, so that few returnees went back to farming by choice, except as a hobby.

At least initially, returns were relatively few, necessarily so if remittances were to remain source of cash to sustain the islands' remaining population at an improved standard of living beyond the poverty, unemployment and poor material conditions that afflicted the island at an earlier period. For Nevis, early studies by Manners (1965) and Frucht (1968) recorded that remittances had become by far the main source of cash income on the island, replacing a rapidly declining agriculture. Such remittances reflected moral and family obligations towards the island and, in most cases, a longer-term intention to return. In the meantime, temporary return visits became an occasion – and an obligation – to bring gifts and to demonstrate the success and worldliness of being a migrant. As one returnee described to Karen Fog Olwig, "I am a big woman now, since I have been outside Nevis, and I must behave accordingly, when I come home" (Olwig, 1993: 171). The same informant continued: "When you go home ... it is necessary to carry a big bag of money and six suitcases of clothes. They all come and ask you right to your face to give you something." Another migrant, whom Olwig knew when she was abroad, was scarcely recognizable to the author when they met up on the island: she had undergone a transformation, parading around in "elaborate costume jewellery and a garish outfit" (Olwig, 1993: 171). The fact that migration is seen as the source of all material and luxury goods which are brought back or imported serves only to depress the islanders' belief in the capability of the island to develop itself. There is also the sense that trying to attain socio-economic mobility within the confines of a small island society, without emigrating, can only be achieved by damaging others; the "neighbour's grudge" therefore becomes a social sanction against individual progress which occurs at the expense of the local community. Only by leaving the island can Nevisians escape the local grudge and accumulate wealth, which can then be legitimately displayed on return (Olwig, 1993: 173-175).

By the 1970s, returns were becoming more numerous. In a large village in St. Vincent, Rubenstein (1979: 24) found that nearly 60 per cent of adult males were return migrants. On both Nevis and Montserrat the growth of tourism and expatriate residences (both largely geared to the North American and British markets) provided opportunities for employment as construction workers, gardeners, porters, cooks etc., as well as possibilities for opening small businesses such as taxis, bars and night clubs. On Montserrat both return migration and the development of tourism were brutally halted, and sent into reverse, by the repeated eruption of the Soufrière volcano in the late 1990s; most of the island's population was evacuated (Philpott, 1999). On Nevis the return phenomenon has continued and grown over recent decades. Indeed Byron (1994) predicts a considerable growth of retirement return for Nevis, and the rest of the "British" Caribbean, based on her analysis of the age structure of the emigrant population in Britain.[7]

Byron's (1994: 168-197) field research on return migration to Nevis reveals a diversity of return types and paths. Britain is by no means the dominant destination country: numerous returns have also taken place from the United States and from the economically booming tourist islands of the Caribbean – the US and British Virgin Islands and St. Martin. Many returnees are sustained by British pensions.[8] Successful return is evidenced by large concrete houses, comfortable lifestyles and, for working-age retirees, small businesses. Self-employment is seen as the ideal for pre-retirement returnees – much of this is linked to tourism, as noted above. Although many returnees engage in spare-time farming on the garden land attached to their new houses, real investment in agriculture is rather rare, whilst industrial initiatives are practically non-existent.

A wider range of employment and social outcomes is evident when we shift our focus to the larger islands of the Caribbean, such as Jamaica. Although in earlier years return was seen as problematic because of the still backward economy and social tensions (Davison, 1968; Patterson, 1968), in more recent decades return has gathered pace and made a more thorough contribution to the reshaping of the Jamaican economy and society. Nutter (1986) interviewed 93 returnees in Kingston in 1983: most had emigrated to Britain in the 1950s and 1960s, and returned to Jamaica in the 1970s and early 1980s. He found that returnees tended to cluster and be over-represented in certain sectors of business activity such as food and beverages and the financial sector, in which they also tended to have larger-scale

---

[7] Between 1981 and 1991 the Caribbean-born population enumerated by the British census fell by more than 30,000; according to Byron (1994: 168-169) 90 per cent of this is accounted for by return migration (the rest by mortality). With 50 per cent of the Caribbean-born in Britain aged over 50 in 1991, most of the return is a return of retirement.

[8] Although these cease to be index-linked if the pensioner moves abroad.

concerns and be occupied in more senior positions than the average for those sectors in the city. The return was seen partly as a function of the returnees' original intention to return, and partly as a response to Jamaica's shortage of skilled manpower. On the other hand, whilst this type of return, selective of the more ambitious and successful emigrants, places returnees at the forefront of Jamaica's modern economic development strategy, doubts can be expressed about the long-term viability of that strategy, particularly in the light of the collapse of several Jamaican banks in the early 1990s. Questions also need to be asked as to whether a type of return based on individual personal success exacerbates polarization and inequality within the country (Nutter, 1986: 209-210).

The story is brought up to date in a recent paper by Thomas-Hope (1999). Return to Jamaica accelerated through the 1990s and brought many types of returnees back, the majority from Britain and the United States (the latter having replaced Britain as the main destination for migrants from the Anglophone Caribbean in the 1960s). Remittances continued to be vital to the Jamaican economy, outstripping the income from the traditional foreign currency earners, sugar and bauxite. Growing awareness of the potential of the overseas community and of return migration for the development of the Jamaican economy induced the government to establish programmes and incentives to facilitate return. In 1992 customs relief was introduced on imported consumer goods, and in 1995 IOM supported the "Return of Talent" programme, designed to encourage the return of skilled people.

Complementing Nutter's work in Kingston, Thomas-Hope collected survey data in rural Jamaica. Here the general trend was for migrants to move into a lower socio-occupational status whilst abroad, compared to their pre-migration educational and employment background, but then to achieve occupational and status mobility after return, often by becoming independent or semi-independent workers and business-owners. Hence emigration was seen in the short term as a means of accumulating capital and some "experience" (although generally the foreign employment was un-skilled or semi-skilled), and in the longer term as the route to socio-economic advancement at home. Returnees from the US were particularly active in buying land for farming and for more speculative purposes, although houses were a more universal investment. Professionals were most likely to return after a short spell abroad, up to five years; a finding with clear policy implications. Returnees are generally able to enjoy a pleasant lifestyle in a warm climate and with a range of investment options. For those with children there are high-quality educational facilities which are often thought to offer a better schooling environment than inner-city schools in Britain or America. On the other hand, the high crime rate and episodes of governmental instability are seen as negative factors by returnees. Demographic-ally, return contributes to the ageing of the population of Jamaica and the Caribbean populations.

The research data on Barbados are more ethnographic but they generally reinforce the findings for Jamaica. For instance, Gmelch's (1987) study of returning students/professionals and returning la-bour migrants found that the former, especially, were responsible for introducing new techniques into the workplace and for introducing new social values. The returning labour migrants had a more re-stricted impact, being more orientated to a quiet life of semi-retirement. Returning students settled in Bridgetown and suburban areas, where they took up professional careers. Most of the returning workers, on the other hand, settled in rural areas whence they came.

FROM HISTORICAL GENERALIZATION
TO THEORY

Virtually all the literature on return migration is empirical or de-scriptive in nature. The tendency has been to examine each return migration group as a distinct entity and to make little attempt at cross-national comparison or theoretical synthesis. To a certain ex-tent, the lack of much theoretical formulation surrounding return migration reflects the situation of migration studies generally. Steps towards theorizing return migration have been taken in two rather different directions: first, attempts to formulate law-like statements *à la Ravenstein* on the basis of empirical and statistical evidence; and second, attempts to understand return migration within more general epistemologies of studying migration and human behaviour. Part of the difficulty of generalizing and theorizing about return migration is that there are many types of return, just as there are many types of migration; this was explored in the section on typologies of return at the beginning of this chapter.

Reviewing the historical evidence, the following "propositions on return migration" can be made (cf. Campbell and Johnson, 1976; Richmond, 1984; Rogers, 1984):

- For every emigration stream, there will be a return stream, to the extent that return is possible (and desired).
- Most emigrants intend to return when they emigrate. Although not all intentions are subsequently realized (and although some intending permanent emigrants do in fact return), much return migration is simply the fulfilment of the original intention to return.
- The propensity to return is greatest soon after migration; the longer the migrant stays in the destination, the less likely he or she is to return, except possibly at retirement.
- Return migration is more likely from short-distance migrations than from long-distance ones.
- The return flows will be large, relative to the emigration flow, to the extent that the origin and destination are economically and socially similar.
- The return stream will be small, relative to the emigration, if the original forces giving rise to the emigration were negative or push factors from the country or place of origin.
- The return will vary in response to economic conditions in the host country: it will be small in times of prosperity and larger during depressions.
- Similarly return will vary in response to economic conditions in the country of origin: in particular return will grow if there are positive developmental processes under way, and it will be small if economic conditions remain depressed.
- Return will also vary according to social and political conditions in both the origin and destination countries: it will grow if these conditions turn against migrants in the destination country (racism, anti-immigrant policies or legislation), and it will grow if there is an improvement in the socio-political environment of the home country (restoration of democracy, social stability etc.).
- Nevertheless, at the individual scale, most return takes place for personal and social reasons rather than economic or political ones.
- The stronger the web of interpersonal ties with the country of origin, the higher the probability of return migration, assuming there are no sanctions against returning.
- Return will be higher amongst those who have experienced no social mobility or occupational promotion in the destination country; and low amongst those who have experienced upward mobility (it might also be low amongst those who have suffered downward

41

mobility because of sanctions of shame and failure in the home country).

- However, generalizations about "successes" and "failures" are difficult to make, not least because definitions of the criteria for "success" may differ between the country of origin and that of destination. Insofar as some generalization is possible, the return flow contains a disproportionate number of migrants with "low personal effectiveness", and of migrants who are single, separated and divorced. On the other hand, some recent studies note that returnees tend to have higher levels of education, skill and income than non-returnees, particularly where opportunities for professional advancement exist in the home country.
- Finally, returnees tend to be older than emigrants, with obvious demographic consequences for the home country.

The second main approach to a more theoretical understanding of return migration has been to try to place return migration (and migration, since return should be logically derivable as a subset of a more general theory of migration) in a wider framework by looking at various social science epistemologies which have relevance to the study of migration. Following and extending the remarks of Wiest (1979) and Richmond (1984), five such epistemologies can be identified:

- functionalist or equilibrium models, which have their philosophical roots in Malthus and in classical economics;
- behavioural or psychologistic models, including the study of individual conflict;
- the Marxist perspective, which also involves conflict analysis, but on a larger scale, as well as historical-structuralist models;
- the general systems framework, which in some respects attempts to combine all of the above three approaches;
- the transnational communities perspective, which sees migration as less of a phenomenon simply concerned with movements between origins and destinations, and more as a reflection of globalization and the cultural geography of diasporas.

By no means all (return) migration studies can be placed in these theoretical pigeon-holes, but the theoretical traditions listed above are valuable in indicating the possible directions that return migration theory might take.

The functionalist equilibrium approach has characteristically viewed migration as a mechanism for restoring the balance between population and resources. Central to this perspective is the conceptualization of migration as a voluntary action based on a rational calculation of the economic costs and benefits, with only passing reference to political and cultural factors. Studies of return migration from a functionalist point of view focus on factors such as the changing fortunes of the areas of origin and destination, poor integration in the receiving society, family ties to the homeland and an economic desire to invest savings upon return. In the equilibrium model, remittances are seen as the means of restoring the balance of payments between migrant-sending and receiving nations, whilst the ideas and skills acquired abroad by the migrants are also channelled back to the origin country via return migration in order to raise living standards and boost development there. This perspective tends to be ahistorical, concentrating on the relationships between variables over limited periods of time; and it fails to address underlying structural conditions and contradictions.

The psychological approach, common in studies by anthropologists, psychologists and other behavioural scientists, assumes that migration is governed by an individual's motivation to achieve certain desired ends. It has produced many detailed studies of the urban adaptation of migrants and, on their return, of migrants' reintegration patterns, including role conflict and ambiguity. The individual scale of this type of analysis tends to lead to a positive evaluation of the migration process, since individuals generally judge migration to be a positive experience, a view substantiated by their improved standards of living after return. Shortcomings exist in this approach, however. It ignores the relevance of factors outside the control of individual migrants and, like the first approach, it tends to obscure the underlying causes and consequences of geographic mobility (Wiest, 1979: 182).

The Marxist or historical-structuralist approach to migration has a number of well-known devotees and has spawned several important overviews of international migration (Castles and Kosack, 1973; Cohen, 1987; Piore, 1979; Potts, 1990). Unlike the equilibrium model which sees migration as a beneficent phenomenon aiding both the sending and receiving economies, as well as the individual migrant, the Marxian interpretation focuses on the essential conflict between the interests of the sending and receiving countries. Nor does the migrant necessarily benefit: often he or she is portrayed as an exploited, defeated and demoralized individual, a pawn in a game whose forces he or she does not understand and cannot control. The essential features of this approach are that social phenomena like migration be placed in their true historical context and that the structure of production relations be delineated. The approach is macro-level and is focused on the role of monopoly and dependent capitalism in shaping international migration patterns. It compels us to ask questions about the underlying causes and effects of migration, and to go beyond return migration's superficial effects on income, consumption and minor social changes. Above all, return is seen as the discarding of labour back into the "reserve army" when not required by the dictates of capital.

Fourthly, as Mabogunje (1970) first pointed out, migration and return migration can be profitably examined within a systems framework. Modern systems theory has its roots in both the functionalist and conflict traditions. Social and regional systems are understood to be open, flexible and to involve exchanges and interactions with other systems and subsystems. Migration is of course one of the most important of these interchanges. Using a systems framework, Hoffmann-Nowotny (1981) sees migration as the transfer of "structural tension" from one society to another. But in the case of most recent mass migrations, immigrants have been relegated to low-status positions within the destination society; hence the tension builds up again and leads to return migration. Return migration can also be seen as a "feedback loop" from the society of destination to that of the origin country. Information conveyed by this feedback process, as well as the demonstration effect of returnees' behaviour, may act to stimulate (or depress, if the feedback is negative) further migration. Some elements of systems thinking also lie behind the recent popularity of social networks theory in studying migration (Boyd, 1989; Fawcett, 1989), and this provides a link to the final perspective.

Nowadays, the study of migration is seen less and less as the study of a single relocation event. Migration is increasingly regarded as a socially embedded process (Castles and Miller, 1998: 19) and as a phenomenon which also has to be understood within long-range personal (even cross-generational) biographies and family histories. In this more overtly historical methodological approach, "emigration" and "return" are seen less and less as discrete events and increasingly as part of wider ongoing processes of global mobility. Hence historically migration is part of the genesis (and a reflection of the existence) of transnational communities and diasporas. Traditionally return is seen as the "closure" of the migration cycle. But as transnational communities become more widely established and firmly embedded in the cultural geography of world population distribution, notions of "home" and "abroad" become blurred, as do definitions of migration, return, mobility, travel and so on.

This chapter opened with a stricture on the lack of attention paid to return in the history of migration. It closes with a plea that studies of return not be isolated around the return decision or event, but be built around a more holistic and theoretically informed appreciation of the nature of migration and mobility in this globalized era. As people migrate, return, circulate and commute, they increasingly lead global lives. Moreover, in a world increasingly dominated by fast transport and a multitude of other communication media, mobility is both real and virtual. Transnationality replaces the fixedness of emigration and return.

REFERENCES

Abadan-Unat, N.
1974 "Turkish external migration and social mobility", in P. Benedict, E. Tümertekin and F. Mansur (Eds), *Turkey: Geographic and Social Perspectives*, E. J. Brill, Leiden: 362-402.
1976 "Migration as an obstacle for re-integration in industry: the Turkish case", *Studi Emigrazione*, 13(43): 319-344.
1977 "Implications of migration for emancipation or pseudo-emancipation of Turkish women", *International Migration Review*, 11(1): 31-58.

Adepoju, A.
1974 "Migration and socio-economic links between urban migrants and their home communities in Nigeria", *Africa*, 44(4): 383-396.
1981 "Migration and socio-economic change in tropical Africa: policy and research", in J. Balán (Ed.), *Why People Move*, UNESCO, Paris: 317-336.

Ahlburg, D.A.
1994 "Return migration from the United States to American Samoa: evidence from the 1980 and 1990 censuses", *Pacific Studies*, 17(2): 71-84.

Anwar, M.
1979 *The Myth of Return: Pakistanis in Britain*, Heinemann, London.

Appleyard, R.
1962 "Determinants of return migration: a socio-economic study of UK migrants who returned from Australia", *The Economic Record*, 38(83): 352-368.

Arif, G.M., and M. Irfan
1997 "Return migration and occupational change: the case of Pakistani migrants returned from the Middle East", *Pakistani Development Review*, 36(1): 1-37.

Asch, B.J. (Ed.)
1994 *Emigration and its Effects on the Sending Country*, RAND, Santa Monica.

Athukorala, P.
1990 "International contract migration and the reintegration of return migrants: the experience of Sri Lanka", *International Migration Review*, 24(2): 323-346.

Axelrod, B.
1972 "Historical studies of emigration from the United States", *International Migration Review*, 6(1): 32-49.

Baines, D.
1991 *Emigration from Europe 1815-1930*, Macmillan, London.

Ballard, R., and C. Ballard

1977 "The Sikhs: the development of South Asian settlements in Britain", in J. L. Watson (Ed.), *Between Two Cultures: Migrants and Minorities in Britain*, Blackwell, Oxford: 21-56.

Barrett, A., and F. Trace

1998 "Who is coming back? The educational profile of returning migrants in the 1990s", *Irish Banking Review*, Summer: 38-51.

Bennett, B.C.

1979 "Migration and rural community development in central Dalmatia (Croatia)", *Papers in Anthropology*, 20(1): 75-83.

Böhning, W.R.

1975 "Some thoughts on emigration from the Mediterranean Basin", *International Labour Review*, 111(3): 251-277.

1979 "International migration in Western Europe: reflections on the past five years", *International Labour Review*, 118(4): 401-414.

1986 *Bibliography on International Return Migration*, International Migration for Employment Working Paper 16 (rev.), International Labour Office, Geneva.

Bovenkerk, F.

1973 "On the causes of Irish emigration", *Sociologia Ruralis*, 13(4-5): 263-275.

1974 *The Sociology of Return Migration: A Bibliographic Essay*, Publications of the Research Group on European Migration Problems 20, Nijhoff, The Hague.

Boyd, M.

1989 "Family and personal networks in international migration: recent developments and new agendas", *International Migration Review*, 23(3): 638-670.

Brettell, C.B.

1979 "Emigrar para voltar: a Portuguese ideology of return migration", *Papers in Anthropology*, 20(1): 1-20.

Buijs, G. (Ed.)

1993 *Migrant Women: Crossing Boundaries and Changing Identities*, Berg, Oxford.

Byron, M.

1994 *Post-War Caribbean Migration to Britain: the Unfinished Cycle*, Avebury, Aldershot.

Campbell, R.R., and D.M. Johnson

1976 "Propositions on counterstream migration", *Rural Sociology*, 41(1): 127-145.

Caroli, B.B.

1970 *Italian Repatriation from the United States, 1900-1914*, Center for Migration Studies, New York.

Castles, S., and G. Kosack
  1973 *Immigrant Workers and Class Structure in Western Europe*, Oxford University Press, Oxford.
Castles, S., and M.J. Miller
  1998 *The Age of Migration: International Population Movements in the Modern World*, Macmillan, London.
Cerase, F.P.
  1970 "Nostalgia or disenchantment: considerations on return migration", in S.M. Tomasi and M.H. Engel (Eds), *The Italian Experience in the United States*, Center for Migration Studies, New York: 217-239.
  1974 "Migration and social change: expectations and reality. A study of return migration from the United States to Italy", *International Migration Review*, 8(2): 245-262.
Cinel, D.
  1991 *The National Integration of Return Migration*, Cambridge University Press, Cambridge.
Cohen, R.
  1987 *The New Helots: Migrants in the International Division of Labour*, Avebury, Aldershot.
  1995 *The Cambridge Survey of World Migration*, Cambridge University Press, Cambridge.
Condon, S.A., and P.A. Ogden
  1996 "Questions of emigration, circulation and return: mobility between the French Caribbean and France", *International Journal of Population Geography*, 2(1): 36-50.
Connell, J., B. Dasgupta, R. Laishley, and M. Lipton
  1976 *Migration from Rural Areas: the Evidence from Village Studies*, Oxford University Press, New Delhi.
Connell, J., and R. King
  1999 "Island migration in a changing world", in R. King and J. Connell (Eds), *Small Worlds, Global Lives: Islands and Migration*, Pinter, London: 1-26.
Dahya, B.
  1973 "Pakistanis in Britain: transients or settlers?", *Race*, 14(3): 241-277.
Davison, B.
  1968 "No place back home: a study of Jamaicans returning to Kingston", *Race*, 9(4): 499-509.
Del Campo, S., and J.A. Garmendia
  1974 "The return of the emigrants", in G. Tapinos (Ed.), *International Migration*, CICRED, Paris: 210-221.
Díaz-Briquets, S., and S. Weintraub (Eds)
  1991 *Migration, Remittances and Small Business Development: Mexico and Caribbean Basin Countries*, Westview, Boulder.

Eikaas, F.T.

1979 "You can't go home again? Culture shock and patterns of adaptation amongst Norwegian returnees", *Papers in Anthropology*, 20(1): 105-115.

Entzinger, H.

1978 *Return Migration from West European to Mediterranean Countries*, World Employment Programme Working Paper 23, International Labour Office, Geneva.

Fawcett, J.T.

1989 "Networks, linkages and migration systems", *International Migration Review*, 23(3): 671-680.

Foeken, D.

1980 "Return migration to a marginal area in north-western Ireland", *Tijdschrift voor Economische en Sociale Geografie*, 71(2): 114-120.

Form, W.H., and J. Rivera

1958 "The place of returning migrants in a stratification system", *Rural Sociology*, 23(2): 286-297.

Frucht, R.

1968 "Emigration, remittances and social change: aspects of the social field of Nevis, West Indies", *Anthropologica*, 10: 193-208.

Gaillard, A.M.

1993 *A Bibliographical Overview of Return Migration*, Center for Migration Studies, New York.

Ghosh, B.

1996 "Economic migration and sending countries", in J. van den Broeck (Ed.), *The Economics of Labour Migration*, Edward Elgar, Cheltenham: 77-114.

Gilkey, G.R.

1967 "The United States and Italy: migration and repatriation", *Journal of Developing Areas*, 2(1): 23-35.

Glaser, W.A.

1978 *The Brain Drain: Emigration and Return*, Pergamon, Oxford.

Gmelch, G.

1980 "Return migration", *Annual Review of Anthropology*, 9: 135-159.

1986 "The adjustment of return migrants in the west of Ireland", in R. King (Ed.), *Return Migration and Regional Economic Problems*, Croom Helm, London: 152-170.

1987 "Work, innovation and investment: the impact of return migrants in Barbados", *Human Organization*, 46(2): 131-140.

1992 *Double Passage: the Lives of Caribbean Migrants Abroad and Back Home*, University of Michigan Press, Ann Arbor.

Gmelch, G., and R.E. Rhoades

1979 "Bibliography on return migration", *Papers in Anthropology*, 20(1): 187-196.

Gopinathan Nair, P.R.
1999 "Return of overseas contract workers and their rehabilitation and development in Kerala (India)", *International Migration*, 37(1): 209-242.

Gorter, C., P. Nijkamp, and J. Poot (Eds)
1998 *Crossing Borders: Regional and Urban Perspectives on International Migration*, Ashgate, Aldershot, UK.

Gould, J.D.
1979 "European inter-continental emigration. 1815-1914: patterns and causes", *Journal of European Economic History*, 8(3): 593-679.
1980 "European inter-continental emigration. The road home: return migration from the USA", *Journal of European Economic History*, 9(1): 41-112.

Griffin, K.
1976 "On the emigration of the peasantry", *World Development*, 4(5): 353-361.

Griffiths, S.L.
1979 "Emigration and entrepreneurship in a Philippine peasant village", *Papers in Anthropology*, 20(1): 127-144.

Gunatilleke, G. (Ed.)
1991 *Migration to the Arab World: Experience of Returning Migrants*, United Nations Press, Tokyo.

Hammar, T., G. Brochmann, K. Tamas and T. Faist (Eds)
1997 *International Migration, Immobility and Development*, Berg, Oxford.

Hernández Alvarez, J.
1966 "A demographic profile of the Mexican immigration to the United States", *Journal of Inter-American Studies*, 8(3): 471-496.
1967 *Return Migration to Puerto Rico*, Population Monograph 1, Institute of International Studies, University of California, Berkeley.

Hoffmann-Nowotny, H.-J.
1981 "A sociological approach to a general theory of migration", in M.M. Kritz, C.B. Keely and S.M. Tomasi (Eds), *Global Trends in Migration*, Center for Migration Studies, New York.

Kayser, B.
1972 *Cyclically-Determined Homeward Flows of Migrant Workers*, OECD, Paris.

King, R.
1978 "Return migration: a neglected aspect of population geography", *Area*, 10(3): 175-182.
1979 "Return migration: a review of some case studies from Southern Europe", *Mediterranean Studies*, 1(2): 3-30.
1980 *The Maltese Migration Cycle: Perspectives on Return*, Discussion Paper in Geography 13, Oxford Polytechnic, Oxford.
1986 *Return Migration and Regional Economic Problems*, Croom Helm, London.

1988   *Il Ritorno in Patria: Return Migration to Italy in Historical Perspective*, Occasional Publication 23, Department of Geography, University of Durham, Durham.

1996   "Migration in a world historical perspective", in J. van den Broeck (Ed.), *The Economics of Labour Migration*, Edward Elgar, Cheltenham: 7-76.

King, R., J. Mortimer, and A.J. Strachan
1984   "Return migration and tertiary development: a Calabrian case study", *Anthropological Quarterly*, 57(2): 112-124.

King, R., and A.J. Strachan
1983   *Return Migration: A Sourcebook of Evoluative Abstracts*, Discussion Papers in Geography 20, Oxford Polytechnic, Oxford.

King, R., A.J. Strachan, and J. Mortimer
1983   *Return Migration: A Review of the Literature*, Discussion Papers in Geography, 19, Oxford Polytechnic, Oxford.

1986   "Gastarbeiter go home: return migration and economic change in the Italian Mezzogiorno", in R. King (Ed.), *Return Migration and Regional Economic Problems*, Croom Helm, London: 38-68.

Kosack, G.
1976   "Migrant women: the move to Western Europe: a step towards emancipation?", *Race and Class*, 17(4): 369-379.

Kraljic, F.
1978   *Croatian Migration to and from the United States*, Ragusan, Palo Alto.

Krane, R.E.
1973   "The effects of cyclical international migration upon socio-economic mobility", *International Migration Review*, 7(4): 427-436.

Lawless, R.I., A. Findlay, and A.M. Findlay
1982   *Return Migration to the Maghreb: People and Policies*, Arab Papers 12, Arab Research Centre, London.

Lever-Tracey, C.
1989   "Return migration to Malta: neither failed immigrants nor successful guestworkers", *Australia and New Zealand Journal of Sociology*, 25(3): 428-450.

Levi, C.
1948   "Economic opportunity in Mexico and return migration from the United States", *Demography*, 33(3): 357-374.

Lipton, M.
1980   "Migration from rural areas of poor countries: the impact on rural productivity and income distribution", *World Development*, 8(1): 1-24.

Livi-Bacci, M.
1972   "The countries of emigration", in M. Livi-Bacci (Ed.), *The Demographic and Social Pattern of Emigration from the Southern European Countries*, Dipartimento Statistico-Matematico dell'Università di Firenze, Florence: 7-123.

Lopreato, J.
1962   "Economic development and cultural change: the role of emigration", *Human Organization*, 21(3): 182-186.
1967   *Peasants No More*, Chandler, San Francisco.

Lucassen, J., and L. Lucassen (Eds)
1997   *Migration, Migration History, History*, Peter Lang, Berlin.

Mabogunje, A.L.
1970   "A systems approach to a theory of rural-urban migration", *Geographical Analysis*, 2(1): 1-18.

Manganara, J.
1977   "Some social aspects of the return movement to rural Greece", *Greek Review of Social Research*, 29: 65-75.

Manners, R.A.
1965   "Remittances and the unit of analysis in migration research", *Southwestern Journal of Anthropology*, 21(3): 179- 195.

Mayano, D.M.
1973   "Individual correlates of coffee production in the New Guinea Highlands", *Human Organization*, 32(3): 305-314.

McArthur, H.J.
1979   "The effects of overseas work on return migrants and their home communities: a Philippine case", *Papers in Anthropology*, 20(1): 85-104.

Miracle, M.P., and S.S. Berry
1970   "Migrant labour and economic development", *Oxford Economic Papers*, 22(1): 86-108.

Moltmann, G.
1980   "American-German return migration in the nineteenth and early twentieth centuries", *Central European History*, 13(4): 378-392.

Muschkin, C.G.
1993   "Consequences of return migrant status for employment in Puerto Rico", *International Migration Review*, 27(1): 79-102.

Myers, G.C., and G. Masnick
1968   "The migration experience of New York Puerto Ricans: a perspective on return", *International Migration Review*, 2(2): 80-90.

Nutter, R.
1986   "Implications of return migration from the United Kingdom for urban employment in Jamaica", in R. King (Ed.), *Return Migration and Regional Economic Problems*, Croom Helm, London: 198-212.

Oberai, A.S., and H.K.M. Singh
1982   "Migration, production and technology in agriculture: a case study in the Indian Punjab", *International Labour Review*, 121(3): 327-343.

Olwig, K.F.
1993   *Global Culture, Island Identity. Continuity and Change in the Afro-Caribbean Community of Nevis*, Harwood Academic Publishers, Chur, Switzerland.

Paine, S.
1974   *Exporting Workers: the Turkish Case*, Cambridge University Press, Cambridge.

Papademetriou, D.G.
1985   "Emigration and return in the Mediterranean littoral", *Comparative Politics*, 18(1): 21-39.

Patterson, H.O.
1968   "West Indian migrants returning home", *Race*, 10(1): 69-77.

Pessar, P.R. (Ed.)
1997   *Caribbean Circuits: New Directions in the Study of Caribbean Migration*. Center for Migration Studies, New York.

Phillips, M.
1980   "Welcome home to Jamaica", *The Observer Magazine*, 12 October: 66-70.

Philpott, S.B.
1968   "Remittance obligations, social networks and choice amongst Montserratian migrants to Britain", *Man*, 3(3): 465-476.

1977   "The Montserratians: migration dependency and the maintenance of island ties to England", in J.L. Watson (Ed.), *Between Two Cultures: Migrants and Minorities in Britain*, Blackwell, Oxford: 90-119.

1999   "The breath of the beast: migration, volcanic disaster, place and identity in Montserrat", in R. King and J. Connell (Eds), *Small Worlds, Global Lives: Islands and Migration*, Pinter, London: 137-159.

Phizacklea, A. (Ed.)
1983   *One-Way Ticket: Migration and Female Labour*, Routledge and Kegan Paul, London.

Piore, M.J.
1979   *Birds of Passage: Migrant Labour in Industrial Societies*, Cambridge University Press, Cambridge.

Potts, L.
1990   *The World Labour Market: A History of Migration*, Zed Books, London.

Ramos, F.A.
1992   "Out-migration and return migration of Puerto Ricans", in G.J. Borjas and R.B. Freeman (Eds), *Immigration and the Workforce*, University of Chicago Press, Chicago: 49-66.

Ravenstein, E.G.
1885   "The laws of migration – I", *Journal of the Royal Statistical Society*, 48(2): 167-235.

1889   "The laws of migration – II", *Journal of the Royal Statistical Society*, 52(2): 241-305.

Reyneri, E.
1980:   "Emigration and the sending area as a subsidised system in Sicily", *Mediterranean Studies*, 2(1): 88-113.

Rhoades, R.E.

1979 "From caves to main street: return migration and the transformation of a Spanish village", *Papers in Anthropology*, 20(1): 57-74.

Richardson, A.

1968 "A shipboard study of some British-born immigrants returning home from Australia", *International Migration*, 6(4): 221-238.

Richardson, B.C.

1983 *Caribbean Migrants: Environment and Human Survival on St. Kitts and Nevis*, University of Tennessee Press, Knoxville.

Richmond, A.H.

1966 "Demographic and family characteristics of British immigrants returning from Canada", *International Migration*, 4(1): 21-27.

1968 "Return migration from Canada to Britain", *Population Studies*, 22(2): 263-271.

1984 "Explaining return migration", in D. Kubat (Ed.), *The Politics of Return: International Return Migration in Europe*, Center for Migration Studies, New York: 269-275.

Rogers, R.

1984 "Return migration in comparative perspective", in D. Kubat (Ed.), *The Politics of Return: International Return Migration in Europe*, Center for Migration Studies, New York: 277-299.

Rubenstein, H.

1979 "The return ideology in West Indian migration", *Papers in Anthropology*, 20(1): 21-38.

Saloutos, T.

1956 *They Remember America: The Story of the Repatriated Greek-Americans*, University of California Press, Berkeley.

Sarna, J.D.

1981 "The myth of no return: Jewish return migration to Eastern Europe 1881-1914", *American Jewish History*, 71(1): 267-278.

Segal, A.

1993 *An Atlas of International Migration*, Hans Zeff, London.

Shepperson, W.S.

1965 *Emigration and Disenchantment: Portraits of Englishmen Repatriated from the United States*, University of Oklahoma Press, Norman.

Shumsky, N.L.

1995 "Return migration in American novels of the 1920s and 1930s", in R. King, J. Connell and P. White (Eds), *Writing Across Worlds: Literature and Migration*, Routledge, London: 198-215.

Swanson, J.

1979 "The consequences of emigration for economic development: a review of the literature", *Papers in Anthropology*, 20(1): 39-56.

Tassello, G.

1983 L'emigrazione di ritorno: rassegna bibliografica", *Studi Emigrazione*, 20(72): 459-519.

Taylor, E.
1976   "The social adjustment of returned emigrants to Jamaica", in F. Henry (Ed.), *Ethnicity in the Americas*, Mouton, The Hague: 213-229.

't Hart, M.
1985   "Irish return migration in the nineteenth century", *Tijdschrift voor Economische en Sociale Geografie*, 76(3): 223-231.

Thomas-Hope, E.
1999   "Return migration to Jamaica and its development potential", *International Migration*, 37(1): 183-207.

Toren, N.
1976   "Return to Zion: characteristics and motivations of returning migrants", *Social Forces*, 54(3): 546-558.

Unger, K.
1981   "Greek emigration to and return from West Germany", *Ekistics*, 48(290): 369-374.

Useem, J., and R.H. Useem
1955   *The Western-Educated Man in India*, Dryden Press, New York.

Virtanen, K.
1979   *Settlement or Return: Finnish Emigrants in the International Overseas Return Movement*, The Migration Institute, Turku.

Watson, J.L.
1977   "The Chinese: Hong Kong villagers in the British catering trade", in J.L. Watson (Ed.), *Between Two Cultures: Migrants and Minorities in Britain*, Blackwell, Oxford: 181-213.

Western, J.
1992   *A Passage to England: Barbadian Londoners Speak of Home*, UCL Press, London.

Wiest, R.E.
1979   "Anthropological perspectives on return migration: a critical commentary", *Papers in Anthropology*, 20(1): 167-187.

Wyman, M.
1993   *Round-Trip to America: The Immigrants Return to Europe*, Cornell University Press, Ithaca.

Chapter 2

Return, Readmission and Reintegration: Changing Agendas, Policy Frameworks and Operational Programmes

Khalid Koser

INTRODUCTION

Having traditionally attracted relatively little attention, return migration is now emerging as an important issue on policy agendas, as demonstrated by cases such as those in Bosnia and Kosovo. These recent cases have also brought into focus a number of issues and considerations that are largely relevant to return migration in general. First, these flows have clearly shown how the political significance of return migration can match, and at times even outweigh, its numerical significance. Second, alongside its growing importance, efforts are being made to develop new policy frameworks for return – temporary protection representing one example. Finally, the situation in Kosovo and Bosnia is a reminder that return is by no means always a straightforward process, and it can present significant challenges to operational programmes.

This chapter expands upon these three themes. The first section asks why return migration is of increasing significance to contemporary policy agendas. After reviewing available data on the scale of return migration, it locates these flows within the changing global migration system to demonstrate their increasing political importance. It is in the context of this changing significance that a re-evaluation of existing policy frameworks and operational programmes for return is currently taking place. This is followed by two sections that review the main types of frameworks and programmes which exist, highlighting their strengths and weaknesses. The concluding section considers directions for the development of a more integrated approach to return migration.

THE INCREASING SIGNIFICANCE
OF RETURN MIGRATION ON POLICY AGENDAS

It is possible to suggest two main reasons why return migration has begun to rise towards the top of policy agendas. The first is that return migration now takes place on a very substantial scale. Particularly when they occur suddenly, the management of these movements can present significant challenges both for home countries as well as international and non-governmental organizations. These challenges can range from the practical – relating for example to the logistics of transportation – to the more conceptual, such as changes of citizenship. But besides a growing numerical importance, there are also indications that return migration is assuming increasing political significance due to changes in the global migration system leading to rising pressure, particularly in host countries, to induce – or sometimes even force – migrants to return home.

Before analysing these two trends in greater depth, it is necessary to clarify what exactly is meant by return migration. Few attempts have been made in the literature to identify different kinds of return migration, although a number of approaches are briefly worth mentioning (King, 1978; see also Chapter 1). The typology which is based on geographical criteria captures patterns of movement and return within the country of origin – distinguishing for example migrants who return to their home area from those who return to other areas within the country of origin. This typology is particularly pertinent for returning Bosnian refugees, who in many cases cannot return to their area of origin where they would now form an ethnic minority. On the other hand, the limits of this kind of geographical typology are demonstrated by the "ethnic" returns taking place in Central and Eastern Europe, where people may be "returning" to a "homeland" in which they have never lived.

Another simple classification can be made on the basis of temporal criteria, distinguishing occasional, periodic, seasonal, temporary and permanent return. The importance of return migration types other than permanent return is increasingly recognized by countries of origin seeking to tap the potential of their overseas nationals. While permanent return may be unlikely when it does not suit the career paths of migrants, temporary returns can still yield benefits for the country of origin, for example by facilitating investment of foreign capital, and providing for a means of maintaining transnational links.

Returns can also be subdivided by their cause into forced, planned and spontaneous movements. These distinctions have gained increasing political significance, particularly in the context of illegal immigrants, where the policy challenge for host countries is to encourage voluntary return rather than to pursue forced expulsions.

Finally, the two distinct traditions discernible in migration studies also apply to studies on return movements. One concerns the "process" of migration, while the other focuses on the "product" or consequences of migration after arrival. This chapter adopts a more inclusive approach, defining a "return cycle" as beginning before departure from a host country and ending after arrival in the country of origin. Particularly for returning refugees, reintegration can be a lengthy process, and, therefore, where relevant the paper extends the "return cycle" beyond the immediate post-arrival period.

The Growing Scale of Return Migration

Data on return migration share many of the problems which characterize data on international migration more generally. Common problems include the difficulties of measuring the time dimension in migration, inconsistencies in recording changes of residence, and complexities in defining and applying the concept of citizenship. Data on international migration have been characterized as patchy, often out-of-date, ambiguous and often incomparable across countries – and it is generally accepted that those relating to return migration are especially poor (Salt and Singleton, 1994).

A particular problem is that the measurement of return migration has traditionally not been a priority in either countries of origin or in host countries. This stems from the fact that for neither set of countries has return migration generally been considered a "problem" in the same way that the emigration of nationals or immigration of non-nationals often has. Even where host and origin countries do purport to have recorded the same return flow, there can be significant differences in their estimations. As mentioned in Chapter 1, during the 1970s German data on Italian repatriation exceeded Italian statistics on return migration from Italy by a factor of at least two (King, 1978). Part of the reason for this sort of inconsistency can be gleaned from a more recent example from Poland, where return migration during this decade has been substantial but has remained uncounted in official statistics, simply because most Polish emigrants during the 1980s left without registering as emigrants (Stola, 1998). Similarly, in Turkey there are no institutions which record data concerning the emigration or return of migrant workers – estimates on return rely only on data collected in host countries (Honeköpp and Tayanç, 1998).

Data deficiencies of this kind preclude any accurate global estimation of return migration. At the same time, certain official statistics on both outflows of non-nationals and inflows of nationals can at least provide an indication of general trends in return migration. Five data sets are briefly reviewed here, namely the voluntary repatriation of refugees worldwide; the immigration of nationals into selected European countries; the return of "ethnic nationals" following the political changes in the former USSR; the emigration of non-nationals from selected European countries; and finally expulsions from selected European countries. Combined, these data confirm that return migration occurs at a substantial rate, and suggest that it may be increasing.

Table 2.1 lists the numerically most significant voluntary repatriations of refugees during 1998 – the most recent year for which complete data are available.

Table 2.2 provides longitudinal data on the immigration of nationals into EU and EFTA countries for the 1990s up to 1996, after which comprehensive data are not yet available. These data relate to long term or permanent return, and are collected from a range of sources which vary across reporting countries. Although data are not available from all reporting countries, the table does provide an approximate indication of the scale of return migration to EU and EFTA countries. The data are distorted by the volume of return to Germany, particularly at the beginning of the decade, which is largely accounted for by the return of *Aussiedler* (immigrants of German descent). Data are also available for the return of nationals to a number of other countries. To illustrate, in 1995 Czech citizens accounted for nearly 5,000 of a total of 10,500 long term entries, and

Finn nationals for 5,800 of a total of 13,300. In 1996 Mexico had a total of 9.5 million of which 2.5 million were nationals (SOPEMI, 1998).

TABLE 2.1

SIGNIFICANT VOLUNTARY REPATRIATIONS WORLDWIDE (1998)

To	From	Number
Afghanistan	Pakistan	107,000
Angola	Congo-Kinshasa, Zambia	15,000
Bosnia and Herzegovina	Germany, Yugoslavia and others	128,000
Burundi	Congo-Kinshasa, Tanzania	25,000
Cambodia	Thailand	40,000
Congo-Brazzaville	Congo-Kinshasa	25,000
Congo-Kinshasa	Tanzania, Uganda, Zambia and others	56,000
Croatia	Yugoslavia	8,400
Ethiopia	Djibouti, Sudan and Kenya	11,000
Georgia (South Ossetia)	Russian Federation (North Ossetia)	1,500
Ghana	Togo	1,000
Guatemala	Mexico	3,900
Iraq	Iran	9,200
Liberia	Ghana, Sierra Leone and others	240,000
Mali	Algeria, Niger and others	240,000
Mauritania	Senegal, Mali	10,000
Niger	Algeria	5,000
Sierra Leone	Guinea, Liberia	20,000
Rwanda	Congo/Zaire	200,000
Somalia	Djibouti, Ethiopia, Kenya and others	50,000
Sudan	Congo-Kinshasa	15,000
Tajikistan	Kyrgyszstan, Afghanistan and others	3,800
Togo	Ghana	4,000

Source: USCR (1999).

TABLE 2.2

IMMIGRATION OF NATIONALS TO SELECTED EU AND EFTA COUNTRIES
(1990-97)

	1990	1991	1992	1993	1995	1996	1997
Austria	-	-	-	-	-	-	13,277
Belgium	12,193	13,330	11,713	10,707	9,812	9,638	9,609
Denmark	21,000	21,445	21,893	22,921	24,042	22,918	22,694
Germany	809,229	273,633	290,850	287,561	303,347	251,737	225,335
Greece	17,043	10,993	17,197	11,090	-	-	-
Spain	20,236	13,767	20,663	17,665	16,554	13,209	22,261
France	-	-	-	-	-	-	-
Ireland	-	227	256	200	-	17,700	20,500
Italy	70,035	56,004	54,849	-	15,865	-	28,816
Liechtenstein	-	-	-	-	-	-	-
Luxembourg	-	-	-	-	735	792	966
Netherlands	36,086	35,912	33,904	31,581	29,127	31,572	109,860
Portugal	-	-	-	-	-	-	-
Finland	7,066	5,763	4,204	3,921	4,877	5,755	5,417
Sweden	6,728	5,805	5,814	7,038	9,808	10,577	11,399
UK	105,562	117,162	102,718	91,799	91,395	98,565	97,000
Iceland	2,055	2,281	1,980	1,749	-	2,406	2,584
Norway	9,800	10,209	9,581	9,416	9,196	-	9,931
Switzerland	31,465	31,673	25,299	22,083	23,010	-	22,083
Total	1,148,498	598,204	600,921	517,731	537,768	464,869	601,732

Notes: "-" signifies no data available.

Source: Eurostat, 1998.

62

The return, particularly of "ethnic nationals", following the political changes in the former USSR and Central and Eastern Europe, represents a special but significant form of return migration, for which partial data are also available on a country-by-country basis (Council of Europe, 1997; SOPEMI, 1998). The most significant returns have been from the former USSR during this decade, although in general numbers have now declined. Among the return flows have been: 5.4 million ethnic Russians between 1990 and 1995; 290,000 Ukrainians in 1992; 240,000 Tatars to Crimea by April 1996, 10,000 people of Latvian origin; 15,000 Finns between 1990-96; two million *Aussiedler* between 1987-94, and 6,000 Pontian Greeks in 1996. In many cases, the trend has continued in more recent years. For example, in 1999 104.916 *Aussiedler* returned to Germany exceeding the number (103.0800) for 1998.

Table 2.3 provides 1996 data on the emigration of non-nationals from selected EU and EFTA countries. The data are disaggregated to show the three numerically most significant citizenships for each broad region of origin. A very important caveat is that these data record departures only, not subsequent arrivals, and it cannot necessarily be assumed that all departing non-nationals are returning to their countries of origin. Two points are worth highlighting from the Table. The first is the significant scale of emigration by citizens of former Yugoslavia, many of whom probably have returned to their various countries of origin following the Dayton Peace Accords in 1995. A second is that there is a low rate of emigration by nationals of poorer countries.

A final source of available data on return migration is the record of expulsions from various OECD countries (Table 2.4). Although expulsions have generally not been at a high rate, their political significance outweighs their numerical significance, which makes them worth including. Caution once again is required in interpreting these data, as in several countries data include individuals simply escorted to the border of the host country, and it cannot be assumed that these people necessarily have returned to their country of origin. Moreover, in some cases the data refer only to the notice of leave (see also Chapter 4).

TABLE 2.3
EMIGRATION FROM SELECTED EU AND EFTA COUNTRIES BY CITIZENSHIP (1996)

	Total	B	DK	D	L	NL	FIN	SE	UK	IS	CH
Total	**507,717**	**7,296**	**6,114**	**400,210**	**878**	**11,069**	**1,905**	**5,005**	**47,986**	**214**	**27,040**
Non EU & EFTA											
Europe	**331,008**	**1,105**	**1,966**	**303,258**	**222**	**2,787**	**1,065**	**1,659**	**5,051**	**89**	**13,806**
of which:											
Former Yugoslavia	**101,138**	**23**	**630**	**89,242**	**89**	**423**	**884**	**801**	**14**	**9,032**	-
Poland	73,336	275	285	71,824	29	287	61	211	0	52	312
Turkey	50,374	311	247	45,030	6	1,537	31	204	424	-	2,584
Asia	**80,594**	**1,653**	**1,413**	**49,354**	**196**	**2,973**	**340**	**1,385**	**18,061**	**32**	**5,187**
of which:											
Japan	11,276	829	196	5,015	52	1,202	37	233	2,837	3	872
China	7,706	175	148	4,740	42	250	105	184	1,437	11	614
India	6,851	120	115	4,824	41	147	24	65	902	1	612
Americas	**47,667**	**3,091**	**1,701**	**22,885**	**387**	**2,766**	**295**	**1,373**	**9,386**	**75**	**5,708**
of which:											
USA	28,179	2,270	1,215	13,915	333	1,647	211	719	4,929	50	2,890
Canada	6,115	263	201	1,535	10	286	47	100	2,940	12	721
Brazil	3,984	166	109	2,276	27	132	16	63	588	1	606
Africa	**34,129**	**1,318**	**720**	**22,992**	**58**	**2,167**	**170**	**400**	**4,364**	**4**	**1,936**
of which:											
Morocco	4,380	389	57	2,518	6	1,121	8	24	0	-	257
Algeria	3,000	61	8	2,753	5	20	5	6	0	1	141
South Africa	2,783	-	-	917	4	234	1	12	1,485	2	128
Oceania	**14,319**	**129**	**314**	**1,721**	**15**	**376**	**35**	**188**	**11,124**	**14**	**403**
of which:											
Australia	9,579	108	243	1,083	13	287	31	155	7,329	8	322
New Zealand	4,320	-	69	251	2	81	4	31	3,795	6	81

TABLE 2.4

STATISTICS ON EXPULSIONS
FROM SELECTED OECD COUNTRIES (1996-97)

Host country from which expelled	Total
France	14,400
Greece	19,000
Hungary	14,000
Italy	5,100
Japan	54,300
Netherlands	51,500[1]
Norway	2,000
Poland	5,000
Romania	12,000
UK	5,300

[1] Includes voluntary returns encouraged by the Government.

Source: SOPEMI (1998).

Return Migration
and the Changing International Migration System

As noted earlier in this chapter, alongside the growing numerical scale of return migration, a number of major trends in the changing global migration system have lent increasing political importance to the issue of return; and this in turn is demanding a revaluation of existing policy frameworks and programmes. Some of these trends are briefly noted below.

Return of skills

The so-called "brain drain" has been a major concern for many countries in Africa, Asia and Latin America over the last few decades – and it is a more recent concern for countries in Central and Eastern Europe and of the former USSR (Ardittis, 1992). In addition to efforts that discourage the migration of skilled nationals in the first place (Abella, 1995), many countries of origin have initiated programmes to encourage the return of skills – often in combination with IOM's Return of Qualified Nationals Programme. The success of such programmes has been varied[1]. What has perhaps added impetus to

---

[1] Logan (1992), see also Chapter 5 in this volume.

initiatives for return has been the more recent engagement of host countries in return programmes, partly in response to unemployment and recession, but also in recognition that assisted return can form an important part of broader development policy.

Irregular migration

Although data are scarce, there is a consensus in most industrialized countries that irregular migration is increasing.[2] This includes not only irregular entries, but also people who overstay their visas or residence permits. Such movements affect both host and transit countries since migrants may become "stranded" before they reach their destination. Irregular migration is also associated with the growing phenomenon of human trafficking which preys on the vulnerability of migrants. The return of trafficked migrants is widely viewed as a deterrent to further outflows and an essential element in anti-trafficking efforts (IOM, 1995). In addition to a raft of policies designed to prevent irregular migration, the question of how to humanely return irregular immigrants who have been apprehended is becoming an important issue of public debate.

Asylum seekers

Although the number of asylum applications in Europe has declined since a peak in 1992, they continue to be substantial, amounting to some 437,400 in 28 European countries in 1999. High application rates have coincided with falling refugee recognition rates, increasing backlogs of unresolved applications, and significant stay rates for rejected asylum seekers. In this context, the return of unsuccessful asylum seekers – again if possible on a voluntary basis – has become a pressing issue in most OECD countries (SOPEMI, 1998).

Refugees

The end of the Cold War precipitated optimism that many global conflicts would wind down, and that a significant proportion of refugees worldwide would be able to return home. The United Nations High Commissioner for Refugees (UNHCR) predicted that the 1990s would *be* the "decade of repatriation". Although repatriation has proved a more elusive solution than was initially expected, it has

---

[2] See in this connection Ghosh (1998).

nevertheless proceeded on a significant scale, as demonstrated by Table 1 above. UNHCR still considers voluntary repatriation to be the optimal durable solution for refugees, and return is therefore a policy being actively pursued (Koser and Black, 1999). Refugee repatriation has also attracted attention in many European countries, which have experienced in quick succession the two largest influxes of refugees – Bosnians then Kosovars – since the Second World War. Drawing particularly on the Bosnian experience, there are an increasing number of commentators arguing that some form of "temporary protection" should constitute the basis of a reformulated international refugee regime – of which return is envisaged as one of the central elements (Hathaway, 1997).

Ethnic returns

As illustrated above, the collapse of the former USSR has precipitated very substantial return flows of "ethnic" nationals to countries in Central and Eastern Europe and also to various states of the former USSR. While return rates have declined since a peak at the beginning of this decade, "ethnic" returns do continue and they have elicited an impressive range of return and readmission programmes in the countries of origin. There also remain a number of "potential" "ethnic" return movements, such as ethnic Koreans, of whom it is estimated that two million currently live in China, 500,000 live in both Central Asia and Russia, and 660,000 live in Japan (Council of Europe, 1997).

Returns driven by global economic changes

Structural and technological changes in the global economy have drastically reduced demands for labour migrants other than the highly skilled. In the Gulf States and South East Asia recently, these have resulted in return of considerable numbers of labour migrants, often overwhelming the receptive capacities of their countries of origin (Amawi, 1998). Further returns have been widely predicted (SOPEMI, 1998). As recession, restructuring and retrenchment continue in countries in Western Europe, attention there too has gradually turned to the return migration of less-skilled labour migrants.

POLICY FRAMEWORKS FOR RETURN
AND READMISSION

Amid the rapid development of policies governing conditions for entry over the past decade, return migration received relatively little policy attention. In response to its growing relevance, however, policy-making efforts relating to return and readmission have recently surged. On the one hand, a raft of new policy frameworks has been evolving as illustrated by the emerging regime of temporary protection – while at the same time existing frameworks are being re-evaluated, and reforms have been suggested.

A Typology of Policy Frameworks

This section identifies seven main policy frameworks pertaining to return and readmission policies, namely: expulsion and readmission agreements, safe country of asylum rules, temporary protection, refugee repatriation, the withdrawal of residence and work permits, the recovery of citizenship, and the return of qualified nationals. The coverage is by no means comprehensive, however these are all frameworks which are particularly relevant to contemporary policy debates.

The selection of these particular frameworks is also intended to be representative. Figure 2.1 locates each of these frameworks within the context of a basic typology of migrants, each framework broadly applying to a different migrant "type". This perhaps illustrates one of the challenges of revising current frameworks, which is to streamline procedures through the adoption of common approaches, while still respecting the varying needs and rights of different migrant types. The typology also categorizes the main country "types" involved in each framework. Most are centred on host countries, although in recognition of the administrative and procedural difficulties surrounding return, agreements including not just host and origin countries, but also transit countries, are evolving. For the origin country a main policy issue concerns the recovery of citizenship. The final framework considered covers the return of qualified nationals, which at the international level, is organized notably by IOM, in cooperation with origin and host countries.

FIGURE 2.1

A TYPOLOGY OF POLICY FRAMEWORKS PERTAINING TO RETURN AND READMISSION

Framework	Migrant "Type"	Parties
Expulsion, Readmission Agreements	Irregular migrants, unsuccessful asylum seekers	Origin, host and transit countries
"Safe country of asylum" rules	Asylum seekers	Origin, host and transit countries
Temporary protection	Displaced people	Host country
Refugee repatriation	"Convention refugees"	Host country
Withdrawal of permits	Labour migrants, seasonal workers	Host country
Recovery of citizenship	Returning (ethnic) nationals	Country of origin
Return of qualified nationals	Skilled migrants	International organizations

Expulsion and Readmission Agreements

As the two separate issues of irregular immigration and growing proportions of unsuccessful asylum seekers have attracted increasing attention in the industrialized nations, legal frameworks for their expulsion from host countries have become important (SOPEMI, 1998). Expulsion remains a politically sensitive issue, and has often failed to be realized because of obstacles which include: the lack of an international instrument to provide the basis for political consensus between host and origin countries; the lack of established administrative procedures for removal and readmission; political and sometimes humanitarian considerations; and uncertainty about the general situation in the country of origin.[3]

One response to such obstacles has been the conclusion of readmission agreements. These agreements stipulate procedures for the return of individuals from a host country and for their readmission either into a transit country or directly into their country of origin. Since 1993 there has been a marked proliferation of readmission agreements, especially in Central and Eastern Europe, targeted on the removal of irregular immigrants and unsuccessful asylum seekers (see Chapter 4 in this volume; also Ghosh, 1998).

---

[3] Secretariat for a Working Meeting on Policies and Practices with Respect to Rejected Asylum Seekers (1992).

Although European countries do have readmission obligations under certain provisions of multilateral agreements (e.g. the Schengen Agreement, the Nordic Passport Union Agreement and the Benelux Agreement), the majority of readmission agreements are bilateral. In addition, readmission provisions can be contained in other agreements – in particular in visa exemption agreements – in which the contracting parties commit themselves to readmit their nationals from the territory of the other contracting party. Finally, the EU's general cooperation agreements with third countries increasingly also incorporate clauses on the readmission of irregular migrants (Budapest Group, 1995).

The scope of bilateral readmission agreements differs considerably. Broadly, there are two types – those which exclusively cover nationals of state parties, and those which apply to nationals of third countries as well. The rationale for the former is to facilitate the return of nationals illegally present in a host country to their origin country. These agreements reaffirm the obligation in international law that a state readmit its citizens, and the agreements simply provide an opportunity to regulate procedural questions. Readmission agreements incorporating third country nationals are normally concluded between a transit country and a host country, and are considered as one element of the "burden-sharing" concept. While there is no obligation in international law for a transit country to readmit nationals of a third country, these agreements substantially create the obligation to readmit. Readmission agreements usually contain procedural provisions regarding return procedure, transit return arrangements, responsibility criteria, standard of proof, time limits and cost distribution, although the exact nature of these procedures can vary significantly (Noll, 1998).

In general, readmission agreements between neighbouring countries tend to be more inclusive than those between non-neighbouring countries, which typically only allow for the readmission of nationals. Western European countries, in view of their growing concerns over irregular immigration, favour agreements which are all-inclusive, whereas Central and Eastern European countries prefer to limit the scope of agreements, to guard against the possibility of becoming overburdened with irregular migrants returned from Western Europe. The motivations of countries to sign readmission agreements clearly vary according to whether they are host or transit countries. Countries of the EU have generally been willing to assist transit countries, for example by providing financial reimbursement for the consequences of illegal immigration (Budapest Group, 1995). Table 2.5 shows an approximate overview of readmission agreements between states in Western Europe and those in Central and Eastern Europe.

TABLE 2.5

READMISSION AGREEMENTS BETWEEN SELECTED EU STATES
AND CENTRAL AND EASTERN EUROPEAN STATES (1995)

	Czech Rep.	Estonia	Hungary	Lithuania	Poland	Romania	Slovenia
Austria	x		x		x	x	x
Belgium					x		x
Denmark		x		x			
France					x		x
Germany					x	x	
Italy					x		
Luxembourg					x		x
Netherlands					x		x
Spain					x		

Source: ICMPD (1995).

At the same time, and in response to the concerns of countries in Central and Eastern Europe, Western European countries have also sought to conclude readmission agreements with non-European countries of origin. In some cases financial and material assistance also form part of these agreements. Table 2.6 provides an overview of readmission agreements signed with non-European origin countries by the end of 1996. Most EU countries continue to negotiate readmission agreements with the main countries from which illegal immigrants originate (SOPEMI, 1998).

TABLE 2.6

READMISSION AGREEMENTS BETWEEN SELECTED WESTERN EUROPEAN STATES
AND SELECTED NON-EUROPEAN COUNTRIES OF ORIGIN.

Country	Chile	India	Morocco	Sri Lanka	Viet Nam
Belgium		x	x		
Denmark				x	
France	x		x		
Germany					x
Netherlands			x		x
Spain			x		
Switzerland				x	

Source: Budapest Group (1996).

Some Central and Eastern European states have also begun to sign readmission agreements with countries of origin. For example, Poland has signed agreements with Bulgaria, the Czech Republic, Croatia, Greece, Hungary, Moldova, Romania, the Slovak Republic, Slovenia and Ukraine. Negotiations are also in progress with Albania, Algeria, Bangladesh, Estonia, India, Kazakhstan, Latvia, Lithuania, Pakistan, Russia, Sri Lanka and Viet Nam (Budapest Group, 1995).

The pursuit of readmission agreements on a bilateral as opposed to multilateral level has resulted in a certain degree of "disfunctionality". Lithuania, for example, has been faced with a growing number of aliens because Belarus has been unwilling to readmit any category of migrants (Budapest Group, 1995). However, the meeting of the Expert Group of the Budapest Group in 1995 concluded that the network of readmission agreements was not yet sufficiently evolved for the systematic development of multilateral agreements (Budapest Group, 1996).

Doubts have also been raised about the effectiveness of readmission agreements. On the one hand they do provide a framework for overcoming some of the obstacles which have traditionally surrounded the removal of irregular migrants and unsuccessful asylum seekers, particularly those pertaining to coordination between host, transit and origin countries. On the other hand, they have often been unable to address obstacles to return of a more procedural nature, including identification, obtaining travel documents, bearing transport costs, and arranging escort and transit routes (Budapest Group, 1995).

Safe Country of Asylum Rules

In contrast to readmission agreements which focus on the removal of unsuccessful asylum seekers, safe country of asylum rules have evolved specifically in Europe and North America to determine the allocation of responsibility for hearing an asylum claim in the first place.

Three policy frameworks arise from the "safe country of asylum" concept (Abella, 1995). One concerns the definition of a "safe country of origin". EU member states have determined by law countries where the occurrence of persecution on political grounds, or of inhuman treatment, is deemed unlikely. A citizen of these countries is therefore excluded from invoking the right of asylum. The classification of a country as "safe" is a matter of governmental discretion in each member state, and there has been criticism of the criteria used in various countries to arrive at this judgement (Cornelius, 1994). As has been the case for irregular immigrants and unsuccessful asylum seekers, the return of asylum applicants to a safe country of origin has proved procedurally difficult, although this category of individuals is also included within certain readmission agreements between EU and non-European states.

A second framework encompasses the definition of a "first country of asylum", and applies specifically to the EU. This determines that the first country within the EU entered by a claimant will accept responsibility for considering their asylum claim. This provision exists in both the Dublin and Schengen Conventions. According to these texts, responsibility for considering asylum claims is determined as follows: if the applicant has a visa, the state which issued the visa is responsible; if the applicant has several visas, the state which issued the visa with the longest period of validity is responsible; and if the applicant has no visa, the first member of the Dublin or Schengen Conventions at whose frontier the applicant arrives is responsible.

"Safe third country" is yet another concept which is included in legislation in the EU and Canada. It means that asylum seekers who have travelled through other countries before reaching the country in which they are claiming asylum will not have their asylum claims examined, but instead will be returned to the transit country. A number of readmission agreements have been signed, mainly between states in Western Europe and those in Central and Eastern Europe, to provide for the return of asylum seekers to transit countries. A series of criteria are determined by various jurisdictions for the prescription of a safe third country, which mainly try to ensure that it is a country to which the asylum seeker can safely be returned. Criticisms have nevertheless been raised concerning the treatment of asylum seekers returned to certain transit countries, particularly if they are countries where the capacity for processing asylum claims may not yet exist (ECRE, 1995).

In order to ensure the protection of asylum seekers being returned to a safe third country, it has been proposed that a series of safeguards should be established (Noll, 1998). These include:

- a transit state should be required to prove that the asylum seeker would have access to proper asylum procedures and protection;
- provisions should be made relating to the responsibility of the transit state to examine the asylum applications of the returned asylum seekers;
- the transit state should be informed of the decision to return the asylum seeker in order to avoid summary rejection of the asylum claim or summary removal, and
- the asylum seeker must be informed of the opportunity to apply for asylum in the country to which he or she is being returned.

Temporary Protection

Since the early 1990s, the concept of "temporary protection" has developed to cover a range of regimes for the temporary admission of displaced people. It is a concept grounded in international and humanitarian law, and was ratified by the Executive Committee of UNHCR in 1980 and 1981. Temporary protection can be offered to people either in need of protection but not satisfying the strict criteria for refugee status, or in situations where individual screening of applicants is not possible.

In Europe the concept has most widely been applied to Bosnians – and more recently to the far smaller numbers of Kosovars who have been admitted to EU countries. Given that the administration and evolution of these regimes has been uneven across the EU, "temporary protection" can hardly be considered a consistent legal category (IGC, 1995; Marx, 1994; Thorburn, 1996). However, underpinning the various legal statuses offered in different countries, one concept was at least common to most European countries – that is, the notion that the protection offered was indeed "temporary". Thus unlike asylum under the 1951 UN Convention on the Status of Refugees, which has in practice come to represent a quasi-permanent status, the granting of temporary protection to Bosnians was based on the implicit assumption of their return after the end of the conflict (see Chapter 5 for a discussion of some of the issues involved).

In the Bosnian case, the relationship between "temporary protection" and return has proved far more complex than originally envisaged (Koser et al., 1998). Even after the Dayton Peace Accords in 1995, and the declaration by the UNHCR that temporary protection for Bosnians should now end, return has not been the major policy option in most EU member states. Instead, with the exception of Germany (Table 2.7), in most cases, the policy has been *de facto* regularization of the status of Bosnians who had initially been granted temporary protection. Arguably, it this experience that may have made EU states generally reluctant to resettle large numbers of Kosovar refugees.

TABLE 2.7

NUMBER OF BOSNIANS WITH TEMPORARY PROTECTION
AND AS A PERCENTAGE OF THE TOTAL BOSNIAN POPULATION
IN EU MEMBER STATES (as of 1 July 1997)

Country	Numbers	Percentage
Austria	8,609	9.7%
Belgium*	5,704	95.1%
Denmark	1,421	6.6%
Finland	0	0%
France*	7,394	49.3%
Germany	275,000	80.3%
Greece	250	6.3%
Ireland	16	1.8%
Italy*	8,827	100%
Luxembourg	466	34.6%
Netherlands	6,000	24.0%
Portugal	-	-
Spain	0	0%
Sweden	3,441	5.7%
United Kingdom*	3,340	55.6%

* In Belgium, France and Italy and the UK the regularization of the majority of the indicated populations is expected.

"-" = no data available.

Source: UNHCR (1997).

Provisions for the regularization of the status of Bosnians have fallen into two main categories. In Austria, Finland and Luxembourg provisions were made simply to transfer Bosnians with temporary protection *en groupe* to a more permanent status of residence. In contrast, in Denmark and the Netherlands, asylum applications which were originally suspended during the granting of temporary protection, have been assessed. For the majority the outcomes have been positive, with Bosnians being granted either full refugee status or some form of humanitarian status.

In both these cases of regularization, the change of status of temporary refugees applied only to Bosnians fulfilling certain criteria. Figure 2.2 lists these criteria for the countries concerned. This explains why a minority of Bosnians in Austria (8,609), Denmark (1,421), Luxembourg (238) and the Netherlands (6,000) still hold temporary protection. These groups , along with the vast majority of Bosnians in Germany, are now the targets of assisted return programmes.

FIGURE 2.2

VARIOUS CRITERIA FOR THE TRANSFERRAL OF BOSNIANS
WITH TEMPORARY PROTECTION TO A PERMANENT STATUS

Country	Criteria
Austria	• regular employment • private accommodation • no criminal record
Denmark	• subject to individual asylum applications
Finland	• arrival pre-Dayton • resident for 2 years
France	• subject to individual asylum applications
Luxembourg	• regular employment • private accommodation • no criminal record
Netherlands	• arrival before 1 January 1994
Sweden	• subject to individual asylum applications

Source: Black et al. (1997).

Refugee Repatriation

Voluntary repatriation is often considered the best so-called durable solution for the problem of refugees. However, in many industrialized states permanent residence rights have historically been conferred upon people recognized as Convention refugees. This contrasts with the position in most countries in Africa, for example, where refugees are expected to repatriate voluntarily when it is safe to do so.

The most important legal instrument pertaining to the repatriation of refugees is the principle of *non-refoulement*, that is, protection against forced repatriation. Article 33 of the 1951 UN Convention prohibits "the involuntary return of refugees "in any manner whatsoever" to the frontiers of territories where their lives or freedom would be threatened. However, as already indicated, this legal provision has not prevented sizeable involuntary repatriation movements.

Withdrawal of Permits

Legal frameworks also exist in EU member states concerning the withdrawal of residence and work permits from long stay migrants (Council of Europe, 1991). The four main criteria used by member states for the withdrawal of residence permits relate to: prolonged absence and voluntary departure from the host country, long term unemployment, lack of means, termination of employment contract and criminal offences. These criteria vary between the member states – for example, a permit can be withdrawn following three months of continuous absence from Greece, compared with three years of continuous absence from France.

Most OECD countries require seasonal workers to leave the country on expiry of their contract. Exceptional criteria can be applied, for example in Switzerland where seasonal workers who have resided in the country for a total of 36 months over four consecutive years can request that their temporary residence permit be converted into an annual permit.

The actual deportation of people from whom permits are withdrawn nevertheless remains a sensitive issue. The courts of most member states have weighed the impact of an expulsion with respect to Article 8, concerning respect for private and family life, of the European Convention on Human Rights. It is rare for the national of another EU member state to be expelled when he or she has been residing lawfully in a member state. This is not generally the case for nationals of non-member states (see Chapter 3).

Recovery of Citizenship

The legal frameworks pertaining to the readmission of nationals into their country of origin are far more straightforward than those that concern their removal from a host country or their readmission into a transit country. This is because of an obligation in international law to readmit nationals. As noted above, readmission agreements between host and origin countries are one method of overcoming the more administrative obstacles that can arise during readmission.

One more complex issue of current relevance, however, concerns the recovery of citizenship for returning nationals who have been absent for long periods. In the case of most EU countries, permanent return demonstrated by a period of residence in the country of origin is normally the main criterion for the recovery of citizenship. In November 1995, as part of a new migration policy framework, Spain amended its legislation for the recovery of Spanish nationality, by suspending the requirement of ten year legal residence (SOPEMI, 1998).

The recovery of citizenship has been a more pressing issue for repatriating "ethnic" nationals in the wake of the political changes in the former Soviet Union and Central and Eastern Europe. There are a number of procedural differences between these countries centring on criteria for recovering citizenship and the repatriation decision-making process. For example, in Germany, Russia, Latvia, Lithuania, Greece and Romania, the right to citizenship is recognised on arrival, whereas in Finland and Ukraine the right is recognised after a period of residence. In Germany, Poland, Finland and Greece, the repatriation decision is made by the state. The decision is normally taken in the candidate's current country of residence. This provides the opportunity to control the repatriation process, for example by restricting the number of returnees and staggering arrivals – although Germany is the only country to have placed a ceiling on the number of arrivals at 225 000 a year since 1992. In contrast, in Russia, Ukraine and Latvia, the initiative for return generally rests with the individual. It is not compulsory to file a repatriation application in the country of residence, and there is no centralized decision-making process (Council of Europe, 1997).

The Return of Qualified Nationals

A final policy framework worthy of consideration is that organized at an international institutional level notably by IOM, to target the return of qualified nationals. While the return of qualified nationals was originally conceived as a specific programme in 1974, it has since developed into a broader policy framework which now encapsulates a whole range of programmes (Pires, 1992).

The framework aims to provide a cost-efficient multilateral mechanism for channelling the highly-skilled personnel required in priority development sectors of the economy in the country of origin. It provides specialized "job broker" services and administers support facilities for the assisted individuals. The specific tasks include:

- identification of specific posts which cannot be filled by qualified personnel available locally but could be filled by an expatriate national;
- implementation of recruitment campaigns in host countries to locate, advise and inform potential returnees;
- pre-selection of candidates on the basis of an evaluation of their professional training and experience, and
- support and assistance during the return and reintegration phase.

Within these broad parameters, a variety of programmes now exist. The original programme was targeted on return to Latin America generally from a range of European host countries, including most significantly Switzerland, Germany and Italy. It was followed in 1981 by a return programme to Africa, which included host countries in both Europe and North America. Alternative programmes within the framework have targeted individual origin countries – for example Nicaragua in 1991 – often in response to specific development needs, as well as specific host countries – for example the framework has been used for the return of qualified Bosnians from Germany.

Various evaluations of earlier programmes show that they have usually scored at least a qualified success. Despite difficult prevailing social and economic conditions in many origin countries, qualified nationals have returned, often permanently. While matching jobs and skills have always been a basic objective of these programmes, more recent ones are giving even closer attention to the demand-led criteria, reflecting priority needs of the country, in the selection of candidates, thereby enhancing their development impact (see Chapter 5 for further discussion). A criticism which was often levelled against earlier programmes was that they failed to sufficiently orient return towards the specific development requirements of the country of origin. In response, more recent programmes have used demand-led criteria in the selection of candidates.

OPERATIONAL PROGRAMMES FOR RETURN AND REINTEGRATION

Within the context of policy frameworks such as those above, there exists a wide range of operational programmes for return and reintegration. While some programmes have existed for many years, there has also been a recent proliferation of new programmes. In many cases these have been targeted on a specific migrant group – for example "ethnic returnees" – or on a specific migrant "type", such as displaced persons granted temporary protection. There have also been changes in the organization of certain programmes, including an increasing number of new bilateral partnerships between host countries and countries of origin.

Typology of Return Programmes

It is possible to devise a typology of return and reintegration programmes on the basis of numerous distinctions, perhaps the most important of which are between voluntary and involuntary return, permanent and temporary return, and assisted and unassisted return. Given the overall aim of this chapter, this section concentrates on programmes aimed at voluntary, permanent and assisted return. Attention is focussed in turn on the roles and contributions during return programmes of host countries, countries of origin, bilateral partnerships between these two sets of countries, and international organizations. To lend coherence to the discussion, four specific case studies are used which illustrate the roles of these various parties (Figure 2.3). Each case study also covers a different migrant "type", thus allowing reflection on the extent to which different initiatives are appropriate for different migrants. The case studies are intended to be representative of the range of operational programmes for return and reintegration, rather than comprehensive.

FIGURE 2.3

A TYPOLOGY OF OPERATIONAL PROGRAMMES
PERTAINING TO ASSISTED RETURN AND REINTEGRATION

Parties	Case Study	Migrant "type"
Host countries	Bosnian return from the EU	Refugees
Country of origin	Ethnic returns to Central and Eastern Europe and states of the former USSR	"Ethnic returnees"
Host country-country of origin	Germany-Eritrea Professional Reintegration Programme	Skilled return
International organization	IOM Assisted Return Programmes	Unsuccessful asylum seekers, irregular migrants, transit migrants

The first case study concerns the return of Bosnian refugees from EU countries, and focuses specifically on the role of the host countries. The second case study is of the return and reintegration of "ethnic nationals" to Central and Eastern Europe and the republics of the former Soviet Union. Most of the programmes have been coordinated by the countries of origin. The third case study illustrates the increasing preponderance of partnerships between host countries and countries of origin, illustrated through the example of the bilateral agreement between Germany and Eritrea targeting the return of skills. Finally, attention is turned to international initiatives, focusing particularly on IOM Assisted Voluntary Return Programmes for unsuccessful asylum seekers and irregular migrants, including transit migrants.

The Role and Contribution of Host Countries: Assisted Return from the EU to Bosnia

In organizing the return of Bosnians, important roles have been assumed by international organizations such as IOM and UNHCR, international NGOs, and by the Bosnian authorities (Black et al., 1997). At the same time, host countries have been particularly active in such programmes The wide range of programmes initiated by the various member states provide a fairly comprehensive overview of the types of contributions that host countries can make.

Within the range of programmes developed by EU countries to assist the return of Bosnians after the Dayton Peace Accords in 1995, it is possible to identify three clear sets of distinctions, each of which pertain to policy-making for return and reintegration in a wider context. First, a distinction can be made between "passive" and "active" approaches followed by the various host countries, although the difference has often been one of degree. More passive approaches tend to rely on pre-existing schemes for return and reintegration – for example current IOM Assisted Return Programmes. More active approaches have involved the development of new programmes specifically for Bosnians. These include efforts to link return with rehabilitation through the return of talent or area development schemes, a strong monitoring component, and a firm engagement with Bosnian community representatives.

Secondly, it is possible to distinguish between three different policy debates. The first concerns whether simply to facilitate or actively to promote return. The second concerns whether policies orientated towards inclusion or exclusion in the host country are more likely to achieve lasting return. The third concerns the type of assistance provided and particularly the relative merits of cash incentives to individuals versus more comprehensive repatriation programmes.

A third and final distinction worth drawing is between those programmes organized by the state, and those by non-governmental organizations. In practice the two parties have often acted in partnership over the return of Bosnians, although normally there has been a division of labour, with each taking responsibility for different elements of assistance. NGOs have particularly made a contribution to reintegration activities, such as house reconstruction. Non-governmental organizations based in host countries which have been especially active in the Bosnian return include Edinburgh Direct Aid (UK), Surviving the Winter (Germany) and Equilibre (France).

Return assistance

Three main types of return assistance have been provided by the host countries, namely organized travel (e.g. Austria and Sweden), the payment of travel costs (e.g. various German Länder), and one-off additional payments or instalment grants (e.g. the Netherlands). The exact nature of each of these assistance types has varied considerably.

Organized travel in countries such as Denmark has incorporated not just logistical arrangements but also pre-departure counselling. Organized return from the UK includes special provisions for the return of large household items and sometimes motor vehicles. Organized return from Germany and Austria also incorporates a post-return monitoring element.

By far the greatest differences in approach have related to additional instalment payments. The exact relationship between the availability and the level of these grants, and the return rate, remains unclear. A report from the Swedish Immigration Board (1997) stated that increased grants resulted in an increased number of applications for return, although closer analysis suggested that in practice returnees had been planning to return in any case, but as the intention to increase instalment grants was widely known, they waited until it was enacted to submit their application. Neither is there conclusive evidence that those German Länder which have paid higher grants have achieved higher rates of voluntary return. Moreover, grants are reported to have had a minimal effect on long-term reintegration, as returnees have often spent them quickly on consumable items, household goods, and rent (Black et al., 1997).

Reintegration assistance

In addition to direct cash payments, the most common forms of assistance given to Bosnian returnees are help in housing and employment. Germany, Sweden and Austria all offer assistance to returnees for housing reconstruction. The type and level of assistance vary between available programmes. For example, some programmes only provide construction materials for returnees to make the repairs themselves. Another approach has been adopted by Caritas Sweden which is conducting relevant training in Sweden for returnees to enable them to carry out necessary repairs on their houses. In the shorter term, there are a number of projects in Germany targeting the construction of shelters, for example for returnees whose homes have been destroyed or are inaccessible.

It does not appear that the offer of housing reconstruction is a significant incentive to return voluntarily, or a guarantee that returnees will remain in the return area. Part of the reason may be that housing reconstruction still remains minimal. Between Hilfswerk and Caritas, only 100 houses were reconstructed in 1997 for 8000 returnees from Austria. In 1997 Caritas Sweden only had the budget to repair a total of 200 flats in Sarajevo. The Swedish International Development Agency (SIDA) programme in Sanski Most had a budget for the reconstruction of only 120 houses.

Projects linked to employment for returnees in Bosnia have mainly been coordinated by the IOM, for example through the Return of Qualified Nationals Programme. At the same time, there are a number of programmes initiated by host country governments and NGOs which have run in parallel. The Nordic Pilot Project, implemented by Denmark, Sweden and Norway, organizes the temporary return of qualified Bosnian nationals to posts within their professional fields. There are other examples of private initiatives, mainly from the Nordic countries, which variously focus on training or provide business loans to qualified returnees. Renningsborg, a non-profit company in Sweden, has contributed start-up capital and equipment to entrepreneurs.

Area reconstruction

To varying degrees, host countries have recognized that the key to lasting return is to secure safe and adequate conditions upon return. Reconstruction assistance and, more broadly, development assistance, are increasingly viewed as laying the foundations for return migration. In conjunction with wider UNHCR programmes, a number of host countries have identified target areas for reconstruction within Bosnia, largely reflecting the origins of the Bosnian populations they host. Reconstruction assistance programmes have tended to integrate various elements, including shelter reconstruction, infrastructure, employment (including micro-enterprise schemes), and in some cases technical cooperation with local authorities.

A particular type of reconstruction assistance gaining currency with host governments and Bosnian municipalities is municipal twinning. One of the first twinning projects was initiated by the Danish Ministry of Interior and the Danish municipalities of Holmegaard and Otterup which had hosted refugees from the Kljuc area. The project involved relocating two Bosnian villages to Kljuc. Fourteen refugees from Kljuc who had been living in Holmegaard and Otterup, returned with the houses in which they lived in Denmark, and lived in them while reconstructing their own homes in Bosnia. The programme has also included direct support to the municipality and the exchange of delegations from Kljuc and the Danish municipalities (Black et al., 1997).

Information

A final form of return assistance for Bosnians in the EU has been the provision of information to assist refugees to make an informed decision on whether to return. Two main types of information have been provided. First, many host countries have established information centres, published information reports and organized public information campaigns. The main aim of these initiatives is to provide information on existing return programmes, including the benefits associated with them.

A second type of information provided has related to current conditions in Bosnia, and it is upon this information that refugees are to make an informed decision about whether, when and where to return. Attempts by governments and NGOs to provide this information have often been received with distrust. In response, host countries now permit refugees to return to Bosnia temporarily to assess conditions for themselves. In certain countries, such as the Netherlands, these programmes simply permit these return visits by allowing Bosnians to return to the host country without loss of status within a specified time period. In other countries, such as Denmark and Sweden, these visits are more proactively encouraged, and grants are available to meet the cost of the visit.

The Role and Contribution of Countries of Origin: the Return of "Ethnic Nationals" to Central and Eastern Europe and the States of the Former USSR

In recent years a wide variety of programmes have been developed in countries of Central and Eastern Europe and the former USSR. One of these concerns a very specific type of return flows – namely, "ethnic" return migration. Assistance provided has often covered both return and reintegration.

Return assistance

It is possible broadly to distinguish between direct and indirect return assistance offered by countries of origin. Direct assistance takes two main forms. One is organizing and physically transporting return migrants back to their country of origin. This has been the case in a number of Central and Eastern European states, particularly where return has been from a neighbouring country (Council of Europe, 1997). A second form of direct assistance is to pay for returnees to organize their own transportation back to the country of origin. This form has also been offered by most European countries affected by ethnic returns. In 1991, for example, the Czech authorities paid a total of 49 million crowns for the transportation of Volhynian Czechs from Russia to the Czech Republic (Bubeník and Lupták, 1991). Transport costs are normally only paid where the decision to return has been made in the country of departure – they are not made in retrospect upon arrival. A less obvious form of direct assistance from a country of origin is the pre-departure preparation offered to returning "ethnic Greeks" by the Greek state, which includes Greek language instruction.

One form of indirect return assistance provides incentives designed to encourage potential returnees to return. Common measures include: tax incentives to attract back investments; grants and subsidies to cover the initial costs of resettlement, and a guarantee of accommodation in the short term. All of the countries of Central and Eastern Europe affected by "ethnic returns", as well as Russia, offer various types of incentives to potential repatriates (Council of Europe, 1997).

In general, the costs of both direct and indirect return assistance have been met by the countries of origin themselves. There are however a few examples where aid is received from abroad – normally on a bilateral basis and for specific programmes. In Latvia, for example, the Skrunda Fund, supported by Sweden, grants assistance for those returning from Russia. Greece and Lithuania both receive limited aid from the Council of Europe's Social Development Fund.

Reintegration assistance

Key elements common to most reintegration assistance packages offered by countries of origin are accommodation, access to the labour market, and social welfare. The nature of the assistance for accommodation varies widely across different countries of origin, although the range of assistance types is well illustrated in the single case of Greece, which offers different forms of assistance to different categories of returnees (Glytsos, 1995).

For Greek emigrants returning home (mainly labour migrants from Western Europe), easy access to mortgages and housing allowances are offered, provided the house is bought with foreign exchange. Housing cooperatives have also been established to provide information and assistance. For Greek political refugees returning home, every effort is made to identify and return confiscated property, and these returnees are given priority for mortgages. The most comprehensive accommodation assistance is offered to returning "ethnic Greeks". Immediately upon return they are housed in "Hospitality Centres", where they are entitled to 15 days of free accommodation and food, as well as assistance on bureaucratic matters. For the following six months they live in "Reception Villages", which are self-contained communities providing training and education, as well as subsidized food. In the next stage returnees move to houses in the community for which the Greek state pays the rent for two years. The final stage is permanent settlement, and even at this stage rent subsidies are available.

Common obstacles to integration in the labour market include the language barrier, access to employment and the geographical concentration of returnees (Council of Europe, 1997). Assistance programmes can take various forms, but normally cover training, initial support during a period of unemployment, and assistance in finding employment (Council of Europe, 1991). A number of countries offer vocational training, for example Germany, Greece, Russia and Finland. Germany, Greece and Finland also offer language training, which can be particularly essential for returning "ethnic nationals" or for children brought up abroad.

Most of the countries in Central and Eastern Europe affected by "ethnic returns" also provide unemployment benefits for fixed periods until employment is found. Focusing on assistance in finding employment, a distinction exists between initiatives targeting employees and the self-employed. For employees, the Czech state makes a commitment to returnees from Russia to locate a job for at least one member per family within one year of return (Bubeník and Lupták, 1991). In Russia, the state offers potential employers incentives to employ repatriates in the form of tax concessions and compensation payments (Council of Europe, 1991).

While the primary focus of reintegration assistance programmes is on the migrants themselves, countries of origin often attempt to gear the potential of returnees towards the wider needs of the national economy. One way of achieving this is through the geographical dispersion of returnees, particularly into less developed areas. In Greece, a lump sum is paid to those returnees who choose to settle in the countryside (Glytsos, 1995). In both Poland and Germany, the entire reception process is decentralized, with the dual objective of integrating repatriates by dispersing them throughout the territory and of ensuring the payment of costs by both the state and the regions (Council of Europe, 1991). Another method is to concentrate returnees in particular sectors of the economy. In Germany, incentives are provided in order to encourage the activities of self-employed returnees in specific economic sectors, particularly agriculture, trade and research.

A third element of reintegration assistance commonly offered to returnees by countries of origin covers social welfare – including health, counselling, social security and education. The Czech Republic, for example, offers a health check-up and free health insurance to "ethnic returnees" (Bubeník and Lupták, 1991). Germany and Russia both offer psychological support to returnees in need (Council of Europe, 1991). Greece also offers counselling of a more general nature, including on overcoming cultural barriers (Glytsos, 1995).

A specific aspect of social welfare concerns the pension and social security rights of returnees. In most countries, returnees enjoy the same social rights as other citizens, but an issue which is of importance to returnees is the extent to which their social security and pension payments in the host country are transferable. Generally, these rights are lost upon leaving the host country, unless a bilateral agreement is signed between the host country and country of origin. Such agreements are still not widespread, although Russia is exceptional in having concluded several agreements – with Tajikistan, Latvia, Turkmenistan, Estonia, Georgia, the Kyrgyz Republic and Belarus (Council of Europe, 1997).

Most countries of origin in Central and Eastern Europe, as well as Russia, offer a range of educational services to returnees, particularly focused on children and students. Germany offers language courses and study grants, Russia offers language assistance, Finland offers bilingual teaching in Finnish and repatriate's mother tongue, Greece offers language and cultural courses, and Lithuania has established a school for the children of repatriates in Vilnius (Council of Europe, 1991).

The role of private associations, including non-governmental organizations and churches

Origin country initiatives for return and reintegration are often supported by the activities of private associations, NGOs and the church. In some cases, associations are involved even outside the country of origin. The Society of Ingrian Finns, for example, is well established in the regions where populations of Finnish origin live. Apart from promoting rights in the country of residence, the society takes part in the repatriation process, advising candidates on the procedure to follow and registering applications for departure.

In most cases, associations concentrate their activities in the country of origin. Examples from within Finland include the Ingrian cultural society, which helps repatriates rediscover their cultural identities, and the legal advisory centre for refugees. In Poland, the Polish Association complements government action by putting municipalities in touch with candidates for repatriation, by assisting repatriates to make a decision by inviting a member of the family to the municipality in question, and by providing financial and legal assistance. Associations are similarly active in other countries, including Germany and Latvia.

The Role and Contribution of Bilateral Partnerships: The Professional Reintegration Programme between Germany and Eritrea

Bilateral partnerships between host countries and countries of origin are becoming an increasingly popular method of organizing and assisting return and reintegration. Usually they are signed between host countries in Europe or North America, and countries from which significant populations of either labour migrants, asylum seekers or refugees originate. In most cases, these agreements focus on the return of skilled or qualified people – although in particular cases, such as between Germany and Turkey and the Netherlands and Morocco, bilateral agreements have a broader scope. Well documented examples of return agreements include those between: Austria and Chile, the Netherlands and Angola, France and Senegal, and Sweden and Bosnia (Werth, 1995; SOPEMI, 1998; Diatta, 1998).

Here, the focus is on one specific case study – the Professional Reintegration Programme between Germany and Eritrea (Black et al., 1997; see also Chapter 5). Germany has been particularly active in the realm of bilateral agreements, and has signed similar reintegration agreements with over 20 countries, including Chile, Turkey, Viet Nam and Mozambique. The specific policy instruments used in the Germany-Eritrea case are broadly the same as those used for all the other agreements. The programme is also fairly extensive, covering for example both employees and the self-employed, and provides a reasonable overview of the policy tools available to bilateral agreements on return and reintegration.

Overview of the Professional Reintegration Programme

The Professional Reintegration Programme consists of two sub-programmes: a salary subsidy programme and a business start-up programme. The salary subsidy programme involves the payment to people returning from Germany to employment in Eritrea of a supplement to their local salary. The payment is made directly from a budget in Germany established by the Ministry for Development, to a local bank account in Eritrea. There are two types of subsidy available. The first is the "standard" subsidy, which involves payment of a supplement of DM 800 per month, for a period of one year. The second is the "expert" subsidy, involving the payment of a supplement of 60 percent of the net salary earned in Germany immediately prior to return, for a period of two years. There is a local office to which subsidized returnees can refer in case of problems.

Business start-up loans are made from a revolving credit fund, equally funded by the German and Eritrean Governments. Loans amount up to DM 100,000, and in exceptional cases up to DM 200,000. In Germany loans are managed through the Deutsche Ausgleichbank (DtA), and in Eritrea through the Commercial Bank of Eritrea (CBE). The loan periods last from three to 15 years depending on the size of the loan and the nature of the business. Interest on loans is charged at 8 percent. There is also a grace period for repayments of up to two years. The equity ratio is 30-40 percent. People eligible for loans fall into two broad categories. The first consists of Eritreans returning from Germany, on whom the German contribution to the fund is intended to be concentrated. The second consists of Eritreans returning from neighbouring countries, and internally displaced people, these being the focus of the Eritrean contribution to the fund.

An important additional element of the programme is the possibility of combining salary subsidies with business start-up loans. Subsidized employees can apply for loans to start their own enterprises after the end of their subsidy period. The programme provides for a one-off payment to subsidized employees to allow them to hire local consultants to assist in preparing a feasibility study for a business start-up loan.

In addition to the credit fund for loans, DtA has established a local consulting office in Asmara. The office serves two main functions. First, it monitors through regular visits, and trains entrepreneurs. This training includes regular seminars (in 1997, these covered book keeping, cultivation planning, workshop management and herb gardening). The second function is to train CBE staff (particularly on credit issues). Both sets of training are organized via local consultants who are initially trained by DtA staff and visiting experts from Germany, with the intention that, after a limited period, DtA should be able to close its local consulting office and leave behind trained local bank officials, entrepreneurs and also instructors.

Since returns began in 1993, 482 returnees had been subsidized by the Professional Reintegration Programme by the end of June 1997, and 65 loans had been disbursed. While the Professional Reintegration Programme has been evaluated in greater depth elsewhere (Black et al., 1997), it is worth briefly focusing on those strengths and weaknesses that arise specifically from the bilateral nature of the programme, in order to emphasize the applicability of this particular case study to the wider context of bilateral agreements (see also Chapter 5).

One of the programme's key strengths has been to ensure local participation in Eritrea. This is one way that the programme has secured a longer-term benefit for Eritrea than that provided by the return of skilled nationals alone. The programme has fostered the development of a local institutional capacity, through the provision of training for entrepreneurs, for bank and other staff, and for local instructors, and by the location in Asmara of the consulting office to monitor the programme. Specific aspects of the programme also support opportunities for longer-term reintegration, for example the possibility of combining a salary subsidy with a business start-up loan, and the provision of a budget for assistance in writing feasibility studies.

At the same time, key weaknesses arise from a lack of coordination. At one level this lack of coordination has been between Germany and Eritrea. For example, criteria for subsidized returns determined in Germany have sometimes been so strict that this has prevented the return of perfectly capable Eritreans under the programme. Moreover, insufficient attention has been paid to defining qualifications and skills in the context of local labour market conditions in Eritrea. At another level, the lack of coordination has been between the programme as a whole and its "users", namely the migrants themselves. In particular, a failure to address the employment and other needs of family members has significantly reduced the number of returns of skilled nationals with families.

The role and contribution of international organizations:
IOM Assisted Return Programmes

The two main international organizations with operational programmes for return and reintegration are UNHCR – focusing mainly on refugees and displaced people – and IOM. In addition to the Return of Qualified Nationals Programme (already discussed above and in Chapter 5), IOM runs several other return programmes. Among these are Assisted Return Programmes, targeted on illegal immigrants, unsuccessful asylum seekers, and also "stranded" migrants in Eastern and Central Europe.

All these programmes consist of three basic stages: pre-departure, transportation and post-arrival (IOM, 1998). Pre-departure assistance covers three main categories: information (dissemination and counselling), medical (medical examinations and documentation, a health care availability database and medical care) and transportation (pre-departure assistance, travel allowances and return grants). The transportation stage may include transport (movement coordination, transit assistance, escort assistance, unaccompanied baggage, documents and formalities) and medical aspects (pre-embarkation medical checks and medical escorts). Finally, the post-arrival stage may include inland transport (reception, return grants), medical elements (medical and accident insurance, rehabilitation of health care infrastructure) and reintegration assistance (often in cooperation with development agencies and NGOs).

General Assisted Return Programmes

There are three main categories of programmes generally available to unsuccessful asylum-seekers and irregular migrants. These are: programmes financed by one host country and aimed at countries of origin worldwide, programmes financed by one host country and aimed at one country of origin, and programmes financed by a group of host countries and aimed at a single country of origin. Programmes of the third type, between multiple host countries and single countries of origin, were still being developed by IOM. In late 1994, IOM circulated a draft proposal for a pilot programme for the assisted return of 2,000 Pakistani nationals from Belgium, Canada, Germany, Switzerland, UK and USA. The outcome of this pilot study was yet to be known.

Assisted programmes for irregular transit migrants

The IOM has two main programmes targeted on irregular transit migrants – the Stranded Student Return Programme and the Programme for the Assisted Return of Migrants Stranded in Eastern and Central Europe (SMIT).

The Stranded Student Return Programme (SSRP) – formerly the Emergency Humanitarian Return Programme (EHRP) – was initiated in the wake of the collapse of the former Soviet Union, which resulted in the suspension of the provision of governmental assistance to some 120,000 foreign scholarship holders – mostly from Africa, Latin America and Asia. These students found themselves stranded without means to complete their studies or return home. EHRP, and then SSRP, were designed to facilitate the return of the students and of their direct dependants. The programmes principally provide: counselling, transportation arrangements, tickets, assistance with other travel documents, transportation, transit assistance and a small travel allowance (IOM, 1998).

The Programme for the Assisted Return of Migrants Stranded in Eastern and Central Europe (SMIT) offers assistance to principally illegal immigrants from Asia, Africa and Middle East, who are stranded in transit countries in Eastern and Central Europe. The programme provides direct counselling, return transportation assistance and also funds information campaigns.

CONCLUSIONS

It is worth reiterating that the preceding overview of operational programmes is far from exhaustive. This is because in the course of the last twenty years or so, numerous return programmes have evolved. Often these have been on a small scale, and designed for specific groups of returnees. The overall impression is of inadequate coherence and integration, and this observation can equally be made of policy frameworks. Indeed, as the preceding analysis of typologies has shown, there are big differences between both policy frameworks and operational programmes. It has also been possible to distinguish between both sets of approaches on the basis of which countries or organizations are involved. Furthermore, it has been shown that policy frameworks and operational programmes cater to specific migrant "types". Although there is a strong case for maintaining flexibility so that policies and programmes can be tailored to suit particular circumstances, there is a drive within certain policy circles to develop a more integrated approach to return migration. In the search for a more integrated approach, the preceding analysis indicates a number of priorities.

One priority is to fill a series of "gaps" that have been shown to exist within and between policy frameworks. One might be described as a "humanitarian gap", as reflected in the criticisms levelled at safe country of asylum rules. It is clearly important that policy developments should not be at the expense of the basic rights of all migrants. Part of the reason why this "humanitarian gap" can develop relates to policy differences between countries that are nevertheless included in single frameworks. A good example is readmission agreements, which risk returning migrants and asylum seekers to transit countries that have not yet developed adequate safeguards. The implication is that a properly integrated migration system needs to support the development of a similar policy baseline in all countries involved. At the same time, it is apparent that a gap also exists between *de jure* and *de facto* return policies. Examples of this gap include, on the one hand, the practical difficulties associated with the expulsion of irregular immigrants, and on the other, the difficulties associated with preventing large-scale involuntary repatriation. The implication is that any system aiming to achieve orderly migration flows needs to respond to problems of procedure and administration, as well as those of formal policy and law.

Analysis of selected operational programmes has emphasized the importance of comprehensive return assistance. The case study of ethnic returns, for example, demonstrated the success of approaches which targeted assistance on all stages of the "return cycle" – from pre-departure through travel to reintegration in the country of origin. Analysis of the weaknesses of the Professional Reintegration Programme highlighted the importance of targeting assistance not just on individual migrants, but also on their families too. And the Bosnian case study showed how assistance targeted on the area to which returnees plan to return is one way of encouraging successful return

– the model being to incorporate return assistance into local development assistance (see also Chapter 5).

Local development assistance is one example of how to overcome a lack of interest convergence between the priorities of host, transit and origin countries for return migration. In the changing global migration system, much of the impetus for return migration originates in host countries, which are keen to remove form their territories unsuccessful asylum seekers or illegal migrants, or to encourage the return of labour migrants as job markets shrink. In contrast, transit countries are far less motivated to accept the burden of dealing with asylum applications, and countries of origin are less willing to accept returning migrants who may swell the ranks of the unemployed and whose return will reduce flows of remittances. How to balance these divergent attitudes, and how to achieve a degree of interest convergence, are pressing priorities in the search for a truly integrated approach to return.

A final observation is simply to highlight the difficulties that are involved in making return successful. This has clearly been the case in the Bosnian context, where the complexity of return has been one of the main factors which has persuaded most EU countries to regularize the status of Bosnians. It has also proved to be the case more generally for refugee repatriation, which has not proceeded at the scale expected at the turn of this decade. A final example lies in the relatively low rates of return which have tended to characterize programmes for the return of qualified nationals under bilateral agreements, including the one between Germany and Eritrea. One implication would seem to be that policy-making should be based on a better understanding of the motivations of migrants themselves, through closer cooperation with migrant representatives and associations.

REFERENCES

Abell, N.A.
1995   "Safe country of asylum policies", paper presented at the Conference on Migration and Nation in Southern Europe.

Abella, M.
1995   "Policies and institutions for the orderly movement of labour abroad", in ILO, *Orderly International Migration of Workers and Incentives to Stay: Options for Emigration Countries*, ILO International Migration Papers 5, Geneva.

Amawi, A.
1998   "Realizing the development potential of return migration: the case of Jordan", paper presented to the Technical Symposium on International Migration and Development, United Nations ACC Task Force on Basic Social Services for All Working Group on International Migration, The Hague, June-July.

Ardittis, S.
1992   "The new brain drain from Eastern to Western Europe", *The International Spectator*, 27(1): 79-96.

Black, R., K. Koser and M. Walsh
1997   *Conditions for the Return of Displaced Persons, Final Report*; Brussels: Office of Official Publications of the European Community.

Brown, R.P.C
1994   "Migrants remittances, savings and investments in the South Pacific", *International Labour Review*, 133:3.

Bubeník, J., and M. Lupták
1991   "Emigration of Czechs to Volhynia and their later reemigration back to Czechoslovakia", unpublished paper.

Budapest Group
1995   *Report of the Expert Group on the Five Themes Selected for Examination by the Budapest Group*, Report by the Expert Group at the Third Meeting of the Budapest Group, Zurich, 14-15 September.
1996   *The Need for Reinforced Cooperation between all European States to Tackle Illegal Migration*, General Report by the Expert Group, Ljubljana, June.

Cornelius, W.
1994   "Spain: the uneasy transition from labour exporter to labour importer", in W. Cornelius, P. Martin and J. Hollifield (Eds), *Controlling Immigration: a Global Perspective*, Stanford University Press, Stanford: 352-69.

Council of Europe
1991   *Report on the Legal Situation of Long-Stay Migrants in Host Countries*, Council of Europe, Strasbourg.
1994   *Report on Europeans Living Abroad*. Council of Europe, Strasbourg.

1997   *Repatriation of Persons following the Political Changes in Central and Eastern Europe*, Council of Europe, Strasbourg.

Diatta, M.A.S.

1998   "Realizing the potential of return migration: the case of Senegal", paper presented to the Technical Symposium on International Migration and Development, United Nations ACC Task Force on Basic Social Services for All Working Group on International Migration, The Hague, June-July.

European Council on Refugees and Exiles (ECRE)

1995   *Safe Third Country: Myths and Realities*, ECRE, London.

Eurostat

1998   *New Cronos Database*, Eurostat, Luxembourg.

1999

Ghosh, B.

1998   *Huddled Masses and Uncertain Shores. Insights into Irregular Migration*, Kluwer Law International, The Hague.

Glytsos, N.P.

1995   "Problems and policies regarding the socio-economic integration of returnees and foreign workers in Greece", *International Migration* 33(2): 155-76.

Hathaway, J.C. (Ed.)

1997   *Reconceiving International Refugee Law*, Martinus Nijhoff, The Hague.

Honeköpp, E., and T. Tayanç

1998   "Realizing the potential of return migration: the case of Turkey", paper presented to the Technical Symposium on International Migration and Development, United Nations ACC Task Force on Basic Social Services for All Working Group on International Migration, The Hague, June-July.

ICMPD (International Centre for Migration Policy Development)

1995   *Towards Collective European Cooperation with Respect to the Movements of People*, Report prepared for the Vienna Process in 1993, reprinted for the Salzburg Seminar Session on Involuntary Migration.

ILO

1985   *The Assisted Return of Qualified Nationals to their Countries of Origin: The UNDP and IOM Multilateral Programmes*, International Migration for Employment Working Paper, ILO, Geneva.

Inter Governmental Conference (IGC)

1995   Paper on temporary protection in Europe, North America and Australia, Geneva: IGC.

IOM

1992   *IOM Programme Experience: Return and Reintegration of Qualified Nationals from Developing Countries Residing Abroad*, Paper No. 7 at the Tenth IOM Seminar on Migration, Geneva.

1995   *Trafficking in Migrants*, Quarterly Bulletin No. 6, March.

1998   IOM Assisted Return Programmes in Europe and North America, IOM, Geneva.

King, R.

1978   "Return migration: a neglected aspect of population geography", *Area* 10(3): 175-82.

Koser, K., M. Walsh and R. Black

1998   "Temporary protection and the assisted return of refugees from the European Union", *International Journal of Refugee Law*, 10(3): 444-61.

Koser, K., and R. Black

1999   "The end of the refugee cycle?", in R. Black and K. Koser (Eds), *The End of the Refugee Cycle: Refugee Repatriation and Reconstruction*, Berghahn, Oxford.

Knerr, B.

1992   "Methods for assessing the macro-economic impact of emigration and policy interventions in the source country", unpublished paper.

Logan, I.B.

1992   "The brain drain of professional, technical and kindred workers from developing countries: some lessons from the Africa-US flow of professionals (1980-1989)", paper presented to the 10th IOM Seminar on Migration: Migration and Development, Geneva.

Marx, R.

1994   *Temporary Protection: international protection or solution orientated approach?*, ECRE, London.

Nair, G.

1998   "Realizing the development potential of return migration: the case of Kerala, India", paper presented to the Technical Symposium on International Migration and Development, United Nations ACC Task Force on Basic Social Services for All Working Group on International Migration, The Hague, June-July.

Noll, G.

1998   "Readmission and the protection of refugees – bilateral arrangements and NGO surveillance", in K. Hakola (Ed.) *Migration and Refugee Policy on the Eastern Border of the European Union*, University of Jyväskylä: 27-39.

Perez, J.C.

1991   "Return migration and economic growth: the case of Spain", paper presented to the International Conference on Migration, Second Session on Economic Development and Job Creation: National and International Policies, OECD, Paris.

Pires, J.

1992   "Return and reintegration of qualified nationals from Developing countries: the IOM programme experience", *International Migration* 30(3/4): 353-75.

Salt, J., and A. Singleton

1994 "International migration: data availability", in R. van der Erf and L. Heering (Eds), *Causes of International Migration*, NIDI, The Hague: 77-93.

Secretariat for a Working Meeting on Policies and Practices with Respect to Rejected Asylum Seekers

1992 *Towards International Recognition of the Need for Consistent Removal Policies with Respect to Rejected Asylum Seekers*, Working Paper.

SOPEMI

1998 *Trends in International Migration. Annual Report 1997.* OECD, Paris.

Stola, D.

1998 "Poland as a migration middle zone at the EU eastern border", in K. Hakola (Ed.) *Migration and Refugee Policy on the Eastern Border of the European Union*, University of Jyväskylä: 84-91.

Swedish Immigration Board

1997 *Report on SIVs Work with Re-Immigration and Repatriation*, 1 January - 1 August 1997, Stockholm.

Thorburn, J.

1996 *Conflict Prevention: The Role of Temporary Protection and Safe Areas*, paper presented to the IPPR Seminar on Human Rights, Refugees and the Restoration of Stability: The Role of the EU, London, March.

United Nations High Commissioner for Refugees (UNHCR)

1993 *Overview of Readmission Agreements in Central Europe*, UNHCR, September, Geneva.

1997 *Bosnia and Herzegovina Repatriation and Return Operation 1997*, UNHCR, Geneva.

United States Committee on Refugees (USCR)

1999 *World Refugee Survey*, Washington.

van Selm-Thorburn, J.

1998 *Refugee Protection in Europe: Lessons of the Yugoslav Crisis*, Martin Nijhoff: The Hague.

Werth, M.

1995 *Review of Official Aid Programmes for the Reintegration of Migrants*, European Committee.

Chapter 3

Protecting the Dignity and Human Rights of Different Categories of Returnees

Gregor Noll

INTRODUCTION

Undoubtedly, the return of persons not entitled to stay in a given host state is a critical element in the discussion of a regime regulating migratory processes at the international level. The "principle of regulated openness", being the normative core of the NIROMP project[1], means a number of things in the return context. As movement is not free and unfettered, provision has to be made for those actors (individuals or states) not in compliance with the regulatory framework. But to strive for the efficiency of return means also to strive for its acceptability. And the acceptance of return activities by both returnees, states and the public hinges first and foremost on the compliance of such activities with the prescriptions of international law. This puts the protection of the individual at the heart of deliberations on this issue. Properly understood, incorporating protection issues into a migratory regime, as envisaged under the NIROMP process, would certainly contribute to the *predictability* of outcomes – a value cherished by lawyers and politicians as well as by migrants and states.

---

[1] For background information on the project see Introduction, including footnote 1.

The need for a protection-sensitive regulation has been high-lighted by a number of tragic events in the near past. Within the period of one year, three separate incidents occurred where undocumented migrants were suffocated when resisting deportation attempts from European states.[2] These incidents represent the visible tip of a little-noticed iceberg consisting of harsher removal policies by receiving states, a persistent reluctance to cooperate by some sending states and the increasing resort of unauthorized migrants to desperate forms of resistance. While the legal responsibility for these incidents remains with the state effectuating return, the responsibility for protection-sensitive return policies is a shared one. Without genuine cooperation between returning states and countries of origin, the spiral of ever more desperate solutions will not be broken. The question remains how international human rights law may guide such policies of cooperation. This question is at the heart of the following reflections.

The present chapter is concerned with the protection of undocumented migrants before, during and after return. Undocumented migrants have been defined in the 1994 Cairo Programme of Action as "persons who do not fulfil the requirements established by the country of destination to enter, stay or exercise an economic activity".[3] Within this group, both undocumented migrant workers and rejected asylum seekers form numerically important subcategories. Undocumented migrant workers have been defined as persons not being in compliance with the conditions "to enter, to stay and to engage in a remunerated activity in the State of employment pursuant to the law of that State and to international agreements to which that

---

[2] On 22 September 1998, a rejected Nigerian asylum seeker, Ms. Semira Adamu, died of asphyxia, after Belgian police officers had pressed a cushion in her face during a deportation attempt at Brussels Airport. Less than half a year later, on 1 May 1999, Mr. Marcus Omofuma died during a deportation attempt by the Austrian authorities. His death was caused by suffocation; his mouth had been covered with adhesive tape and he had been tied to his passenger seat. Twenty-eight days later, a rejected Sudanese asylum-seeker, Mr. Aamir Ageeb, died due to suffocation during a deportation attempt by German authorities. A full-faced motorcycle helmet had been placed on his head to prevent him form hurting others and himself, and a German border guard held down his head during take off. In 1994, another Nigerian deportee died during a flight after having been administered sedatives by the German authorities. In 1991, a rejected Tamil asylum seeker died at the hands of the French police during an attempt to return him forcibly.

[3] International Conference on Population and Development, Cairo, 5-13 September 1994, Programme of Action, para 10.15, UN Doc. No. A/CONF.171/13. It should be noted however that the failure to meet the requirements may also relate to the laws of the sending country. See Bimal Ghosh (1998: 1-3).

State is a Party".[4] The term "rejected asylum seekers" has been "understood to mean people who, after due consideration of their claims to asylum in fair procedures, are found not to qualify for refugee status, nor to be in need of international protection and who are not authorized to stay in the country concerned."[5] Thus, the return of documented migrants[6] as well as of refugees[7] or persons enjoying other forms of regularized territorial protection[8] is excluded from the scope of the present inquiry.

The discussion of protection hinges largely on how the concept of return is delimited. Conceiving return as a mere physical process of transportation will confine our discussion to rather technical matters: may a police officer counter the resistance of a deportee with force? If yes, within which limits? While these issues are important, they represent only one facet of a much larger problem. Rather, we would propose to conceive return as a comprehensive concept spanning over a period from the manifestation of illegal stay in the returning country to a lasting reintegration in the country of origin. The choice of perspective is intertwined with the goals pursued by return. Is speedy return intended as a political objective in the domestic arena of a host state, demonstrating the government's capacity to control the composition of its population? Or does the returning state subordinate the expeditiousness of return to the preservation of stability in the country of origin? Apparently, there is a tension between a short-term and a long-term perspective on return, mirroring the divide between a particularist and an universalist perspective. Given the fact

---

[4] International Convention on the Protection of the Rights of All Migrant Workers and Members of their Families, 18 December 1990, GA Res. 45/158 [hereinafter Migrant Workers Convention], art. 5. This instrument is not yet in force.

[5] Memorandum of Understanding between the United Nations High Commissioner for Refugees (UNHCR) and the International Organization for Migration (IOM), May 1997, para. 29. It should be noted that IOM also uses the term "unsuccessful asylum seekers", including those persons who have chosen not to further pursue an asylum claim once filed.

[6] As defined in para. 10.9 of the Cairo Programme of Action. See supra note 1.

[7] As defined in art. 1 A. (2) of the 1951 Refugee Convention as amended by art. 1 of the 1967 New York Protocol. Convention relating to the Status of Refugees, 28 July 1951, 189 UNTS 137 [hereinafter 1951 Refugee Convention]. In this text, reference to the 1951 Refugee Convention covers the Convention as modified by the Protocol relating to the Status of Refugees, 31 January 1967, 606 UNTS 267. Such movements are usually referred to as repatriation, which, in principle, must be voluntary. See further UNHCR (1996: 10).

[8] Such forms of protection may be based either on international law (inter alia on art. 3 CAT, art. 7 ICCPR or on regional instruments) or on municipal law. For the purposes of this inquiry, such forms of protection imply as a minimum that expulsion is stayed for protective reasons.

that the NIROMP process shows affinity to the development of return as a functional component of an emerging regime of orderly migration, it appears appropriate to regard return not merely as a question of logistics, but also as a *sustainable* process. Thus, for the purposes of this chapter, the concept of return stretches over a pre-departure stage, a transportation stage and a post-arrival stage.

The chapter will be structured as follows. The next section features an analysis of the interests held by various actors involved in return. In Section 3, the most common problems associated with return will be described. Drawing on the framework provided by international law, protection at various stages of the return process is examined. At the end of each subsection, proposals for promoting protection in the scrutinized area are made. As all involved actors can be assumed to strive for integrating an enhanced protective component in existing return policies, Section 4 will suggest three themes for further consideration. Finally, Section 5 will offer conclusions drawn from previous sections.

THE ACTORS

Introductory Remarks

As the presence of an undocumented migrant in a host state becomes known to its authorities, he or she will be normally asked to leave its territory. In an ideal world of orderly migration, the individual would comply with this order voluntarily, the country of origin would receive back its citizen, and the *status quo ante* would be restored.

In reality, a number of problems occur at the point of return. The individual may refuse to comply with an order to leave, returning states may use excessive means in enforcing it or countries of origin may obstruct readmission. Before moving on to the legal aspects of these problems, the differing interests of actors involved should be made clear. The simple sketch of return problems drawn up above suffices to identify three main actors: the returning state, the individual and the country of origin. With regard to returning states, a further distinction can be drawn between states being the final destination of migrants and transit states. As will be seen from the discussion below, their interests are not necessarily identical in all aspects.

Apart from states and returnees, intergovernmental organizations as well as non-governmental organizations hold a stake in return. All these actors have different types of interests. Any system regulating migration needs to strike a viable balance between these interests.

States

A common interest

A common interest for returning states, transit states and countries of origin is controlling the composition of their populations. However, as discussed below, this common interest may articulate itself in conflicting positions and practices.

Returning states

Following the reasoning of affluent states, the necessity to implement return is usually motivated by the integrity of migration control systems. If norms governing the presence of aliens were not implemented, it is said, the credibility of migration control would be called into question. This is especially pertinent in the case of rejected asylum seekers. The investment of time, financial resources and effort into the operation of complex determination procedures is only deemed justifiable if states actually enforce negative decisions. Moreover, non-implementation may represent a factor of attraction as such, because persons having no substantive protection claim would use asylum procedures as a way of entering the country. Thus, the credibility of the systems of migration control and of asylum protection is a primary interest of returning states.

Secondly, returning states are interested in operating their systems of migration control and asylum protection with a minimum of financial, social and political costs. Implementing return is not without cost, especially if non-voluntary forms are used by the returning state. However, the one-time expense related to return is considered to be lower than the long-term financial costs accrued by non-implementation. It is difficult, if not impossible to verify this argument in the case of continued illegality of the migrant in question, as the costs triggered by illegality are hard to quantify.[9]

A quite different matter is a cost-benefit analysis of social factors. It is feared that non-implementation promotes the emergence of a new social strata of illegal aliens. Being beyond the protective mechanisms and benefits of the welfare state, this class would be open to exploitation, abuse and criminality.

Of course, such negative social effects can be buffered by the introduction of amnesties, which legalize the stay of certain groups of illegal aliens. Nevertheless, amnesties raise an important question of principle: why should states be involved in determination procedures at all, if it is possible to bypass them by staying illegally for a certain period. While aliens staying illegally import global inequality into host societies, amnesties are an attempt to level out such inequality again, and to reaffirm the image of a non-discriminatory social organization. However, the egalitarian logic of amnesties puts migration control at large into question.

The political costs linked to return issues are not easily determined either. If the electorate is in favour of a restrictive approach vis-à-vis aliens at large, it may appear attractive for politicians to implement return in a rather strict fashion. On the other hand, public acceptance for forcible return in individual cases can be low, particularly if families with children are involved and the media coverage is intense.

Until now, return has been considered to be a sensitive political and administrative issue. While statistics on asylum application are readily published and widely dispersed by asylum countries[10], statistics on return are hard to obtain for most countries. The amount of secrecy engulfing return is considerable, and the question must be

---

[9] However, the situation is different if the stay of the undocumented migrant is legalized on the grounds of e.g. an amnesty or the development of family ties. In such cases, as he or she is allowed to enter the welfare system, it should be possible to quantify the costs connected with his/her stay. This would ultimately allow for carrying out a cost-benefit analysis. With regard to the rather comprehensive Swiss program for Bosnian nationals residing under Temporary Protection, the absolute costs and benefits of assisted return would be recovered after approximately 10-11 months for a family of three persons. IOM Voluntary Return Programme for Bosnian Nationals Residing under Temporary Protection. A Sample Convention, Prepared for the IGC "Best Practice" Workshop on Readmission Agreements and Assisted Voluntary Return Schemes, Geneva, 21-22 September 1998: 5.

[10] See for example the regularly updated and rather detailed statistics on asylum claims on the Internet site of the Inter-governmental Consultations on Asylum, Refugee and Migration Policies in Europe, North America and Australia (IGC). Available at: http://www.igc.ch. Accessed 4 May 1998.

asked whether this secrecy rather augments than decreases the political costs of return.

In spite of all return efforts, some immigrants simply cannot not be returned, for example, for logistical reasons or because the country of origin does not readmit them. It follows that, for the sake of credibility of control and reasons of economy, states will try to keep such non-returnable immigrants off from their territory. In this regard, safe third-country mechanisms are an important tool. In the long run, however, safe third-country mechanisms lead not only to an unequal distribution of the protection responsibility, but also of the return burden.[11] And , yet seen from a Western European perspective, this double exoneration is certainly in the interest of potential destination states.

Finally, attention should also be devoted to the interest of returning states vis-à-vis uncooperative countries of origin. If return is especially desirable for individuals from a specific country in a short-term perspective, the returning state might feel tempted to compete with other returning states by offering greater benefits to the country of origin than the latter. However, if the returning state takes a long-term perspective, it might be more prone to cooperate with other returning states and form a negotiating cartel. This puts the group of returning states into a more powerful position and minimizes the costs of bargaining with uncooperative countries of origin.

Transit states

Transit states hold a position of intermediaries in the process of migration. With returning (destination) states, they share the wish to maintain the integrity of migration control as well as to reduce costs. This does not mean, however, that their interests cannot conflict. Where returning states have involved transit states in safe third country arrangements, the latter may experience increasing demands on their own migration systems, and as already noted, a considerable part of the return burden may be passed on to them. Moreover, the latter are often not in an as favourable economic situation as returning states, which increases their relative costs of return.

This divergence of interests between returning (destination) states and transit states becomes particularly clear in the negotiation of re-admission agreements providing for the return of third country

---

[11] Cf. Gregor Noll (1997: 405-437) and Gregor Noll and Jens Vedsted-Hansen (1999).

nationals. A pertinent example of such divergence concerns the setting of time limits for return. Short time limits reduce the number of potential returns, while the absence of such time limits have the opposite effect. For obvious reasons, returning states are interested in long time limits or the absence of time limits. The opposite is true for transit states.

A comparison between the EU specimen agreement[12] and the Czech Draft Principles[13] mirrors the difference in perspective. The EU specimen agreement lets the time limits for making readmission requests and answering such requests run from the point of time "the Contracting Party [noted] the illegal entry and presence of the said national of a third country on its territory". Furthermore, it provides that "the application for readmission must be submitted within a maximum of one year of the Contracting Party noting the illegal entry and presence of the said national of a third country on its territory".

The Czech Draft Principles recommend "to stipulate in the readmission agreement of a time limit within which it is possible to carry out the readmission and to set the moment of illegal entry as the beginning of this time limit".[14] Such a rule is, of course, to the detriment of a potential requesting/returning state, as time starts to run from the actual moment of entry, and not when the authorities learn of the presence of the person to be returned.

Transit states have no influence on the attraction of destination states for undocumented migrants. Often, they perceive that their territory is abused in a double sense – firstly, by the migrants themselves, who need a hub on their way to destination states, and, secondly, by states of final destination, shifting over a caseload of which a considerable group is expensive or logistically impossible to return. Most exposed to the consequences of this negative perception

---

[12] Recommendation concerning a specimen bilateral readmission agreement between a Member State of the European Union and a third country, adopted 30 November and 1 December 1994, SN 10339/94 [hereinafter EU specimen agreement]. The EU Council adopted this recommendation in 1994, which spells out that the specimen is to be used flexibly and as a basis for negotiation with third countries on the conclusion of readmission agreements. While earlier drafts of the specimen contained substantial provisions safeguarding rights and interests of protection seekers, those are lamentably absent in the finalized text. See E. Guild and J. Niessen (1996: 407).

[13] In the area of readmission agreements, the Expert Group of the Budapest Group has prepared a report containing what became known as the Czech Draft Principles. The named report is part of the preparations for the forthcoming Ministerial Conference in Prague. Working Group of the Budapest Group, *Report on the Implementation of Readmission Agreements*, Doc. No. BG11/96 C.

[14] Supra, at footnote 6.

of the transit states and the relative lack of their resources is, of course, the undocumented migrant.

Countries of origin

As discussed above, returning states are highly interested in regulating the composition of their population. So are countries of origin. The latter may regard certain groups as less desirable elements of its population. Thus, return may appear as unattractive in the light of demographic policies pursued by the country of origin. Such considerations exist regardless of justifiability under international law. It should be recalled that a state's denial to readmit one's own citizens represents a human rights violation[15] and can as such amount to persecution in the sense of article 1 (A) (2) of the 1951 Refugee Convention.

Something quite different is the economic interest pursued by countries of origin within the migratory framework. Expatriates may be the source of considerable transfers of remittances to the country of origin.[16] Thus, emigration may be seen as something inherently positive by countries of origin, and return regarded as something inherently negative.

Secondly, the country of origin may itself experience difficulties with its domestic economy. There may be problems of large-scale unemployment, obstructing the reintegration of returnees into the home society. The problems may be exacerbated if the country of origin has just witnessed armed conflict or other forms of serious crises. During the phase of recovery, the return of large groups of nationals may adversely affect its social and economic stability. In such situations, countries of origin are interested in a phasing of return, allowing for a smoother reintegration.[17] They are also interested in financial aid, which may mitigate the economical difficulties of reintegration, thus alleviating social tensions associated with it.

While returning states tend to regard return as an isolated problem, the solution of which is to be found in international law,

---

[15] See "Denial of readmission by the country of origin" in the section on Protection.

[16] On the role of remittances, see generally Edward Taylor (1999: 63-88); Bimal Ghosh (1996: 97-102).

[17] Some readmission agreements contain provisions on phased return, limiting the number of returnees during a specified period of time. See, for example, the agreements between Germany and Viet Nam and between Sweden and the Federal Republic of Yugoslavia. It should be remembered that both agreements not only cover rejected asylum seekers, but also other nationals not or no longer allowed to remain on the territory of the returning state.

countries of origin tend to put it in a wider perspective, involving elements of internal stability, development policies, access to foreign labour markets, remittances and distributive justice.

The Individual

First, as a prime beneficiary of human rights norms, the undocumented migrant has a clear interest in their implementation. This interest surfaces in his or her relationship with the country of origin as well as the returning state and stretches over the right to return to the right not to be treated in an inhuman manner.

Second, the individual to be returned is interested in preserving his/her dignity, which makes all forms of coercion and force principally undesirable for him/her.

Third, the undocumented migrant has invested a considerable effort into the attempt to migrate and enter a new community. Clearly, a paramount interest is to succeed in this effort. Faced with an order to leave, continued, albeit illegal, residence may appear as a better option than return. The choice between illegality and return is contingent upon the goal pursued by the migrant. As we will see below, it is precisely at this point, where returning states seek to promote voluntary return by meeting some of the overarching interests of the undocumented migrant.

Depending on the length of their stay in the host country, undocumented migrants may have integrated to a certain degree into the host society. Accordingly, it is also in their interest to preserve the value of these integrative efforts. Especially in cases where family ties have been established, this interest can be shared with members of the host society. A similar consideration applies to the assets accumulated and benefits for which the migrant qualifies. Making theses assets and benefits transferable to the country of origin lowers the threshold of return.

Organizations

Three determinants

Both intergovernmental and non-governmental organizations have been involved in return issues. In general terms, organizations are interested in consolidating and expanding their role. This interest is shaped, first, by the organizations' mandate, second, by states' willingness to involve the organization into specific return operations and third, by the costs for the organization emanating from involvement. Where the organization has a choice between involvement and non-involvement, an analysis of costs against benefits plays a crucial role: is the amount of control achieved by involvement sufficient to curb risks for the organization flowing from such involvement? Not getting involved means leaving choices to other actors, while getting involved may imply bearing the responsibility for any failures which may occur. As we will see, these three determinants are relevant for intergovernmental and non-governmental organizations.

Non-governmental organizations

Although only involved indirectly, migrant organizations and NGOs monitoring human rights can play an important role in the formulation and implementation of migration policies. Human rights-focused NGOs, as for example Amnesty International or Human Rights Watch, are concerned with any state practice impacting on the enjoyment of human rights. Thus, such organizations may reverberate and amplify the interest undocumented migrants take in the observance of their human rights. However, different from migrant organizations, human rights-focused NGOs are not catering for migrant interests at large. A strict confinement to human rights issues allows them to be perceived as a neutral third party.

The strength of migrant organizations is that they often represent a whole array of interests held by a certain group of migrants, including those going beyond the observance of human rights. Apart from the single migrant's easily disregarded voice, migrant organizations often represent the position of those most affected – the migrants themselves. Apart from the two types of organizations named above, a wide array of other NGOs – like charitable, religious or interest organizations – may be involved in providing assistance to undocumented migrants through various stages in the return process.

Given that migrants themselves are to a large extent excluded from the process of positing norms regulating migration [18], all these organizations play an important role in influencing the perception of legitimacy of the migration regime. Some states have already operationalized this insight and accorded NGOs roles as providers of

---

[18] For an analysis of the exclusionary logic of refugee law and the legitimacy problems entailed by it, see Gregor Noll (1997: 429-451).

information and services.[19] Without distracting from the state's prerogative to exclude non-citizens, such cooperation sends out a signal that the state is interested in negotiating the manner by which exclusion is implemented.

While it is true that not all states are in favour of involving NGOs in return, not all NGOs are willing to be involved either.

The primary function of such organizations is not to serve state interest, but to represent the voice of those affected in the formulation and implementation of migration law. Therefore, a close cooperation with the authorities of returning states may compromise the credibility of NGOs. In this context, credibility means an organization's capacity to dissociate itself from state policies, where those contravene the legitimate interests of migrants.

Intergovernmental organizations

Contribution potential

Migration as well as human rights are such broad issues that a number of different intergovernmental organizations are in a position to contribute to the area in one way or another.[20] As concerns the issue of return, it is of special interest to two of them – IOM as a provider of services within the international migration system and UNHCR as a stakeholder in the good functioning of the asylum institution.

IOM

IOM is mandated to deal exclusively with migration issues. This organization operates assisted return programmes, which offer various categories of undocumented migrants an opportunity to return in dignity to their country of origin[21] (see also Chapters 2 and 5 in this volume).

---

[19] By way of example, information on a Swiss assisted return programme implemented in collaboration with IOM was disseminated through a Bosnian-language newspaper published by an NGO in Switzerland. IOM Voluntary Return Programme for Bosnian Nationals Residing under Temporary Protection. A Sample Convention, Prepared for the IGC "Best Practice" Workshop on Readmission Agreements and Assisted Voluntary Return Schemes, Geneva, 21-22 September 1998, p. 3.

[20] In the field of human rights, a major contribution is made by the UN Human rights Commission as well as by the treaty monitoring bodies under universal and regional instruments. With regard to migration, mention should be made of the contributions offered *inter alia* by DESIPA, DPCSD, ILO and FAO.

[21] For a categorization, see IOM, IOM Return Policy and Programmes. A Contribution to Combating Irregular Migration, 5 November 1997, MC/INF/236, para. 11

What are the legal ramifications of these activities? According to article 1 of its Constitution, one of the purposes and functions of IOM is "to provide services [...] for voluntary return migration, including voluntary repatriation".[22] The express requirement of voluntariness was introduced into the Constitution in 1989. In the original Constitution, this requirement was implied in article 2(b) of the Constitution which stipulates as a requirement for membership "a demonstrated interest in the principle of free movement of persons".[23] It follows that any involvement of IOM into the return of rejected asylum seekers presupposes voluntariness on the part of the returnee.

This becomes particularly clear in the stance IOM takes on return systems for irregular migrants. In the view of IOM, such systems should provide for two options:

- Assisted voluntary return, through IOM, for which the migrant may opt, should it be available and offered to him/her.
- Forced return by government authorities, under national law enforcement procedures, if the person does not leave the country by his/her own means or under IOM auspices before the deadline for return.[24]

How, then, does IOM define the decisive criterion of voluntariness? The organization "considers that voluntariness exists when the migrant's free will is expressed at least through the absence of refusal to return, e.g. by not resisting to board transportation or not otherwise manifesting disagreement. From the moment it is clear that physical force will have to be used to effect movement, national law enforcement authorities would handle such situations."[25]

---

[22] Constitution of the International Organization for Migration, art. 1 (1) (d).

[23] IOM, IOM Return Policies and Programmes. A Contribution to Combating Irregular Migration, 5 November 1997, MC/INF/236, para. 6.

[24] Ibid., para 8. IOM has made it clear that the organization will not assume responsibility for transport arrangements for forcibly returned persons.

[25] Elsewhere, IOM observed that "there is often no sharp and clear-cut distinction between forced and voluntary migration". As stated earlier in this chapter, the same goes for forcible return as opposed to voluntary return. For operational reasons, a breaking point must be identified on the gliding scale between the two extremes. This is perfectly understandable. Two aspects of the definition of voluntariness deserve increased attention. First, it is clear that the definition focuses on a physical manifestation of will, namely, physical movement without manifest acts of resistance on behalf of the applicant. It can be objected that the returnee may be unaware of the significance of his entering the means of transportation without resistance. The absence of resistance can be the result of voluntariness, but it might also flow from intimidation or coercion. Clearly, it contributes much more to clarity if traditional means of expression were used, as, e.g. the signing of a declaration

The degree to which states involve IOM in return is certainly impressive. Bilateral programmes on assisted voluntary return have been established with European states (Belgium, Germany, Czech Republic, the Netherlands, Hungary, Romania, Portugal, Slovak Republic, Switzerland) as well as in Asia (where the beneficiaries are unsuccessful asylum seekers from Viet Nam in various host countries)[26] and in North America.[27]

UNHCR

UNHCR was set up for the protection and assistance of refugees as defined in the organization's mandate. Persons determined not to be a refugee by a final decision in a fair and full-fledged procedure as well as persons who never applied for asylum are outside the mandate of UNHCR. Therefore, it was stated in the 1990 Note on International Protection:

> While UNHCR should not be involved in the enforcement of return decisions, it could, if so requested by the Secretary General and in cooperation with other appropriate agencies, assume responsibility outside its traditional mandate but compatible with its strictly humanitarian competence to coordinate the safe and dignified return of rejected asylum seekers.[28]

Since 1990, the position on return has been further developed (see also Chapter 5 for a discussion of related issues). In 1997, the Standing Committee concluded that if the organization's "involvement with return can be shown directly or indirectly to contribute to the fulfilment of its protection and solutions responsibilities stemming

---

of intention. Individual applications for return assistance normally presuppose some form of application by the rejected asylum seeker. Such applications would satisfy the criterion of clarity much more than the interpretation of a person entering a means of transportation. Second, the definition disregards that factors unacceptable under international law may have contributed to the decision of the returnee. Where detention conditions contravene art. 7 ICCPR, one cannot properly speak of a choice between voluntary or non-voluntary forms of return. Coercion has taken place long before the moment a means of transportation is boarded by the returnee. Thus, it should be considered whether the definition of voluntariness could be refined by criteria focussing on factors preceding embarkation.

[26] IOM, Report of the Director General on the Work of the Oganization for the Year 1996, MC 1896, paras 145 and 189.

[27] IOM, IOM Assisted Return Programmes in Europe and North America, 1 July 1998.

[28] Executive Committee of the High Commissioner's Programme, Note on International Protection (submitted by the High Commissioner), 27 August 1990 UN GAOR A/AC.96/750, para. 26 (xi).

114

from UNHCR's Statute, there is no overriding mandate obstacle to involvement."[29] A critical observer will note that an indirect link to protection can easily be constructed, provided that one declares return to be crucial for the maintenance of asylum systems. Given the level of abstraction of such arguments, it has to be asked where exactly the scope of the mandate ends.[30] In the same document, a number of criteria for involvement are set out:

- the involvement of the Office must be fully consistent with its humanitarian mandate to protect refugees;
- return is recognized as being primarily a bilateral matter between the countries concerned and
- UNHCR's role is a supportive one, ideally as part of an interagency arrangement. [...]

Furthermore, UNHCR's protection responsibilities require that the Office's involvement be preceded by its determination that there is no valid protection reason why a group of individuals should not be required to return, and that UNHCR involvement is beneficial to protecting individuals and the institution of asylum.[31]

Accordingly, UNHCR involvement with return programmes will be "preceded by a cost/benefit-analysis for UNHCR" and should be exceptional by nature, giving way to already involved or better suited international agencies.[32] Given these preconditions, the organization's involvement in return has been kept limited, although some affluent states have signalled that they would welcome a more active involvement of UNHCR in return.[33]

Following the terms of the UNHCR's mandate, a crucial criterion for any involvement of the organization is the quality of the refugee determination procedures. If persons screened out in national determination procedures indeed merit international protection, UNHCR would directly contravene its mandate when assisting in their return.

---

[29] Executive Committee of the High Commissioner's Programme, Standing Committee, Return of Persons Not in Need of International Protection, 30 May 1997, EC/47/SC/CRP.28, para 15.

[30] But see Guy S. Goodwin-Gill (1992), arguing that UNHCR's mandate would indeed cover an involvement in the return of rejected cases.

[31] Executive Committee of the High Commissioner's Programme, Standing Committee, Return of Persons Not in Need of International Protection, 30 May 1997, EC/47/SC/CRP.28, paras 15 and 16.

[32] Ibid., para 18.

[33] Executive Committee of the High Commissioner's Programme, Standing Committee, Composite Flows and the Relationship to Refugee Outflows, Including Return of Persons Not in Need of International Protection, as Well as Facilitation of Return in its Global Dimension, 25 May 1998, EC/48/SC/CRP.29, para 15.

Consequently, any involvement presupposes close monitoring of determination procedures in the returning state. In addition, determination procedures could be negatively affected if decision-makers misunderstand the involvement of UNHCR as a signal that the country of origin is generally safe.

An increased involvement with return would mean that UNHCR entered the area of migration management at large. The organization would be caught in state-like dilemmas when balancing protection functions and migration control. Moreover, migration control hosts its own dilemmas, one of them being the opposing interests of returning states and countries of origin.

PROTECTION AT VARIOUS STAGES OF RETURN

Introductory Remarks

From the perspective of returning states, comprehensive return policies are built on five considerations.[34] A primary consideration of return policies is to ensure that an unauthorized individual voluntarily complies with the obligation to leave the host country. Promotion of voluntary return ranges from simple measures informing on the situation in the country of origin to programmes involving financial assistance. Concerning the latter, states are usually anxious not to create unintended incentives, where return assistance would attract further migrants.[35]

A second consideration for returning states is to devise measures responding to non-compliance with the obligation to leave. Some of these measures are intended to secure the preconditions of removal; they relate to the identification (i.e. by means of fingerprinting, database checks or language tests) of the individual; documentation (obligations to assist in travel document procurement); localization (reporting obligations and detention);and, finally, the actual removal (expulsion orders and escorts).

---

[34] For a comprehensive overview on the issue of return and a case study on Germany, see G. Noll (1998).

[35] See the sixth recital in the preamble to the Council of the European Union Decision of 26 May 1997 on the exchange of information concerning assistance for the voluntary repatriation of third-country nationals, O.J. 1997 L 147/3: "Whereas it should be avoided that such assistance leads to undesired incentive effects;…"

Disputes on nationality, delays in issuing travel documents or an outright denial of readmission by countries of origin may also inhibit efficient return practices. Thus, a third consideration of returning states is *to ensure the cooperation of the country of origin*.

A fourth consideration is *to secure the cooperation of third states* in return operations. This may take the form of forming negotiating cartels to exert pressure on recalcitrant countries of origin. To give another example, returning states may also approach potential transit states lying *en route* on the migratory trajectory in order to negotiate agreements on the readmission or the transit of third country nationals.

Finally, a fifth consideration for returning states is *to secure a sustainable return*. In the individual case, this means alleviating the pressures leading to renewed attempts of undocumented migration. The measures taken vary depending on the nature of the emigration pressure. In a wider perspective, this mechanism compels returning states to take an increased interest in the realization of civic and political as well as economic, social and cultural rights in countries of origin.

What role do norms of human rights law play in this context? Which of these norms risk to be violated in the context of return? State activities flowing from these considerations can be divided into three phases – before, during and after return.

Protection before Return

Scope of the problem

In the phase preceding return, a number of protection issues arise which merit discussion. A first one concerns the individuals' right to return to his or her country of origin. Second, there is the question of voluntary vis-à-vis involuntary return. Third, the enforcement activities of returning states such as expulsion decisions and localization need to be examined in the context of human rights protection.

Denial of readmission by the country of origin

Where a country of origin arbitrarily denies entry to a citizen wishing to return, it violates the right to return enshrined in *inter alia* article 12 (4) ICCPR.[36] The right to return extends also to stateless persons and aliens, which have such a close relationship to the country in question that it should be properly termed "their country".[37] It should be noted that this right is not subject to the limitations set out in article 12 (3) of the same instrument.

It is important to recall that returning states cannot invoke this provision to support involuntary return vis-à-vis a recalcitrant country of origin.[38] The right-holder is the individual, not a returning state, and it is within the discretion of this individual to invoke the right to return. From the perspective of the returning state, this is an additional reason to promote voluntary return, as it provides another supportive legal argument in dealing with a recalcitrant country of origin.

The individual's right to return can also be violated indirectly, when a country of origin protracts the issuing of necessary identity or travel documents. However, drawing the dividing line between a reasonable period needed for formalities and politically motivated obstruction tactics is a challenging task. In such cases, the point of departure should be the fulfilment of the obligations flowing from the ICCPR in good faith.[39]

Voluntary versus involuntary return

In comparison to involuntary removal, voluntary return lowers the risk for human rights violations, preserves the dignity of the returnee and incurs less financial and political costs.

Most of the protection problems discussed below arise in the context of involuntary return practices. Where the relationship between the returning state and the returnee can be transformed from confrontation to cooperation, there is no need to detain or use force. Thus, promoting voluntary return is the primary, and probably the most efficient method of human rights protection in a return context, as it eliminates situations where violations may occur.

---

[36] International Covenant on Civil and Political Rights, 19 Dec. 1966, 999 UNTS 171 (hereafter ICCPR). It is to be noted however that the refusal to admit usually comes from the state when it denies that the person involved is a citizen.

[37] Cf. the usage of the possessive pronoun "his" in art. 12 (4) instead of an allusion to citizenship. See further Manfred Novak (1993: 219, para. 48).

[38] For a comprehensive argumentation, see G. Noll (1999: 276-277).

[39] See art. 26 of the Vienna Convention on the Law of Treaties, 24 May 1969, 1155 UNTS 331, codifying a rule of general international law applicable even before the entry into force of the Vienna Treaty Convention.

Even if carried out in strict compliance with the dictates of human rights law, involuntary return disregards the will of the individual and reifies him or her for the sake of migration control. States should see the avoidance of this humiliation as a separate goal to be attained, which suggests an increased focus on voluntary forms of return.

Thirdly, it is generally acknowledged that a voluntary return incurs less financial as well as political costs than a forcible expulsion. In Germany, the average cost for an escorted expulsion by air was US$ 840 in 1995, which should be compared to the price tag of US$ 490 for an assisted voluntary return in cooperation with IOM[40] Other returning states incur even higher costs for forcible removals. In Sweden, the average cost of removal amounted to SEK 24 541 per person (roughly equivalent to US$ 3160) in 1996.[41]

With regard to political costs, it should be recalled that the public acceptance of forcible removal is generally low in returning countries.[42] In individual cases, serious repercussions can flow from mishandled deportations. To illustrate, in October 1998 the suffocation of a deportee by Belgian police agents led to massive demonstrations in Belgium, the resignation of the responsible minister and a temporary halt to forcible removals.[43]

This suggests that a first approach to the problem of return should be to promote voluntary return – on an individual as well as collective basis. Only where such an approach has failed in an unequivocal manner, it would be reasonable to move on to more intrusive and expensive measures. Briefly, this two-pronged approach can be understood as implementing the maxim *in dubio mitius* for the whole area of return. From a human rights perspective, this cautionary rule implies that a less intrusive measure is chosen in case of doubt,[44] thus establishing a preference for voluntary return over forcible removal.

---

[40] Oral information provided by an official within the UN system.

[41] Utrikesdepartementet, *Verkställighet och kontroll i utlänningsärenden*, SOU 1997:128, Stockholm 1997, p. 96.

[42] From a legitimacy perspective, cases of forcible removal may be said to represent a litmus test of public opinion vis-à-vis return policies. While return policies in general seem to be covered by the consent of the electorates in returning states, this is not the case for concrete cases of forcible removal. Here, one might wish to apply a Schmittian perspective. Sovereign is he who decides the exceptional – which suggests that states should carefully reconsider how far their mandate goes in *implementing* strict return policies.

[43] See, also, footnote 1 in this chapter.

[44] Thus, in our particular case, the maxim is used in analogy to penal law. In the context of interpretation of international law, *in dubio mitius* suggests that norms must not be interpreted in such a way as to exceed the intention of the states mak-

It is often claimed by returning states that a return system exclusively built on incentives cannot succeed. The threat of forced return is often perceived as a precondition for voluntary return.[45] However, a caveat seems warranted against the ostensibly clear-cut dichotomy of incentives and sanctions. It is hard to tell *prima facie* whether the withdrawal of basic subsistence benefits should be properly termed as a sanction or an incentive. As long as the threat of imposing a sanction is not realized, it works as an incentive for conduct in conformity with the norm. Moreover, conduct appearing to be voluntary compliance may be the product of an illegitimate threat. Will-formation in these circumstances is certainly not to be judged in the same manner as will-formation in the absence of such threats.

There is no authoritative legal ground for drawing a clear dividing line between voluntariness and non-voluntariness. It must be accepted that any classification involves appreciation and, accordingly, an element of politics. Terming activities as "promoting voluntary return" does not *per se* allow for any deductions concerning their acceptability from a protection perspective. Where undocumented aliens opt for return only to evade the threat of human rights violations by the returning state, the decision cannot be properly termed as a voluntary one.[46] In each case, there is an interplay between elements of persuasion, threat and force. Therefore, a careful assessment of the legality of a specific return activity should be made in its individual context.

---

ing them. In the latter case, the beneficiary of a more favourable outcome is the contracting state, while it would be the individual migrant in our case.

[45] The German policies on the return of Bosnians after the conclusion of the Dayton agreement are a case in point. In the Western European context, Germany initiated return at a comparably early stage after the conclusion of the Dayton agreement. While it has to be acknowledged that Germany invested considerable resources into assisted return programmes and the reconstruction of housing facilities in Bosnia-Hercegovina, the responsible authorities gave a high profile to the threat of forcible return in their rhetoric. In practice, the number of forcible returns remained relatively limited. As of 31 May 1999, 3579 persons had been forcibly removed to Bosnia, while 207.307 persons had returned voluntarily. Source: Bundesministerium des Innern [German Federal Ministry of the Interior], Statistische Übersicht über Rückführungen nach Bosnien und Herzegowina, 31 May 1999.

[46] This situation may arise where the individual would be faced *e.g.* with harsh detention conditions, excessively violent deportation practices or forms of benefit slashing that deny basic subsistence and medical care.

Expulsion decisions

Legal impediments to expulsion

At the outset, it must be recalled that the refusal of an individual to return or to cooperate in securing travel documents necessary for return can be legitimately grounded in human rights law. In spite of the delimitation of this chapter[47], it is worth recalling that asylum seekers may be rejected due to insufficient protection provisions in national law, an overly restrictive interpretation of existing provisions or unfair procedures. In such cases, a denial to comply with an order to leave is perfectly legitimate from the perspective of international refugee and human rights law[48]. Nor is return an option where it would lead to the splitting of family ties. In other cases, the health condition of the individual migrant may inhibit return.[49] As mentioned in the preceding section, such cases should normally lead to the granting of some form of protection, which would bring them beyond the scope of this chapter. At any rate, it is worth reiterating that under certain circumstances a removal decision as such may contravene international law.

As an implemented expulsion decision may constitute in itself a human rights violation, a right to appeal flows from the obligation to provide a legal remedy, enshrined *inter alia* in article 2 (3) of the ICCPR.[50] In the words of the Human Rights Committee, this norm

---

[47] See Introduction to this chapter.

[48] International refugee law: see art. 33 of the 1951 Refugee Convention. International human rights law: see *inter alia* art. 7 ICCPR, art. 3 CAT as well as equivalents in regional instruments.

[49] Two main categories of health-related obstacles to return can be made out, both relating to the protection provided by international law against inhuman treatment (*inter alia* under art. 7 ICCPR). First, where the individual suffers from health defects which would be further deteriorated by the strains of travel, return may be excluded. The deterioration must attain a certain severity to trigger protection under human rights norms. Second, recent case law by the ECHR organs suggest that discontinuing medical treatment for persons suffering from AIDS flowing from return to countries without adequate medical resources may constitute inhuman treatment. *D. v. the United Kingdom*, Judgement of 2 May 1997, ECHR Reports 1997-III, No. 37. Se also *B.B. v. France*, Judgement of 7 September 1998, available at <http://www.dhcour.coe.fr>. Accessed on 29 September 1998.

[50] In the European context, the right to remedy is enshrined in Article 13 ECHR. The Committee of Ministers of the Council of Europe has recommended its Member States to ensure that the right to an remedy is guaranteed to rejected asylum seekers in legislation or practice against decisions on expulsion. Council of Europe, Recommendation No. R (98) 13 of the Committee of Ministers to Member States on the Right to an Effective Remedy by Rejected Asylum Seekers Against Decisions on Expulsion in the Context of Article 3 of the European Convention on Human Rights, 18 September 1998.

entails that "an alien must be given full facilities for pursuing his remedy against expulsion so that this right will in all circumstances be an effective one".[51]

Collective expulsion

Given the fact that some returning countries conduct repatriation flights by chartered aeroplanes in regular intervals, the question has surfaced whether such practices constitute a prohibited collective expulsion or mass expulsion in the sense of human rights law. When considering the French report under article 40 of the ICCPR, the Human Rights Committee welcomed

> the announcement made by the French delegation during the consideration of the report that the practice of deportation of groups of illegal immigrants by chartered flight to their home countries, bearing characteristics of collective expulsion, has been stopped since 1 June 1997.[52]

Collective expulsion is explicitly prohibited by article 4 of the Fourth Protocol to the European Convention on Human Rights and Fundamental Freedoms[53] and article 22 (9) of the American Convention on Human Rights. Article 12 (5) of the African Charter on Human and People's Rights prohibits mass expulsion, defining it as being " aimed at national, racial, ethnic or religious groups". With regard to the African Charter, Plender has stated that there "is good reason to believe that [it] reflects a rule of modern customary law."[54] Moreover, a prohibition of collective expulsion is also included in article 22 (1) of the UN Convention on Migrant Workers What, then, endows an expulsion with the attributes of collective expulsion or mass expulsion?

Plender rightly states that not all expulsions *en masse* constitute collective or mass expulsions.[55] With regard to the expulsion of undocumented aliens, he is of the opinion that "[o]f the principles of

---

[51] Hammel v. Madagascar, Communication No. 155/1983, para. 19.2. For an elaborated account of the right to remedy under the ICCPR and the ECHR, see Richard Plender and Nuala Mole (1999).

[52] Human Rights Committee, Consideration of reports submitted by states under article 40 of the Covenant, 1613th mtg, 60 sess., 31 July 1997, U.N. Doc. No. CCPR/C/60/FRA/4, para. 6

[53] Protocol No. 4 to the European Convention for the Protection of Human Rights and Fundamental Freedoms, securing certain Rights and Freedoms other than those already included in the Convention and in the First Protocol thereto, Strasbourg, 16 September 1963, ETS. No. 46.

[54] Richard Plender (1988: 476).

[55] Ibid., p. 459.

customary international law governing such cases, the prohibition of arbitrary conduct and the rule of proportionality are likely to prove particularly apt; reasons must be advanced which could reasonably and properly lead the expelling state to the conclusion that its action is necessary in the public interest."[56]

As a specification of the prohibition of collective expulsion, article 22 (1) of the UN Convention on Migrant Workers stresses that "[e]ach case of expulsion shall be examined and decided individually".[57] Thus, a first step to the compliance with the relevant legal norms is an individual, fair and full-fledged procedure examining and deciding on the continued presence of an undocumented migrant on state territory. Secondly, actual return practices must be neutral with regard to factors such as race, nationality or religion. By way of example, a practice of returning one or a few nationalities, while refraining from action against others could fall under the concept of collective expulsion, as the inequality of treatment is based on nationality. It follows that returning states must maintain return policies that are non-discriminatory not only in law, but also in practice.[58]

Elaborated standards under the Migrant Workers Conventions

General remarks

The discussion above on the protection-related obstacles to expulsion and the prohibition of collective expulsions based on international treaty law practically exhausts consideration of this subject matter. However, the UN Convention on Migrant Workers provides further and rather detailed guidance on the legal framework of expulsion in its article 22. To be sure, this instrument has not entered into force yet. According to its article 87, 20 states have to ratify the convention before its entry into force. At the time of writing, eight years after its adoption by the U.N. General Assembly, only nine states have done so (Bosnia and Herzegovina, Cape Verde, Colombia, Chile, Egypt, Mexico, Morocco, the Philippines, Seychelles, Sri Lanka, Uganda).[59] It is rather difficult to establish to which extent the Migrant Workers Convention mirrors norms already binding as

---

[56] Ibid., p. 475.
[57] Although this instrument has not entered into force yet, its content may be an expression of ratifying states' *opinio juris*. See section "General remarks" infra.
[58] See also art. 26 ICCPR.
[59] As of 15 September 2000, fourteen states ratified the Convention and six other states were signatories to it. Signature is a preliminary step to ratification. (ed.)

customary international law. The generally low interest in ratification by major returning states of the industrialized world, the outspoken resistance by certain states against the inclusion of rights for undocumented migrant workers[60] and the creative rather than codifying approach in some relevant provisions warrant a very cautious approach to this question. With respect to article 22, a comparison can be made with article 7 of the 1985 U.N. Declaration on the Human Rights of Individuals Who are not Nationals of the Country in which They Live.[61] The latter provision grants certain rights relating to expulsion, but it is expressly restricted to aliens lawfully on the territory of a state. Thus, the consensus on expulsion issues expressed in the General Assembly has definitely expanded from 1985 to 1990. Turning the tables, it cannot be excluded that some of the provisions in the UN convention on Migrant Workers mirror what is or what will soon be an obligation under international law. Therefore, a closer scrutiny of article 22 seems justifiable.

Procedural standards

First, article 22 contains procedural rights in the context of expulsion decisions. Such decisions shall be made by a competent authority in accordance with law and duly communicated to the migrant. Moreover, the migrant shall be informed of these rights before or, at the latest, at the time the decision is rendered. Second, article 22 contains a qualified form of legal redress, namely the right to have one's case reviewed[62] and, pending such review, to seek a stay of the decision of expulsion.

The latter provision does not represent a full-fledged right to appeal. However, it should be read together with the right to a legal remedy enshrined inter alia in article 2 (3) of the ICCPR mentioned earlier in this section.

Third, article 22 states also that an annulled expulsion decision shall not be used to prevent beneficiaries under the Convention from re-entering the state concerned. Moreover, the convention opens up a

---

[60] These countries shared the view that an inclusion of rights for undocumented migrant workers could be taken as an encouraging of irregular migration. See Ryszard Cholewinski (1997: 187).

[61] Declaration on the Human Rights of Individuals Who are not Nationals of the Country in which They Live. General Assembly resolution 40/144 of 13 December 1985.

[62] Art. 22 (4) grants this right unless compelling reasons of national security require otherwise.

limited choice of destination country. "Without prejudice to the execution of a decision of expulsion", article 22 (7) states, a beneficiary under the Convention who is "subject to such a decision may seek entry into a State other than his or her State of origin".

Standards regulating economic aspects in an expulsion context

For undocumented migrant workers, economic aspects deserve consideration in the context of expulsion decision (since they may impact to a very high degree on return). Where legal or practical reasons inhibit the transfer of wages and other entitlements or where returnees are charged the costs of his or her expulsion, the undocumented migrant is denied resources for their reintegration in the home country. Thus, allowing the transfer of wages and other entitlements is a reasonable form of conduct for returning states wishing to promote voluntary and sustainable forms of return.

The 1975 ILO Migrant Workers Convention[63], ratified by 18 states, provides a basic framework for such action. Article 9 envisages equal access to rights arising from past employment and spells out that the worker or his family shall not bear the cost of expulsion.[64]

With due reference to its present status under international law, the 1990 U.N. Migrant Workers Convention can provide further guidance. Starting out with expenditures, article 22 (8) states that the costs of expulsion shall not be borne by a beneficiary under the Convention in case of expulsion. However, the person concerned may be required to pay his or her own travel costs.

Article 17 (8) continues by stating that "if a migrant worker or a member of his or her family is detained for the purpose of verifying any infraction of provisions related to migration, he or she shall not bear any costs arising therefrom".

Concerning entitlements, article 22 (9) states that expulsion from a state of employment shall not in itself prejudice the rights of beneficiaries acquired in accordance with the law of the returning state. Such rights are expressly stated to cover wages and other entitlements. Further, article 22 (6) safeguards the enjoyment of such rights by stating that a beneficiary subject to expulsion shall have a reasonable

---

[63] ILO Migrant Workers (Supplementary Provisions) Convention, C 143, 24 June 1975.

[64] State practice beyond the circle of State Parties does not suggest that this norm is generally followed. By way of example, Section 82 of the German Aliens Act (Ausländergesetz, BGBl. I, p. 1354) provides in para. 1 that the alien has to defray the costs of expulsion. Germany is not bound by the ILO convention.

opportunity before or after departure to settle any claims for wages and other entitlements due to him or her. The same is true with regard to pending liabilities.

Localization

General remarks

As the final step in the chain of events leading to return, states seek to control the physical presence of the alien. The absence of the alien can take three alternative forms – return, onward migration or continued illegal stay at another location in the returning country.

Measures of localization may range from simple address checks to detention. By way of example, the Dutch police conducts checks at the latest known address of the rejected asylum seeker. Similar control effects can be ensured by obliging the alien to report to a local authority at regular intervals. Such measures represent relatively modest intrusions into the integrity of a rejected asylum seeker, while allowing for a rudimentary form of control. Of course, the information gained by this form of control is limited in its value. The absence of the alien can be motivated by three alternatives – return, onward migration or continued illegal stay at another location in the returning country.

As an intermediate step, in some states legislation allows for limitations on domicile or residency, while a large number of states choose to detain aliens to be expelled. Detention ensures a maximum of control, but it is the most intrusive and resource-demanding alternative for locating an alien, and it also raises a number of intricate legal issues.

Detention decisions

As with other forms of deprivation of liberty, detention is subjected to specific norms of human rights law. On a universal level, a pertinent regulation can be found in article 9 ICCPR:

1. Everyone has the right to liberty and security of person. No one shall be subjected to arbitrary arrest or detention. No one shall be deprived of his liberty except on such grounds and in accordance with such procedure as are established by law.
2. Anyone who is arrested shall be informed, at the time of arrest, of the reasons for his arrest and shall be promptly informed of any charges against him.

[…]

4. Anyone who is deprived of his liberty by arrest or detention shall be entitled to take proceedings before a court, in order that court may decide without delay on the lawfulness of his detention and order his release if the detention is not lawful.
5. Anyone who has been the victim of unlawful arrest or detention shall have an enforceable right to compensation.

In its General Comment 8/16, the Human Rights Committee has pointed out that this paragraph "is applicable to all deprivations of liberty, whether in criminal cases or in other cases such as, for example, mental illness, vagrancy, drug addiction, educational purposes, immigration control, etc."[65] The Committee added that "if so-called preventive detention is used, for reasons of public security, it must be controlled by these same provisions, i.e. it must not be arbitrary, and must be based on grounds and procedures established by law (para. 1), information explaining the reasons must be given (para. 2) and court control of the detention must be available (para. 4) as well as compensation in the case of a breach (para. 5).

In the European context, a more specific legal framework exists, confining detention to a narrow rationale of pre-deportation preparation. Decisions to detain rejected asylum seekers must conform with article 5(1)(f) ECHR[66]. This implies not only that such a decision must be based on law and decided under a proper procedure, but that it must also be grounded on purposes which are narrowly circumscribed. A rejectee may only be detained when 'action is being taken with a view to deportation.' Detention for other purposes than those enumerated in article 5(1) ECHR is illegal. Thus, it is of importance to identify the exact content of the wording of article 5(1)(f). Trechsel has pointed out that the purpose of this provision is to allow for the implementation of removal.[67] Thus, a deprivation of liberty in order to prevent that the alien goes into hiding is covered by paragraph 1(f), as well as the deprivation of liberty inherent in forcible removal itself. Trechsel underscores that the serious intention to remove, held by the authority in question, is of decisive importance. If it turns out that actual removal cannot be performed, this does not make past detention illegal. But, by the same token, it would be ille-

---

[65] General Comment 8/16 (Sixteenth session, 1982), para. 1.
[66] European Convention for the Protection of Human Rights and Fundamental Freedoms, 4 November 1950, ETS 5-1950 (hereinafter ECHR). For an overview of the case law under the ECHR, see Nuala Mole (1997: 41-44).
[67] Stefan Trechsel (1994: 43-59).

gal to continue detention in spite of the fact that removal is rendered impossible.[68]

Thus, for State Parties to the ECHR, it is illegal to detain an undocumented migrant when removal proceedings have come to a halt. This can be the case if there are legal obstacles to removal (e.g. under article 7 ICCPR or article 3 CAT[69]), or if factual impediments render repatriation impossible (e.g. if the home country declines to receive its nationals, or if it is logistically impossible to transport the individual to his or her country of origin). It should be underscored that the turning point is not an absolute impossibility of removal, but its improbability within a reasonable time-frame. In addition, it should be emphasized that detention for the purpose to punish the undocumented migrant for lack of cooperation is illegal.

Leaving aside the fact that the ECHR was adopted earlier than the ICCPR, the requirements flowing from article 5 of the ECHR can be seen as a specification of the prohibition of arbitrariness in detention provided for under article 9 (1) of the ICCPR.[70] It follows that even those state parties to the ICCPR which are not bound by the ECHR should respect these requirements.

Detention conditions

The living conditions of aliens held in detention facilities have been a recurrent theme of observations directed at state practices. To name but one example, the 1996 Annual Report of the Committee on Civil Liberties and Internal Affairs of the European Parliament criticized the "deplorable conditions" under which asylum seekers are kept in detention for expulsion purposes in Member States of the EU.[71] In states where various categories of aliens are not separated, the criticism of detention of asylum seekers covers the conditions under which deportable undocumented migrants are kept *mutatis mutandis*.[72] Moreover, the European Commission for the Prevention of Torture and Inhuman or Degrading Treatment or Punishment (CPT)

---

[68] Ibid.

[69] Convention against Torture and Other Cruel, Inhuman or Degrading Treatment or Punishment, 10 December 1984, UN Doc. No. A/Res/39/46 (hereinafter CAT).

[70] This prohibition exists apart from the requirement of legality provided for in art. 9 (1) ICCPR. See further Novak, supra note 33, p. 172.

[71] EP Doc. A4-0034/98, at para. 26.

[72] For a regional overview of detention of asylum seekers, see J. Hughes and F. Liebaut (1998).

has scrutinized the detention conditions of deportable aliens and pointed out a number of shortcomings in European countries.[73]

Article 10 of the ICCPR offers basic guidance with regard to the treatment of detainees:

1. All persons deprived of their liberty shall be treated with humanity and with respect for the inherent dignity of the human person.
2. (a) Accused persons shall, save in exceptional circumstances, be segregated from convicted persons and shall be subject to separate treatment appropriate to their status as unconvicted persons;

[...]

Based on the case law of the Human Rights Committee, the consequences flowing from the general protection rule in paragraph 1 have been summarized by a commentator as follows: "Regardless of economic difficulties, the State [...] must provide detainees and prisoners with a minimum of services to satisfy their basic needs (food, clothing, medical care, sanitary facilities, communication, light, opportunity to move about, privacy, etc.)."[74] He goes on to stress that "the requirement of humane treatment under article 10 goes beyond the mere prohibition of inhuman treatment under article 7 with regard to the extent of the necessary "respect of the inherent dignity of the human person".[75] Thus, the protection rule spelt out in article 10 (1) is comprehensive, but of considerable abstraction.

Article 10 (2) (a) specifies that separation of categories is part of the treatment owed to the detainee. While this separation relates to the categories of non-convicted and convicted persons, the UN Convention on Migrant Workers goes further in article 17 (3):

Any migrant worker or a member of his or her family who is detained in a State of transit or in a State of employment for violation of provisions relating to migration, shall be held, in so far as practicable, separately from convicted persons or persons detained pending trial.

---

[73] See,e.g., Report to the German Government on the visit to Frankfurt am Main Airport carried out by the European Committee for the Prevention of Torture and Inhuman or Degrading Treatment or Punishment (CPT) from 25 to 27 May 1998, CPT/Inf (99) 10, paras 19-32.
[74] Novak, supra note 33, p. 188-189, para. 14.
[75] Ibid.

In reality, undocumented migrants are not always separated from other groups in detention.[76] The CPT has been noting inadequate state practices with regard to the holding of "immigration detainees". In its seventh General Report, the CPT underscores that persons deprived of their liberty for an extended period under aliens legislation should be held in centres specifically designed for that purpose.[77] Neither the UN Convention on Migrant Workers nor the findings of the CPT are binding as such, but the separation of categories required by both sources is based on a principle which has found a specific expression in article 10 (2) (a) of the ICCPR.

Countries of origin have an important role to play in the monitoring of compliance. Article 36 of the Vienna Convention on Consular Relations[78] provides for communication and contact with detained nationals in returning countries. Moreover, a state's consular officer has the right to be informed about detention of its nationals upon request. The rights to communication and contact also apply to the detainee, who is to be informed about them by the returning state.[79]

Protection During Return

General remarks

Given the fatal incidents mentioned earlier in this chapter, it should be underscored that the alien's right to life, enshrined *inter alia* in article 6 ICCPR, must be guaranteed at all stages of expulsion.

Another important issue relating to the removal is the prohibition of torture, inhuman or degrading treatment or punishment, contained in article 7 ICCPR as well as a number of thematically focussed or regionally confined human rights instruments.[80] This norm is not only applicable to detention conditions, but also to the use of force when actually enforcing removal. As the Human Rights Committee has noted, the ICCPR does not contain any definition of the concepts

---

[76] Taking the example of Germany, it has been established that three federal states generally separate rejectees from other groups, while four states do not maintain any separation of categories. See R. Göbel-Zimmermann (1997: 25, 59).

[77] European Committee for the Prevention of Torture and Inhuman or Degrading Treatment or Punishment, *Seventh General Report* (CPT/Inf. (97) 10), 22 August 1997, para. 29.

[78] Convention on Consular Relations, 24 April 1963, 596 UNTS 261.

[79] Art. 16 (7) of the Migrant Workers Convention replicates some of the rights spelt out in art. 16 of the Vienna Convention on Consular Relations.

[80] See *inter alia* arts. 1 and 16 CAT, art. 3 ECHR, art. 5 ACHR, art. 5 African Charter.

covered by article 7, nor does the Committee consider it necessary to draw up a list of prohibited acts or to establish sharp distinctions between the different kinds of punishment or treatment; the distinction depends on the nature, purpose and severity of the treatment applied."[81]

Protection from these forms of treatment is especially pertinent in situations of forcible removal, where attempts are made to overcome anticipated or actual resistance by the returnee. Rudimentary guidance can be extracted from the practice of international treaty monitoring bodies. The CPT has recognized "that it will often be a difficult task to enforce an expulsion order in respect of a foreign national who is determined to stay on a State's territory. Law enforcement officials may on occasion have to use force in order to effect such a removal."[82] Nonetheless, the CPT concurrently points to the limits of forcible removal: "However, the force used should be no more than is reasonably necessary."[83] By way of example, the CPT has pointed out that "[i]t would, in particular, be entirely unacceptable for persons subject to an expulsion order to be physically assaulted as a form of persuasion to board a means of transport or as punishment for not having done so."[84]

The reasoning of the CPT can be developed further. For the purposes of this text, it is sufficient to focus on the least intrusive of the measures falling under article 7 ICCPR and equivalent norms. Drawing on the case-law of the European organs relating to article 3 ECHR, a refined understanding of the threshold of suffering regarding inhuman measures and the threshold of humiliation regarding degrading measures can be established. In the assessment of suffering or humiliation, it should be asked whether the treatment causing suffering is proportional to legitimate goals the actor (in this case, the returning state) seeks to attain. By way of example, one might resort to cases of solitary confinement, where the additional suffering adduced by solitude has been regarded as motivated by the detainee's exceptional dangerousness. In such cases, the interests of the claimant are weighed against the interests of the state. In other words, a particular treatment or punishment is inhuman or degrading when the

---

[81] General Comment 20/44, 3 April 1992.
[82] CPT, Report to the Swedish Government on the visit to Sweden carried out by the European Committee for the Prevention of Torture and Inhuman or Degrading Treatment or Punishment (CPT) from 15 to 25 February 1998, 3 July 1998, CPT/Inf (99) 4 [EN], [hereinafter CPT Report on Sweden], para. 68.
[83] Ibid.
[84] Ibid.

suffering or humiliation occasioned is disproportional to the legitimate goals the actor seeks to attain by it.[85]

The use of force in deportation should be seen against this backdrop of purposefulness, severity and proportionality. Not all use of force is illegal under article 7 ICCPR and its equivalents. But state obligations under this provision are engaged when there is no proportionality between the legitimate goal of migration control and the measures taken to achieve it. Migration control on the whole is not an all-legitimizing goal.[86] It must be recalled that an individual removal contributes to this goal only as a fraction of total removals. Thus, the use of gags, sedative medication and other intrusive measures in removal cases can give rise to serious legal concerns. In each individual case, the suffering and humiliation effected by it must be weighed against the contribution of the individual's removal to migration control.

Specific practices

In the following, specific practices used to overcome the resistance of deportees shall be examined. It must be underscored, though, that the mesh of norms regulating such practices is still rather fragmentary, although the tragic incidents named initially have given a new impetus to legal developments at the domestic level. The reflections made here are far from being exhaustive, and the fact that a practice is not dealt with here does not imply that it is uncontroversial under human rights law.

---

[85] The European Court of Human Rights also takes into account whether alternative means to pursue that goal exist: "A further consideration of relevance is that in the particular instance, the legitimate purpose of extradition could be achieved by another means which would not involve suffering of such exceptional intensity or duration." *Soering v. U K*, ECHR (1989), Series A, No. 161, 111. In that case, the legitimate goal of bringing a person suspected of murder before a court could be attained by trying him in the UK. Thus, the proportionality test is further supplemented by the maxim *'in dubio mitius'*.

[86] The German instructions to border police officers of 21 January 1998 reflect the principle of proportionality by stating that removals should not be enforced at any cost ("keine Rückführung um jeden Preis"). Quoted in CPT, Report to the German Government on the visit to Frankfurt am Main Airport carried out by the European Committee for the Prevention of Torture and Inhuman or Degrading Treatment or Punishment (CPT) from 25 to 27 May 1998, CPT/Inf (99) 10 [EN] (Part 1) [hereinafter CPT Report on Germany], para. 16.

Gagging

Two of the three fatalities mentioned in the introduction occurred due to gagging. In the Belgian case, the so-called cushion technique had been used on the deportee, while the mouth of the deportee had been taped by police officers in the Austrian case. Earlier cases have been recorded where the method of gagging had caused the death of deportees.

The reason for using gags is usually to prevent the deportee from biting himself or other persons, e.g. the escorting police officers. Another reason is to keep the deportee from shouting, which might cause protest by fellow passengers on commercial flights.[87] Thus, from the perspective of the deporting authorities, there is both a physical and a psychological motivation to use gags.

The risks entailed by gagging are, however, considerable. The CPT has made clear that "to gag a person is a highly dangerous measure".[88] Further, with explicit referral to the suffocation of Semira Adamu mentioned earlier, the U.N. Human Rights Committee has reminded Belgium that "the placing of a cushion on the face of an individual in order to overcome resistance entails a risk to life".[89]

In the reassessment of the use of force during removal, at least the Belgian and Austrian authorities seem to have drawn the conclusion that the risk caused by gagging is always disproportional to the goal of implementing removal. The relevant Belgian directives governing return and repatriation, issued after the death of Semira Adamu, prohibit the usage of any technique obstructing the respiratory ways, even if only in part.[90] In Austria, the relevant rules were also revised

---

[87] The informal monitoring exercized by other passengers delivers an important contribution and should not be underestimated. Therefore, the privatization of removal by using chartered planes does not necessarily contribute to the transparency of removal practices. Recently, Austria has started to deport recalcitrant aliens by chartered aircrafts. Letter of 30 July 1999 by the Austrian Ministry of the Interior to the Belgian Border Police. On file with the author.

[88] CPT Report on Sweden, supra note 79, para. 68. Sweden has expressed its unqualified agreement with this statement. Interim report of the Swedish Government in response to the report of the European Committee for the Prevention of Torture and Inhuman or Degrading Treatment or Punishment (CPT) on its visit to Sweden from 15 to 25 February 1998, transmitted by letter of 3 February 1999, CPT/Inf (99) 4 [EN] (Part 2), para. C.1.

[89] Human Rights Committee, Consideration of Reports Submitted by State Parties under Article 40 of the Covenant. Concluding Observations of the Human Rights Committee. Belgium, 19 November 1998, U.N. Doc. No. CCPR/C/79/Add.99, para. 15.

[90] See the Directives concernant le refoulement et le rapatriement d'étrangers, issued by the Belgian Ministry of the Interior on 2 July 1999 [hereinafter the Belgian Directives], para. 2.1.15.2, prohibiting "toute technique où les voies respiratoires,

after the fatal incident of 1999, prohibiting the use of any material to gag or seal the mouth.[91] Moreover, as a consequence of the German incident, the German border police has been instructed to ensure the deported foreigners' "unimpaired breathing".[92]

An absolute prohibition of techniques impairing respiration also seems to find strong medical support. In the aftermath of Semira Adamu's death, Amnesty International sought the opinion of three prominent forensic pathologists on the application of the cushion technique. The experts made the following observations: "Firstly, as a matter of practicality, there are great difficulties in covering only the mouth but not the nasal passages... Secondly, the method is vulnerable to complications such as presence of vomitus or other mechanical blockage of the airways."[93] The experts concluded that "under no such circumstances should a cushion or other object be used to obstruct the mouth and/or nose. It is an extremely dangerous procedure and can occasionally result in a fatality."[94] As the reader will note, this indicates that not only the cushion technique, but also all methods impairing the normal functioning of the respiratory system should be rejected.

To conclude, strong arguments suggest that such methods are disproportional to the ends states seek to achieve by resorting to them. Therefore, the use of these methods may violate Article 7 ICCPR and its equivalents.

Forced medication and other means of restraint

Cases have been reported where deportees were given sedatives against their will. Clearly, the forcible administration of drugs represents a strong intrusion into the integrity of the individual. As all other means of restraint, it must be subjugated to a strict proportionality test in order not to contravene Article 7 ICCPR and its

---

même partiellement, sont obstruées (par exemple en utilisant un coussin, en poussant le visage de l'intressé sur le siège, en exerçant une pression sur le thorax our sur la gorge, en pressant la poitrine de quelqu'un sur l'accoudoir du siège, en exerçant une pression complète et de longue durée ("plié en deux) sur le siège...);"

[91] *Migration News Sheet*, New Rules on Expulsion, July 1999 issue, p. 8.
[92] *Migration News Sheet*, Halt to Forceful Repatriations is Lifted, July 1999 issue, p. 9.
[93] Amnesty International, Letter to Deputy Prime Minister and Minister of Internal Affairs Mr. Luc van den Bossche of 17 February 1999, annexed to Amnesty International, Belgium. Correspondence with the government concerning the alleged ill-treatment of detained asylum-seekers, EUR 14/01/99, June 1999, available at <http://www.amnesty.it/ailib/aipub/1999/EUR/41400199.htm>. Accessed on 4 August 1999.
[94] Ibid.

equivalents.[95] It is noteworthy that the CPT has paid particular attention to reports of forced medication and requested further information from the governments concerned. In one case, the government stated that such medication is not authorized.[96] In another case, the government underscored that the administration of tranquillizers for the purposes of deportation is only permissible after an appropriate decision by the judicial authorities.[97]

It is probably indicative for the outcome of a proportionality test that the revised Belgian directives contain an absolute prohibition of forced medication. Among the formally prohibited means, the directives enumerates

> the administration of sedative substances or other medicaments, except when expressly demanded by the person concerned, and under medical supervision.[98]

Moreover, the CPT has requested the German authorities to document the use of full-faced motorcycle helmets when put on resisting deportees,[99] and it has pointed out to the Swedish government that the "body chains" used during the transport of deportees are not an approved means of restraint.[100] In both cases, the governments complied by introducing appropriate changes. As the full-faced motorcycle helmet may have contributed to the death of a Nigerian deported by German authorities, caution would suggest that its use be discontinued until medical expertise has clarified the risks entailed

---

[95] It should be noted that the named practices typically do not fall under the prohibition of medical *experimentation* in Article 7 ICCPR, but may very well constitute a form of cruel, inhuman or degrading treatment or punishment.

[96] CPT, Observations by the German Government in response to the report of European Committee for the Prevention of Torture and Inhuman or Degrading Treatment or Punishment (CPT) on its visit to Frankfurt am Main Airport from 25 to 27 May 1998, CPT/Inf (99) 10 [EN] (Part 2), para. 4.

[97] CPT, Response of the Spanish Government to the report of the European Committee for the Prevention of Torture and Inhuman or Degrading Treatment or Punishment (CPT) on its visit to Spain from 21 to 28 April 1998, CPT/Inf (98) 10 [EN], para. 4.

[98] The French original prohibits "l'administration de moyens calmants ou d'autres médicaments, sauf sur demande expresse de l'intéressé et sous surveillance médicale". Supra note 89, para. 2.1.15.2.

[99] CPT Report on Germany, supra note 83, para. 17. Germany has adopted its practices to this recommendation.

[100] CPT Report on Sweden, supra note 79, para. 69. Sweden has abstained from the further use of body chains.

in it. In Austria, the use of such helmets has been prohibited recently.[101]

Another serious issue is the use of any forms of fetters that cannot be removed quickly when the means of transport is exposed to an emergency situation. Such fetters hinder the deportee to leave the craft, and may also inhibit the timely evacuation of other passengers. In the light of a proportionality test, this is unacceptable. It is indicative that the Belgian directives prohibit the use of such means of restraint which cannot be detached immediately in cases of emergency.[102] Reasonably, one can assume that such a prohibition would also flow from the proportionality test under Article 7 ICCPR and its equivalents. Interestingly, Austria has equipped staff escorting removals with cutting instruments to be applied on fetters to secure a quick release of the deportee in cases of emergency.[103]

Protection after Return

So far, this analysis has very much focused on action by returning states. It must be underscored, however, that the situation in the country of origin cannot be excluded from a discussion of sustainable return. Thus, countries of origin bear a major share of the responsibility for securing the respect for human rights of the returnees.

Ensuring protection after return is not easy, as the issue intersects with those norms of international law expressly or implicitly prohibiting "refoulement". Subject to certain conditions, it is mandatory that return shall not take place where human rights are violated in the country of origin. This reflects part of the responsibility of the returning state. But it also reinforces the interest of the latter in the compliance with human rights by the country of origin.[104]

However, in the country of origin, human rights violations may occur which were not anticipated by the returnee (and thus could not have been taken into account in the course of an asylum claim presented to the returning state). Moreover, there are violations which do not reach the necessary intensity required for extraterritorial protection. Nevertheless, these violations diminish both the willingness

---

[101] Letter of 30 July 1999 by the Austrian Ministry of the Interior to the Belgian Border Police. On file with the author.
[102] Belgian Directives, supra note 89, para. 2.1.15.2.
[103] Letter of 30 July 1999 by the Austrian Ministry of the Interior to the Belgian Border Police. On file with the author.
[104] See further section "Voluntary versus involuntary return" supra.

of the individual to return and the prospects for sustainable return. What can be done about such violations?

Clearly, the country of origin is already obliged under international law to refrain from or to suppress such violations. The problem lies more with implementation. In this context, it is of little help that a number of bilateral readmission agreements stipulate that their content does not prejudice the obligations of the parties under other international agreements.[105] A somewhat more specific approach can be envisaged in line with article 6 of the readmission agreement concluded between the Danish Immigration Service and the authorities in North East Somalia[106]:

> Return and readmission of the returnees under this agreement will take place with full respect for human rights by all concerned.

Further, article 1 (3) of the German-Vietnamese readmission agreement[107] states that both parties are obliged to carry out return in an orderly way with regard to the safety and human dignity of the persons concerned. This formulation is clearly less precise than the preceding example.

In the Agreement to Stop Clandestine Migration of Residents of Haiti to the United States,[108] the parties address a much more specific risk:

> The United States Government appreciates the assurances which it has received from the Government of the Republic of Haiti that Haitians

---

[105] See article 14 (3) of the readmission agreement between France and Slovenia. This provision establishes the primacy of the ECHR over the agreement. Accord entre le Gouvernement de la République francaise et le Gouvernement de la Republique de Slovénie relatif à la réadmission des personnes en situation irrégulière, Ljubljana, 1 February 1993, JO, 1995, pp. 9790-9791.

[106] Agreed Minutes Between the Authorities in North East Somalia and the Danish Immigration Service on the Return of Rejected Asylum Seekers from North East Somalia in Denmark. Bosaso, 6 July 1997. This agreement represents an anomaly in that the statehood of North East Somalia is unclear. Thus, one could doubt whether the said agreement is an agreement under international law.

[107] Abkommen zwischen der Regierung der Bundesrepublik Deutschland und der Regierung der Sozialistischen Republik Vietnam über die Rückübernahme von vietnamesischen Staatsangehörigen, 21 July 1995. BGBl. 1995 II p. 744.

[108] Agreement to Stop Clandestine Migration of Residents of Haiti to the United States, Exchange of Letters, at Port-au-Prince, 23 September 1981.

returned to their country and who are not traffickers will not be subject to prosecution for illegal departure.[109]

This shows that readmission agreements can be used to alleviate threats impairing the rights and reintegration prospects for returnees.

In individual cases and beyond formal arrangements, some returning states monitor the fate of returnees through their diplomatic missions. While such practices must never be used as a pretext or compensation for restrictive asylum policies or unsatisfactory determination procedures, they may very well contribute to promoting awareness of human rights-related risks endangering sustainable return.

However, monitoring can also be systematized and integrated into a feedback mechanism leading to intervention where human rights violations are alleged to occur. In a unique tripartite arrangement, UNHCR has assumed a passive monitoring role under the bilateral return activities from Switzerland to Sri Lanka. These activities are based on a readmission agreement concluded in 1994 between the two countries, which regulates the return of rejected asylum seekers from Switzerland. UNHCR is requested to act as a liaison between the returnees and both countries. In addition, each returnee is given a document containing *inter alia* the agreement with the UNHCR. Should the returnee experience personal security problems, he or she could contact UNHCR, which in turn would seek clarifications or intervene with the competent authorities of Sri Lanka. This cooperation started in 1994 and is still on-going. At least in two cases, returnees, who were detained upon arrival, have been released after UNHCR's intervention.

To be sure, the legal devices listed above may prove most effective where activities of the country of origin are the very source of a threat affecting the sustainability of return. Where such threats emanate from non-state agents, it may be useful to remind a country of origin of its positive obligations under human rights law. But where obstacles to sustainable return lie in an imploding economy, inadequate housing facilities or the damages brought to society by armed conflict, the situation is different. Some returning states perceive material assistance to the returnees and the communities readmitting them as a proper solution to improve the prospects for return. In an indirect

---

[109] Letter of 23 September 1981 sent by the Embassy of the United States of America to the Haitian Secretary of State for Foreign Affairs, forming part of the agreement referred to supra, note 107.

manner, such assistance means nothing less than strengthening economical, social and cultural rights.[110]

PROTECTION-SENSITIVE RETURN POLICIES: THEMES FOR CONSIDERATION

Introductory Remarks

A synopsis of protection issues in a return context leaves the observer with a rather complex picture. The discussion in the first section of this chapter, showed that return is principally challenged by the diverging interests of returning states and receiving states. The entrenchment of this conflict may foster a spiral movement towards ever more desperate solutions. Returning states will raise the thresholds of access and choose harsher methods of return, which may be particularly reflected in the length of detention and the early resort to forcible methods. In an attempt to spread the risks and responsibility flowing from such policies, they will seek to involve intergovernmental organizations or even privatize parts of their return practices.[111] Countries of origin may retaliate by open or camouflaged resistance and deny readmission to those forcibly returned. Overall, this scenario would result in a sharply increased and continuing potential for violations of human rights.

Assuming that all actors involved have a strong interest in avoiding such developments, a wide variety of specific proposals to improve protection have already been put forward in the preceding section. The very broad range of issues and their complexity might however be somewhat bewildering. In an attempt to reduce the com-

---

[110] Therefore, one should distinguish between situations where the readmission of undocumented migrants is bought by returning states by linking it to non-earmarked forms of assistance and situations where the allocation of returning states' resources are targeted to make return sustainable. It is quite another matter how the strengthening of remigration communities goes together with overall development goals for the country of origin. It may very well be that return assistance may draw resources from other, much more pressing projects.

[111] Apparently, the Australian Department of Immigration has established a practice of engaging the services of a South African company specializing in "a complete management service in the repatriation of inadmissibles to the individual's country of origin." Eve Lester, Privatizing Deportation from Australia, On the Record, Vol. 2 No. 5 (1998), available at http://www.advocacynet.org/excom/2210.html. Accessed 5 November 1998. The lack of transparency inherent in the privatization of return policies raises delicate issues.

plexity of the matter, this study concludes with proposing three themes for further consideration: promoting voluntary return, filling normative gaps, and monitoring compliance.

Promoting Voluntary Return

Legally, the obligation to return and the obligation to readmit are not conditional on the availability of return assistance. However, for pragmatic reasons, the number of assisted return arrangements is on the increase. One may say that coupling return and assistance has become a middle ground where the interests of returning states, undocumented migrants and countries of origin may converge. From a human rights perspective, this development can only be applauded. Returning states should certainly persevere in the efforts to make voluntary return more attractive by reinforcing existing assistance return programmes and developing further programmes.

If return assistance indeed represents a middle ground for states involved, there are good reasons to broaden the discussion to include international organizations and non-governmental organizations. In the domestic arenas of returning states, one of the greatest challenges is to limit the confrontational tinge attached to return issues. Involvement of a broad group of actors, including those representing migrant's interests, will lead to sound and suitable programmes, but also to a less contentious implementation.[112]

An important aspect is the incorporation of a protection perspective into assisted voluntary return programmes. Where return assistance is merely a way of "acquiring compliance" by the individual and the country of origin, its potential for securing sustainable return is not fully exploited. First, a protection perspective would clearly suggest that any assistance linked to return arrangements should not be made available to the state as such, but rather to the returning individual and the home community. Second, assistance should not only address the economic situation of the individual, but also those threats affecting the sustainability of return. This suggests that part of the assistance should contribute to community-building as an indirect measure to secure the protection of the returnee's human rights.

---

[112] This is especially clear in the area of information on conditions in the country of origin, where informal sources influence the decisions of the individual migrant to a rather high degree. In a climate of distrust and confrontation, there is a high probability that official information will be perceived as politicized by non-governmental actors.

Filling Normative Gaps

As the preceding section has shown, human rights law certainly provides a solid ground for further normative developments within the NIROMP process. But it provides a framework which is at times rather abstract and at times hampered by lacking bindingness. Reducing its abstraction and thereby improving its guiding function in specific return situations is a challenge. Two solutions offer themselves. First, states can elaborate detailed norms. To make these norms binding form would be the preferred solution, while norms guiding the interpretation of existing hard law would represent the second best option. The use of force before and during return as well as the issue of detention should be put first on the agenda of such deliberations. Second, existing norms could be specified by making full use of existing monitoring mechanisms or instituting new ones, focusing on questions of return. *Mutatis mutandis*, the opinions elaborated in single cases by these monitoring bodies may provide valuable guidance in future incidents.

If states indeed were to negotiate new protection norms in a return context, what would be the adequate vehicle for the implementation of such norms? Beyond doubt, a broad multilateral solution is the most desirable one. However, its negotiation will not be a fast process. In the meantime, and without any prejudice to efforts at the multilateral level, the inclusion of protection measures in bilateral readmission agreements could be considered.

In the decade of the 1990s, an amazing proliferation of readmission agreements has taken place. Such agreements and the protocols attached thereto are often rather technical, transforming the question of return from a larger political context into mere logistics. Moreover, where readmission is part of a tit-for-tat deal, linking economic incentives or threats to compliance with readmission obligations, the protection aspect is most often simply forgotten.[113]

Overall, the potential of readmission agreements as carriers of protection obligations has been exploited only to a very limited degree.[114] Until a comprehensive multilateral regime is in place, states

---

[113] Underscoring the necessity of genuine rather than formalized cooperation between returning states and countries of origin: Bimal Ghosh (1998: 144). For a detailed presentation of Germany's strategy for concluding readmission agreements, see Olaf Reermann (1997: 121).

[114] For a list of minimum standards which should be included into all agreements regulating the return of deportable aliens, see Meijers and Fernhout (1997: 105, 111-112).

could consider the interim solution to insert protection clauses into readmission agreements to be concluded; these can subsequently be multilateralised. Further, they could deliberate the modification of existing agreements to the same effect. Where expert committees or other consultative mechanisms are provided for, protection issues should be included as a mandatory item on their agenda.

Such protection clauses should, as a minimum, provide that both returning states and countries of origin ensure full respect for the human rights of the undocumented migrant before, during and after return. It should be underscored that such clauses represent a mere reaffirmation of existing obligations. Their merit lies in drawing the attention of all actors involved in return to the modalities of meeting those obligations regarding human rights.

Some readmission agreements operate with minimum or maximum quotas of persons to be returned during a certain period of time. When the return of Vietnamese citizens under the German-Vietnamese agreement failed to reach the agreed numbers, the German government intervened quite insistently with its Vietnamese counterpart to bring about a better implementation. To underscore their respective responsibilities for sustainable return, an unsatisfactory implementation by either party of a protection clause included in the agreement should also provide grounds for the other party's demand for rectification. In an increasing number of cases, readmission agreements covering nationals are part of larger package deals involving, for example, trade or development cooperation. Where possible and appropriate, such packages could be used to incorporate conditionality into readmission agreements. Thus if a country of origin violates the human rights of returnees after return, other forms of cooperation with this country are discontinued. Today, the threat of non-cooperation is usually limited to situations where countries of origin deny readmission to their citizens. Or, viewed from another angle, where returning states violate the human rights of returnees before or during return, countries of origin would be entitled to suspend the operation of readmission agreements until the matter has been clarified. Clearly, there are risks with such arrangements. Where there is a strong difference in leverage between the parties, conditionality arrangements tend to perpetuate this inequality. Therefore, parity of sanctions should be aimed at.

Finally, it should not be forgotten that rather specific human rights norms have already been negotiated and adopted under the ILO Convention no. 143 and the UN Convention on Migrant Workers. A comparatively simple step towards complementing the abstract provisions in the major human rights instruments is to press for the ratification of these instruments and their effective implementation.

Monitoring Compliance

Monitoring has already been touched upon as a device contributing to the elaboration and refinement of guiding norms in the area of return. But first and foremost, provision for monitoring is a preventive measure, diminishing the number and gravity of violations. Therefore, voluntary compliance by states as well as individuals would be enhanced, if a consistent monitoring of current practices by neutral and impartial actors took place. The transparency resulting from monitoring would enhance the legitimacy of state action, while individuals would be able to put greater trust in the actual legality of state practices. This, in turn, is a factor promoting voluntary return. With regard to returning states, monitoring would cover the scope of protection offered under national law, the quality of detention decisions, the duration and conditions of detention, and actual expulsion practices. With regard to countries of origin, monitoring would embrace the exercise of the right to return as well as the actual reception of the individual concerned and the conditions following return.

A comparatively simple measure is to integrate a complaints procedure into bilateral readmission arrangements, allowing individual to report grievances, which are then followed up by competent authorities. Such arrangements are already in operation in some cases. The U.S.-Mexican cooperation on the return and readmission of undocumented Mexican nationals provides for the reporting and bilateral processing of complaints.[115]

For reasons of credibility, monitoring should ideally be carried out by an impartial actor. Further, efficient monitoring necessitates a certain presence in the field. It could appear tempting to endow such actors with monitoring tasks who are already present in countries relevant for the return process. Within the framework of assisted voluntary return programmes, IOM is often represented both in the returning country and the country of origin. However, its involvement is limited to cases of voluntary return, where the potential for violations is limited. Another problem could be the convergence of interests: where an organization is governmentally funded for its

---

[115] A. Escobar-Latapí (1999: 153-182, 170-171).

logistical involvement in return operations, its capacity for impartial monitoring is, of course, hampered or can be perceived to be so.[116] Briefly put, monitoring presupposes a certain separation of interests. This is why monitoring by diplomatic personnel of involved states must be seen as merely a first step in the right direction. It is of course quite a different matter when an organization is funded by involved states merely to facilitate its monitoring functions. Although this brings in a certain dependency on external resources, it excludes a conflict of interest between different return-related activities within the organization.

Thus, it would be worthy of further scrutiny under which arrangements intergovernmental and non-governmental actors could be involved in monitoring. With regard to intergovernmental organizations, the involvement of UNHCR into return from Switzerland to Sri Lanka could be the object of further study.[117] As regards NGOs, a critical assessment of state activities is already carried out by them as single actors, but this can be improved.[118] For example, it would be useful to link those national NGOs involved in the return process by means of strategic alliances covering the whole of the return process. This means that a NGO present in the returning country would cooperate with a NGO present in the country of origin, sharing information and pooling resources to bring alleged violations to the attention of relevant actors, courts or other monitoring bodies. The experiences accumulated in the monitoring of returns to safe third countries carried out by a European network of NGOs could serve as a model.[119] In principle, such networks may be created and maintained without involving states.

It would also be useful if such monitoring mechanisms would contain a formalized channel to make grievances known to responsible states and to prevent further violations from happening. Therefore, it is desirable that regular consultations take place between monitoring actors and states involved in return, based on the mutual interest of addressing and avoiding human rights violations.

---

[116] Of course, this does not mean that organizations involved into the logistics of return should not carry out human rights-based assessments of return activities – on the contrary. The point is rather that such assessments cannot replace impartial monitoring.

[117] See section "Protection after Return" supra.

[118] See e.g. Human Rights Watch, "Prohibited Persons": Abuse of Undocumented Migrants, Asylum Seekers and Refugees in South Africa, New York, 1998.

[119] The European Council of Refugees and Exiles has coordinated such a network, attempting to follow the norm compliance of state actors involved in the return of asylum seekers to safe third countries.

A further point of discussion is the degree to which a monitoring mechanisms can sanction non-compliance. Ultimately, there is a choice between a purely advisory mechanism and a highly autonomous body entrusted with the power to decide unilaterally whether a violation has taken place and which remedial measures to take. While the first runs the risk of being neglected in practice, the second belongs to the realm of ambitious, but less realistic, solutions.

Finally, a choice between bilateral or, at least, geographically limited solutions and multilateral approaches has to be contemplated. The first may be perceived as more flexible and easier to launch. The second, however, provides the advantage of a greater uniformity in the application of rules and the avoidance of double standards. Consideration may also be given to pursuing a two-pronged approach within a common framework with the prospect that each process could derive support from the other.

CONCLUSIONS

The implementation of return is an important aspect of the construction of a state's demos. Return is an act of physical exclusion with strong symbolic connotations. Answering the question as to who is to be excluded and how exclusion is to be implemented reveals the self-conception of a political community. Needless to say, any state must accept to be judged by its exclusionary practices.

In liberal democracies, exclusion cannot be imposed unilaterally, and its forms may not be chosen freely. To command both respect and acceptance , the framework of exclusion needs to be legitimate. And the legitimacy of the framework, as argued in the second section of this chapter, is enhanced when it is negotiated both within and beyond the national constituencies, bringing together the perspectives of returning states, countries of origins and affected individuals. Used wisely, a forum like the NIROMP could be the launching pad for such a discourse. It is of utmost importance that such negotiations be conducted in an open and transparent fashion. The still widespread secrecy engulfing return is democratically unacceptable and risks to fly in the face of decision-makers wherever individual return cases arouse public interest. Both domestically and internationally, there is a choice between more or less democratic return policies.

However, the legitimacy of outcomes any such exercise hinges on its respect for the norms set by human rights law and the willingness of the parties involved to comply with the protection standards and, where necessary, deepen them. As indicated in the third section, the limits set by these norms have been trespassed in several cases, with negative consequences for the individuals affected as well as for the viability of return policies at large.

The protection problems encountered in return can be positively reformulated in the form of a set of recommendations directed at countries of origin, returning states and international organizations.

Countries of origin should

1. Scrupulously observe the right to return of their citizens as well as other persons falling under the scope of article 12 (4) ICCPR. By consequence, they should also provide sufficient resources for their administrations and diplomatic representations to facilitate the issuing of necessary travel documents to returnees.
2. Eliminate obstacles impeding voluntary return within their jurisdiction, by safeguarding the full implementation of human rights in all parts of their territory.
3. Make use of their rights to contact and communicate with their citizens detained by returning states.
4. Intervene with returning states to protect the interests of citizens having been, or running the risk of being, exposed to excessive force during the process of removal.

Returning states should

1. Strengthen the individual right to return by promoting voluntary return. They should refrain from invoking article 12 (4) ICCPR in the context of involuntary return.
2. Persevere to promote voluntary return to evade the risks associated with forcible return. They should also promote the coordination and harmonization of assisted return programmes on the international level. They should refrain from "manufacturing" voluntariness by the implicit or explicit threat of treatment contrary to human rights norms.
3. Implement their obligations under international refugee law and international human rights law in their domestic legislation, so that expulsion decisions are made in strict compliance with binding norms having a direct or indirect bearing on expulsion. As expulsion decisions may violate international human rights law, domestic law shall provide for an effective legal remedy against such decisions. As a step in the promotion of voluntary return as

well as predictability in return, returning states should give serious consideration to article 22 of the Migrant Workers Convention, regardless of the present legal status of that instrument.

4. Seek to minimize the use of detention to avoid the risk of human rights violations. Decisions on detention as well as detention conditions must conform with the framework set out by international human rights law. They should fully comply with existing reporting obligations under human rights instruments with regard to detention decisions and detention conditions. To augment the transparency of detention practices, they should, whenever possible, also invite interested non-governmental organizations to monitor detention facilities on a regular basis.

5. Seek to minimize the use of force in a removal context to avoid the risk of human rights violations. In cases where force is used, it must be proportional to the means pursued and otherwise conform to relevant norms of international human rights law, especially article 7 ICCPR and its regional equivalents. Clear and precise guidelines for removals should be elaborated to guide domestic authorities seized with the implementation of return. Apart from spelling out the principle of proportionality, such guidelines should prohibit means of restraint impairing respiratory functions, or inhibiting the prompt evacuation of deportees in case of emergency. Moreover, the use of forced medication for the purpose of removal should be banned.

Together, returning states and countries of origin should

1. Negotiate a set of norms on detention, codifying and specifying the existing framework derived from international law. Intergovernmental as well as non-governmental organizations having a stake in return should be associated with such negotiations leading to a binding document.

2. Reiterate and specify those norms of international human rights law having a bearing on the use of force in readmission agreements or other agreements under international law. The negotiation process preceding such agreements should be accessible to *intergovernmental* as well as *non-governmental organizations* having a stake in return.

3. Insert clauses reaffirming the relevance of human rights law in readmission agreements or other agreements under international law. Where specific threats to the returnees are known to exist, such agreements should seek to alleviate them by inserting appro-

priately specified protection clauses. The effectiveness of such clauses should be secured by positing that any benefits flowing from or linked to the agreement are conditional upon their implementation. The negotiation process preceding such agreements should be accessible to *intergovernmental* as well as *non-governmental organizations* having a stake in return.

Moreover, *organizations whose mandate restrict them to deal with voluntary return* should ascertain that voluntariness is not brought about by an implicit or explicit threat of treatment contrary to human rights norms.

Finally, *intergovernmental and non-governmental organizations* having a stake in return should be enabled to monitor the compliance with human rights by countries of origin after return. Wherever possible, they should seek to establish formal channels for bringing cases of violations to the attention of all actors involved.

* * *

It cannot be overemphasized that a comprehensive return policy and individual return cases cannot be unhooked. Inclusionary negotiations on return and a respectful approach to issues touching upon the basic human rights of undocumented migrants remain interdependent preconditions for the development of truly sustainable return policies. If states participate in the NIROMP processes, this process might represent a turning point towards a more protection-sensitive , dignified and efficient regime of return.

REFERENCES

Cholewinski, R.
1997 *Migrant Workers in International Human Rights Law*, OUP, Oxford.

Escobar-Latapí, A.
1999 "Low-skill emigration from Mexico to the United States. Current situation, prospects and government policy", *International Migration*, 37(1): 153-182.

Ghosh, B.
1998 *Huddled Masses and Uncertain Shores: Insights into Irregular Migration*, Kluwer Law International, The Hague.
1996 'Economic Migration and the sending countries" in Julien Van den Brock (ed.), *The Economics of Labour Migration*, Edward Elgar, Cheltenham, United Kingdom.

Göbel-Zimmermann, R.
1997 "Die Anordnung und der Vollzug der Abschiebungshaft", in K. Barwig and M. Kohler (Eds), *Unschuldig im Gefängnis? Zur Problematik der Abschiebungshaft*, ZDWF, Siegburg.
1992 *Refugee and Asylum Procedures. The Return of Rejected Cases: A Role for UNHCR*, revised version of a paper presented to an informal meeting on protection issues at UNHCR in December 1991.

Guild, E., and J. Niessen
1996 *The Developing Immigration and Asylum Policies of the European Union*, Kluwer Law International, The Hague.

IOM
1996 *Report of the Director General on the Work of the Organization for the Year 1996*, MC.
1997 *IOM Return Policy and Programmes. A Contribution to Combating Irregular Migration*, MC/INF/236.
1998 *IOM Voluntary Return Programme for Bosnian Nationals Residing under Temporary Protection. A Sample Convention*, prepared for the IGC "Best Practice" Workshop on Readmission Agreements and Assisted Voluntary Return Schemes, Geneva, 21-22 September 1998.

Meijers, H., R. Fernhout and A. Terlouw
1997 "Forced repatriation: towards minimum guarantees for repatriation treaties", in H. Mejers et al. (Eds), *Democracy, Migrants and Police in the European Union: The 1996 IGC and Beyond*, Forum, Utrecht.

Migration News Sheet
1999 "New rules on expulsion", July issue.
1999 "Halt to forceful repatriations is lifted", July issue.

Mole, N.
1997 *Problems Raised by Certain Aspects of the Present Situation of Refugees from the Standpoint of the European Convention on Human Rights*,

Council of Europe Publishing, Human rights files No. 9 rev., Strasbourg: 41-44.

Noll, G.
1997   "Prisoners' dilemma in fortress Europe. On the prospects of burden sharing in the European Union", *German Yearbook of International Law*, 40: 405-437.
1997   "The democratic legitimacy of refugee law", *Nordic Journal of International Law*, 66 (4): 429-454.
1998   *Unsuccessful Asylum Seekers: The Problem of Return*, paper prepared for the Technical Symposium on International Migration and Development, The Hague, 29 June - 3 July 1998. A revised version is available at www.unhcr.ch/refworld/pub/wpapers/wpno4.htm
1999   "Rejected aAsylum seekers: the problem of return", *International Migration*, 37(1): 276-277.

Noll, G., and J. Vedsted-Hansen
1999   "Non-communitarians: refugee and asylum Policies", in P. Alston (Ed.), *The European Union and Human Rights*, OUP, Oxford.

Novak, M.
1993   *U.N. Covenant on Civil and Political Rights. CCPR Commentary*, N.P. Engel, Kehl.

Plender, R.
1988   *International Migration Law*, Martinus Nijhoff Publishers, Dordrecht.

Plender, R., and Nuala Mole
1999   "Beyond the Geneva conventions: constructing a de facto right of asylum from iInternational human rights instruments", forthcoming in: F. Nicholson and P. Twomey (Eds) *Refugee Rights and Realities: Evolving International Concepts and Regimes*, CUP, Cambridge.

Reermann, O.
1997   "Readmission agreements", in K. Hailbronner and D. Martin and H. Motomura (Eds), *Immigration Admissions: The Search for Workable Policies in Germany and the United States*, Berghan, Providence.

Taylor, E.
1999   "The new economics of labour migration and the role of remittances in the migration pProcess", *International Migration*, 37 (1): 63-88.

Trechsel, S.
1994   "Zwangsmassnahmen im Ausländerrecht", *Aktuelle Juristische Praxis* 1(1994): 43-59.

UNHCR (United Nations High Commissioner for Refugees)
1990   Note of the Executive Committee of the High Commissioner's Programme on International Protection (submitted by the High Commissioner), 27 August 1990, UN GAOR A/AC.96/750.
1996   *Handbook Voluntary Repatriation: International Protection*, Geneva.

1997   Executive Committee of the High Commissioner's Programme, Standing Committee, Return of Persons Not in Need of International Protection, 30 May 1997, EC/47/SC/CRP.28.

1998   Executive Committee of the High Commissioner's Programme, Standing Committee, Composite Flows and the Relationship to Refugee Outflows, Including Return of Persons Not in Need of International Protection, as Well as Facilitation of Return in its Global Dimension, 25 May 1998, EC/48/SC/CRP.29.

Wolf, R.

1997   "Materielle Voraussetzungen der Abschiebungshaft", in K. Barwig and M. Kohler (Eds), *Unschuldig im Gefängnis? Zur Problematik der Abschiebungshaft*, ZDWF, Siegburg.

Working Group of the Budapest Group

1996   *Report on the Implementation of Readmission Agreements*, Doc. No. BG11/96 C.

Chapter 4

Irregular Migration and Return Procedures in Central and Eastern Europe

F. Laczko[1]

INTRODUCTION

It is often argued that an effective migration policy requires that those who enter or reside in a state illegally should be subject to removal from the country, preferably voluntarily, but, if necessary, by a formal procedure of deportation to the migrant's country of origin or to the last country of residence[2]. In practice, states often experience many problems in trying to remove undocumented migrants from their territory because of the lack of cooperation of migrants, countries of origin, and countries of transit. The migrants concerned may

---

[1] I am grateful to Jessica Graf for research assistance in preparing this chapter. The chapter is based on a longer unpublished report entitled "The Return of Irregular Migrants: The Challenge for Central and Eastern Europe", Technical Cooperation Centre, Vienna, International Organization for Migration. This chapter reflects the views of the author and does not necessarily reflect that of the International Organization for Migration.

[2] For example, in 1997 the participants of the Conference of Ministers on the Prevention of Illegal Migration held in the context of the Budapest Process, which brings together states from both Western and Eastern Europe, agreed on "the necessity of efficient return and readmission policies becoming an integral part of immigration systems of participating States and that such policies constitute an essential element in the combat of illegal migration."

disappear before they can be returned. They may have no documents making it difficult for the authorities to identify them, and to know where they should be returned to. Countries of origin may for economic or other reasons not wish to cooperate in the return of their own citizens. Transit states, for their part, may be reluctant to see third country migrants returned to their territory, and the costs of return shifted from destination countries to them.

Although return is often seen simply as a matter of removing the migrant concerned from a given territory, other problems may arise if the return is not sustainable and if little is done to facilitate the re-integration of the returning migrant. Return may also ultimately not be viable in cases where the migrant is removed to a transit state which lacks the means to return the migrant concerned to his or her country of origin. The end result may be that the migrant simply tries to re-enter the destination country illegally.

Forced expulsion, while a necessary component of a comprehensive migration policy, is also viewed by many as an extreme measure. It is sometimes difficult to enforce it humanely and effectively, and it can raise sensitive issues of human rights (see Chapter 3 in this volume). Mass expulsion in particular is often not consistent with respect for fundamental human rights.[3]

However, return policy serves not only purposes of migration control, since it is often argued that CEE countries require effective return policies also to maintain the credibility of their emerging asylum systems.

> The investment of time, financial resources and effort into the operation of complex determination procedures is only deemed justifiable if states actually enforce negative decisions (IOM, 1999: 12).

These are all new kinds of problems for the countries of Central and Eastern Europe (CEE). Ten years ago, there were few unsuccessful asylum seekers and irregular migrants who needed to be returned from the CEE countries. And few irregular migrants arriving in EU countries from CEE states were returned to these countries. Furthermore, there were no readmission agreements between CEE and EU countries to facilitate the return of third country nationals who had travelled through CEE states.

---

[3] "Combating Irregular Migration and Migrant Trafficking: The Elements of a Response", paper submitted by IOM for the Second Regional Conference on Migration, Panama, 11-14 March 1997.

The situation has changed dramatically over the last ten years as large numbers of migrants have entered Western Europe illegally from the CEE region, whilst others have come through illegal channels in search of employment in Central European states. It is therefore likely that return policy will become an increasingly important area of concern for the CEE states in the coming years. CEE states also face new challenges in the area of return policy due to the EU's pressure on the migration policies of the CEE countries, as explained below.

The management of the EU´s future external borders in Central and Eastern Europe has now become one of the most pressing issues on the European political agenda.[4] All CEE states, and especially the candidate countries, are increasingly affected by and seek to adapt to, the emerging European Union (EU) border and migration regime. As the EU´s external border moves eastwards, the new CEE member states will be required to demonstrate that efficient migration controls are in place to combat migrant trafficking and illegal migration. It follows that if this process leads to the apprehension of more irregular migrants, the CEE states will then have to develop more effective return policies. Such policies are likely to include a variety of measures including both involuntary and voluntary means of achieving returns.

Concerns have been expressed, however, that the CEE states will find it difficult to develop effective return policies, because they lack the financial resources required, and because they have had little experience of managing return programmes. It is also argued that many states in Western Europe have difficulties in returning irregular migrants from their territory, and have in recent years increasingly relied on the cooperation of neighbouring transit countries in Central European to facilitate returns by means of readmission agreements. Can these states in turn rely on cooperation from Eastern European and other source countries to implement the return of irregular migrants from their territories?

Other questions concern the role of the EU, and the way in which the policies of EU countries currently influence and will shape the future return policies of the CEE states. As the EU moves towards developing a common migration policy, how is this likely to affect return policies in the candidate countries of Central and Eastern

---

[4] See Judy Batt, Final Report of the Reflection Group on "The Long-Term Implications of EU Enlargement: The Nature of the New Border", European University Institute, Florence, Italy, 1999.

Europe? In short, what will be the likely EU "acquis" concerning return measures that the candidate countries will have to adopt?[5] At the same time, are current EU policies, and in particular the readmission policies of EU states, actually making it more difficult for CEE states to establish effective return measures?

The main focus of this chapter is on the return policy challenges facing four Central and Eastern European (CEE) countries (Czech Republic, Hungary, Romania and Slovakia[6]).[7] It deals with the return of undocumented migrants.[8] Issues related to the return of documented migrants as well as refugees or persons enjoying other forms of protection are excluded from the scope of this chapter.

Some comparisons are made with experiences in EU countries, and in particular Austria, Belgium, Germany, and the Netherlands.[9] The potential contribution of voluntary assisted return programmes, which provide an alternative to forced expulsions, is also discussed with a particular focus on the Hungarian Assisted Return Programme which is the most important programme of its kind in Central and Eastern Europe. Although readmission agreements are often used by many states to achieve returns, they are not the main focus of this chapter since this subject has already been discussed in detail elsewhere.(Noll, 1998; Budapest Group, 1999; IGC, 1999).

---

[5] The acquis communautaire consists of all the real and potential rights and obligations of the EU system and its institutional framework. New members are expected to take on the whole of the acquis communautaire on accession, although transitional periods are often negotiated.

[6] These countries took part in an IOM technical assistance project funded by the EC's Odysseus Programme in 1999.

[7] This chapter is based on a longer report entitled "The Return of Irregular Migrants: The Challenge For Central and Eastern Europe", which was prepared for an IOM project funded by the European Commission's Odysseus Programme in September 1999. The title of the project is "Research, Training and Exchange Pilot Project on Voluntary Return of Migrants in Irregular Situations". The chapter draws on the experiences and views of the officials who are responsible for managing returns, and who took part in this IOM training and exchange programme.

[8] Undocumented migrants have been defined in the Cairo Conference Programme of Action as "persons who do not fulfil the requirements established by the country of destination to enter, stay or exercise an economic activity". Irregularity (lack of documentation) may however also occur in the sending country (see Bimal Ghosh, 1998).

[9] These countries took part in the IOM research and training programme mentioned above.

BACKGROUND: THE EU ACQUIS CONCERNING THE RETURN OF IRREGULAR MIGRANTS[10]

The four CEE countries included in this chapter have all applied for EU membership. Before considering the current return policies and procedures in operation in these countries, it is useful to consider briefly how membership of the European Union may affect the measures taken by such states to return irregular migrants.

Although there are many EU instruments related to return, the majority of them are non-binding, and there is as yet no harmonized Union-wide approach to return. Overall there does not exist any consolidated EU paper on "policies for the voluntary and involuntary return of migrants", only pieces of work relating to various aspects, such as readmission, expulsion, return of temporary persons etc. (Widgren, 1999: 1). Within the EU, policies concerning return vary considerably. Whilst some states have used return as an important instrument of migration control, others have preferred to rely more on alternative measures such as regularization programmes and measures to prevent irregular migration.[11]

Perhaps the area where there is the most common agreement is the one that concerns readmission policies. Since the mid-1990s, an EU model has been developed for Member States to follow when negotiating bilateral readmission agreements (IGC, 1999). The EU has also been exploring the possibility of developing a Community readmission agreement with third countries.

At a binding level, the Treaty of Amsterdam may pose a most significant challenge for the candidate countries in regard to return policy. The Treaty of Amsterdam signed in October 1997 by all EU Member States will establish, five years after it comes into force, common standards and procedures for controlling the EU's external borders. The Treaty will effectively transfer much of migration policy in the EU from the third to the first pillar , that is, from intergovernmental decision making to the community level. According to the Action Plan of the Council and the Commission[12], within two years after the entry into force of the Treaty, a coherent policy on readmis-

---

[10] This section is based mainly on Chapter 3 of the 1999 IOM report on *The Return of Irregular Migrants: The Challenge for Central and Eastern Europe.*
[11] For more details on this, see Grete Brochmann and Tomas Hammar (1999).
[12] Council of the European Union, Action Plan of the Council and the Commission on how best to implement the provisions of the Treaty of Amsterdam establishing an area of freedom, security and justice, 7.12.98.

sion and return should be established and within five years there should be :

> the possibilities for the removal of persons who have been refused the right to stay through improved EU coordination, the implementation of readmission clauses and the development of European official (embassy) reports on the situation in the countries of origin are to be improved.

Although the EU has since 1994 argued in favour of the expansion of voluntary return schemes, noting that they are "cost-effective, when compared with the costs of involuntary repatriation", there are few specific EU instruments concerning such programmes. More recently, there does appear to be a growing emphasis on the need for EU states to develop further voluntary assisted return programmes. For example, in 1998 the EU created a High Level Working Group on Asylum and Migration (HLWG). One of the tasks of this group is to establish action plans with respect to some of the most important source countries of irregular migrants arriving in the EU, such as Afghanistan, Albania, Morocco, Somalia and Sri Lanka. One of the measures under consideration by the HWLG is to explore measures aimed at favouring voluntary return to the countries mentioned above.

To sum up, approaches to the return of irregular migrants vary enormously within the European Union, and although the EU is moving towards establishing a common approach to return issues, there is no clear EU model or established common policy which the CEE states are likely to be expected to adopt in regard to the return of irregular migrants. This may be a good thing for the CEE states for the time being since, as explained below, the pattern and trends of irregular migration in the CEE region are quite different from those in the EU countries.

TRENDS IN IRREGULAR MIGRATION IN THE CEECS: SHARP INCREASE IN THE POTENTIAL RETURN CASELOAD

In this section, we examine the recent trends in irregular migration in the CEE region and the characteristics of the returnee caseload.

Some countries, like Romania, continue to be major source countries for migrants seeking to enter EU countries illegally, whilst others like the Czech Republic, Hungary, and to a lesser extent the Slovak Republic are mainly transit countries, but also increasingly target countries for many irregular migrants from Eastern Europe and the former Soviet Union.

Romania, for example, receives few asylum applications (1,236 in 1998), and reports relatively few apprehensions of illegal migrants at its borders (604 in 1998). However, figures on border apprehensions give only a partial picture of the scale of irregular migration. There are estimates, for example, which suggest that there are 50-55,000 illegal immigrants living in Romania (CDMG (97) 17 rev).

In 1998, 21,600 Romanian nationals were returned to Romania from other countries under readmission agreements. Romania therefore might be expected to be more concerned about the return of its own nationals and how to re-integrate them, than with developing return programmes to combat irregular migration of third country nationals.

By contrast, the situation is very different in the Czech Republic and Hungary. Less than 10 years after the fall of the Berlin Wall, these countries are apprehending more illegal migrants at their borders than many EU countries. Before 1989, thousands of refugees from the CEECs sought asylum in Western Europe and North America. Today the CEECs have themselves become target countries for a growing number of asylum seekers.

For example, in the Czech Republic there were a record number of attempted illegal border crossings in 1998 (44,000).[13] The majority of these migrants were apprehended trying to cross from the Czech Republic into Germany and over half originate from other CEE countries. The Czech figure is actually higher than the respective figures for Austria (19,653) and Belgium (1,220), and even slightly higher than the figure for Germany in 1998 (40, 202). The number of border apprehensions in the Czech Republic in 1998 was also far greater than in other CEE countries such as Hungary (18,017) and the Slovak Republic (8,187).

It is important to note that these figures refer to the number of *apprehensions*, and not to the number of *migrants* trying to cross borders illegally. At some borders the same person may have been apprehended on more than one occasion. Therefore, the high Czech figure may be partly due to the fact that many migrants make several attempts to cross the border illegally. This trend is particularly likely to

---

[13] Some of those included in the statistics are persons readmitted from Germany, but it is not clear how many.

occur when states are unable to return apprehended migrants to their country of origin.

In 1998, 19,137 persons were readmitted from neighbouring countries, nearly 90 per cent from Germany to the Czech Republic. In contrast, only 5,561 persons were readmitted to Hungary and 2,146 to the Slovak Republic. The majority of persons readmitted to the Czech Republic were third country nationals, from the Federal Republic of Yugoslavia (FRY), Afghanistan, the Former Yugoslav Republic of Macedonia (FYROM), and Romania.

In 1997 there were only approximately 10,000 asylum applications in all CEE Associated Countries (IOM/ICMPD, 1999). By 1998 there were more asylum applications in the Czech Republic (4,086) and Hungary (7,386) than in some EU states such as Finland (1,272) and Greece (2,953). During the first nine months of 1999, asylum applications in several CEE Associated countries rose sharply compared to the same period in the previous year. Asylum applications were up by 246 per cent in the Slovak Republic, 238 per cent in the Czech Republic, 112 per cent in Hungary and 82 per cent in Bulgaria.[14]

A combination of factors explain the rise in asylum seeking in Central and Eastern Europe. Partly, this is a consequence of the establishment of new asylum procedures in CEE states in line with EU and international standards, and partly the consequence of the Kosovo crisis. As in Western Europe, most asylum claims in Central and Eastern Europe are rejected, which means that the number of rejected asylum seekers who might be returned to their country of origin or to a third country is rising.

The majority of those who should be returned based on asylum applications[15] and border apprehensions are young males. The majority of migrants apprehended trying to cross CEE borders illegally originate from the CEE region. For example, in the case of Hungary, only 13 per cent of migrants apprehended between 1990 and 1998 were female, and two-thirds were aged 18-29.[16] The majority of migrants apprehended at Hungary's borders since 1990 have come from Romania and the countries of former Yugoslavia.

Despite the increase in the number of asylum seekers in the CEECs, the number of asylum applications in the CEE region remains well below the figure in most EU states. There were nearly 100,000

---

[14] UNHCR, *Asylum Applications: Statistics in Europe*, Third Quarter, Geneva, 1999.
[15] See IOM (forthcoming), *Migrant Trafficking and People Smuggling in Europe*.
[16] IOM study on "Migrant Trafficking in Hungary", unpublished, 1999.

asylum applications in Germany in 1998, 45,000 in the Netherlands, 21,965 in Belgium and 13,805 in Austria.

In EU countries, the challenge for return policy is much more a problem of how to return rejected asylum seekers, who wish to reside in EU countries, whereas this is less of a problem in the CEECs, where there are many more transit migrants who are not interested in claiming asylum in these countries.

Another indicator of the scale of irregular migration in the CEECs is the number of migrants found to be working or living illegally in these countries. Many migrants enter a CEE country legally as a tourist, or on a student or other type of visa, and then overstay. It is difficult to obtain accurate figures, but it has been estimated that the size of this population is large and growing (IOM/ICMPD, 1999). It is relatively easy for workers from poorer Eastern European countries to enter Central European countries legally as no visas are currently required for entry. In Hungary, it is estimated that 6,000-7,000 foreign workers are employed illegally in the construction industry alone (IOM/ICMPD, 1999). This is a relatively high figure given that the total number of foreign workers employed legally in Hungary was just over 20,000 in 1997.

Another significant irregular migration trend has been the growth in the trafficking of women from Eastern European to Central European countries (IOM, 1995). The Czech Republic, for example, is a major target country for women trafficked from Ukraine and Bulgaria.[17] In the case of Hungary, the women are mainly trafficked from Romania and Ukraine. Thus, those responsible for developing return policies in CEE countries also need to bear in mind that some groups of irregular migrants may have special needs – such as victims of trafficking. They may therefore require considerable specialized pre-departure and post-arrival return assistance.

This brief review of trends in irregular migration in the CEE countries suggests that the main return challenge facing the Central European countries, at present, is how to return large numbers of irregular migrants who are transiting through these countries from poorer Eastern European states such as Romania, Ukraine, the Balkan states, and especially the FRY. Nonetheless, the proportion of migrants from non-European countries has been increasing as the number of asylum seekers has grown (IOM/ICMPD, 1999). As ex-

---

[17] See "Profile of Victims of Trafficking from the Czech Republic", Technical Cooperation Centre, IOM, Vienna, 1999 and *Trafficking and Prostitution: The Growing Exploitation of Women From Central and Eastern Europe*, IOM, Geneva, 1995.

plained below, if this trend increases in significance, CEE states are likely to face growing problems in implementing returns. Before considering the likely obstacles that they may face, we should first review to what extent the four CEE countries included in this study have thus far been able to develop effective return policies.

CEE Return Trends

It is difficult to obtain reliable data on the number and type of irregular migrants who are actually removed from CEE states. Return statistics do not always make clear whether someone has actually been returned, or merely given notice to leave the country, and it is rare to find statistics which even distinguish between men and women.

There is little information available on whether or not return has been sustainable and whether the irregular migrant concerned has been able to re-integrate into his or her host society. This is also true for vulnerable groups such as trafficked women. Little is known about the dangers that they may have faced on their return to their country of origin.

What then can we say about return trends in the CEECs? Despite the difficulties involved in obtaining accurate data, it is likely that relatively few irregular migrants who could be returned are actually returned. We estimate that approximately 10-15,000 irregular migrants were returned in 1998 (see Figures 4.1 and 4.2). It is difficult to be more precise, because there are no official data for Hungary or the Slovak Republic on the total number of implemented returns.

Figure 4.1 indicates the number of expulsion orders given, and the number of expulsions implemented in the Czech Republic, Hungary, Romania and the Slovak Republic in 1997 and 1998. Leaving aside the figures for Hungary, which refer only to expulsion orders, the figures available for the Czech Republic, Romania and the Slovak Republic suggest at most 1,500-2,500 returns per country per year. Hungary issued a high number of expulsion orders, 22,553 in 1998, but it is not clear how many of these resulted in implemented returns. Most of these expulsion orders were given to citizens of the FRY and Romania. Only 3,000 expulsion orders were given to Asian and African migrants in 1998.

FIGURE 4.1

1997 AND 1998 EXPULSION ORDERS AND EXPULSIONS BY THE CZECH REPUBLIC,
HUNGARY, ROMANIA AND THE SLOVAK REPUBLIC
(in thousands)

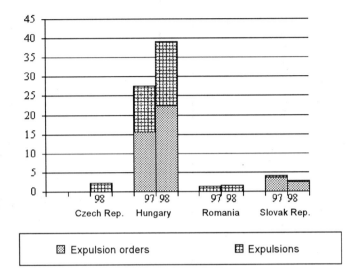

Czech Republic: Data on expulsion orders are not available. Aliens whose residence authorization was terminated, or who were issued an entry and residence ban, receive an exit visa, which notifies the alien within what period s/he has to leave the country. Under this broader range of reasons, 17,289 were given notice to leave in 1997, and 21,935 in 1998. Under expulsions are included expulsions carried out with an escort or controlled departures. Escorts remain very rare. There were 462 returns by air in 1998.

Hungary: Data on expulsion orders only refer to the issuing of these orders. Data on expulsions refer to those expulsion orders which have to be implemented with an escort. There are only estimates on the number of actually implemented returns. In 1998, 342 returns were to be implemented by air, of which 281 were implemented by IOM. Readmission data overlap to some extent with the expulsion data. However, the extent of this overlap cannot be documented, as not all cases to be returned under readmission agreements enter the aliens police procedure, nor are all the aliens who enter the alien's police procedure returned under readmission agreements.

Romania: Data on expulsion orders are not available, as this procedure does not exist apart from the border procedure of issuing exit visas, which may be issued to any alien supposed to leave the country within a given time limit. In 1997, 4,100 aliens were issued an exit visa and 2,830 in 1998. Moreover, the right to stay is cancelled in only a very few cases (23 in 1997 and 28 in 1998) to aliens who committed a serious violation of the Romanian laws, or whose behaviour threatens Romanian national interests The data on expulsions refer to implemented expulsions carried out under escort or controlled departures/transportation. There were 763 expulsions carried out by air in 1997.

Slovak Republic: Data on expulsion orders only refer to the issuing of these orders. It should not be confused with the data on notice to leave, which is issued – amongst others – together with the cancellation of the right/authorization to stay. For instance, in 1998 5,798 aliens were given notice to leave within a certain time period, of which 3,366 were given notice to leave after their right/authorization to stay was cancelled. Controlled departure may take place in case an escort is not ordered, but this practice is not systematically documented. Data on expulsions refer to actually implemented expulsions with an escort or police assistance.

Source: Technical Cooperation Centre for Europe and Central Asia.

FIGURE 4.2

READMISSION TO AND FROM SELECTED CENTRAL EASTERN EUROPEAN COUNTRIES

Persons Readmitted to the Czech Republic, Hungary, Romania and the Slovak Republic, 1998
(in thousands)

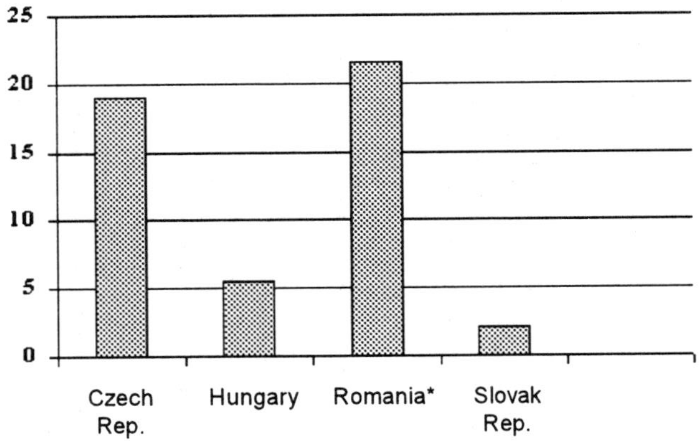

Persons Readmitted from the Czech Republic and Hungary, 1998
(in thousands)

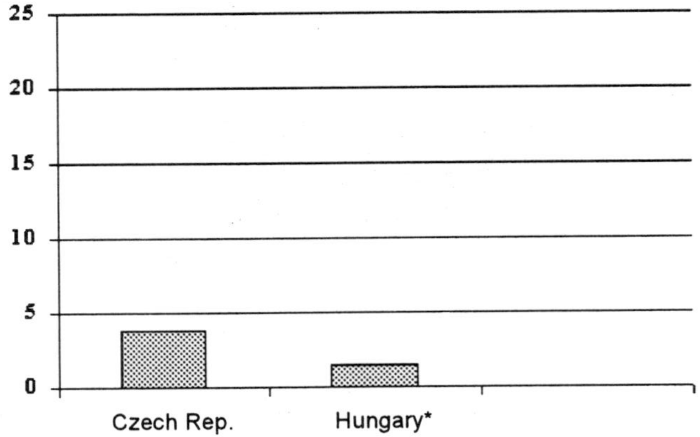

*Only Romanian nationals

*Plus 816 persons returned following an accelerated procedure directly from the border

Another important indicator of the number of returns is the number of persons readmitted to other countries. Here we can see that the number of returns according to readmission agreements is relatively high in the case of the Czech Republic and also relatively high in Hungary (see Figure 4.2). Some 3,818 persons were readmitted from the Czech Republic to other countries in 1998, and 1,452 were readmitted from Hungary to other countries in the same year. Figures for Romania for 1997 suggest that only 107 people were returned from Romania to other countries according to readmission agreements (IOM/ICMPD, 1999). Most of those readmitted from the Czech Republic were persons readmitted to the Slovak Republic, and mainly nationals of the FRY, Afghanistan, FYROM and Romania.

A third interesting aspect that concerns the number of irregular migrants who are returned is the number of returns by air, which usually also provides a good indication of the extent to which returns are to the migrant's country of origin. Here the data are more reliable, and produce some surprising results. Among our four CEE countries, the number of returns by air was highest in Romania in 1998 (763 including escorts). In each of the other countries less than 500 returns by air were organized in 1998.

Of the four CEE countries, only Hungary operates a significant voluntary assisted return programme. In 1998, with the assistance of IOM, 281 returns were implemented, which represents the majority of returns by air of irregular migrants from Hungary in that year. Although the absolute numbers of IOM assisted returns have been relatively low, the numbers are significant because they are usually returns to the migrant's country of origin. The Hungarian scheme is discussed further in the next section.

Given that a relatively low number of migrants are returned from the CEE countries, it seems unlikely that a high proportion of the migrants readmitted from EU states are subsequently removed to a neighbouring country or to their country of origin. Although this is a difficult point to establish with certainty, since some of the third country nationals who are readmitted to the CEECs may be eligible to remain legally in those countries, and some will in fact be CEE citizens.

Comparison with EU Countries and the EU Acquis

Although it is extremely difficult to compare return trends in CEE and EU countries, it is clear that in absolute terms EU states are returning a much higher number of irregular migrants than CEE states. Germany, for example, expelled 38,479 migrants in 1998, Austria, 15,522, the Netherlands, 13,484, and Belgium, 7,016, (IOM, 1999: 27). However, these figures are not so impressive when one considers that there are many more unsuccessful asylum seekers in EU countries, as noted earlier, than in the CEE region. For example, two-thirds of those expelled from Germany in 1994 were rejected asylum seekers. Moreover, a large proportion of the migrants who are being returned from EU countries are being returned to the CEE region and other third countries but not necessarily to the migrant's country of origin. For example, in Belgium over half (56%) of returns were not to the migrant's country of origin in 1998. In the case of Germany, as mentioned earlier, huge numbers of migrants (nearly 20,000 in 1998) are being returned to Central Europe according to readmission agreements.

Another difference between the EU countries and the CEE region is that the use of voluntary assisted return schemes is more widespread in Western Europe. A large number of assisted voluntary return programmes rely on cooperation between the returning state and IOM. They offer unsuccessful asylum seekers and other undocumented migrants a variety of services connected to their return or onward migration. Benefits provided under these programmes typically include return transportation, a travel allowance to cover miscellaneous expenses on the journey, and possible additional baggage allowance over and above that normally offered by the carrier. These schemes provide governments with a significant alternative to forced returns. For example, in Germany, approximately one in five returns are implemented with IOM assistance, and in Belgium the figure is one in eight (IOM, 1999).

CEE Return Policies: The Main Obstacles to Return

There are several explanations for the relatively low number of returns from CEE countries. Perhaps the most obvious is that some CEE states, such as Romania, are mainly source countries, and do not apprehend many irregular migrants at present. This is not to say that irregular migration is not a problem in these countries, merely that few illegal migrants are discovered by the authorities.

A common problem in many European countries is that even among unsuccessful asylum seekers there are many who originate from countries to which they cannot be safely returned. Some irregular migrants simply cannot be returned either for technical reasons, such as proof of identity, lack of travel documents, or because the country of origin is not safe or not willing to readmit them. CEE states are more likely than EU states to share borders with countries which might not be considered to be "safe" countries of return, or with whom they do not have readmission agreements, thus making return potentially more difficult to achieve.

There are also many other technical and political obstacles to implementing returns in the CEECs. Return policy covers many elements and is not limited to the procedures relating to the expulsion of migrants. It also includes measures such as voluntary assisted return programmes and readmission agreements, and procedures relating to preparation for return, such as counselling and the reception of migrants, and programmes which provide assistance to migrants after their return. Return policy also involves issues relating to international cooperation, since it is very difficult for any state to operate an effective return policy without the support of countries of origin and transit.

Costs of Return

It is often argued that CEE countries, unlike EU states, cannot afford to pay for the transportation and other costs required to implement returns. For example:

> Deportation is not widely practised in the (CEE) region, largely because of the costs involved – governments often issue an expulsion order but for financial reasons refrain from physically expelling people. (Hughes and Kessing, 1998: 62).

Even in the case of the Czech Republic, one of the richer countries of the region, it is reported that in 1999 the Aliens Police received only one-third of the amount they required for border control and management and for the operation of the major Balkova detention centre for irregular migrants.

The costs associated with implementing an effective return policy include the cost of providing reception facilities for irregular migrants prior to their return. Such costs can be very high, especially when return proves difficult to organize and migrants spend a long period of time in a reception centre. In Hungary, it is estimated that the costs can amount to US$ 7,000 per year per migrant (more than the minimum wage per year).

Reception facilities for irregular migrants are limited across the region. Among the four CEE countries included in this study the number of centres is greatest in the Czech Republic and Hungary, and lowest in Romania and Slovakia. In Romania there is only one centre for illegal migrants with a capacity to host a maximum of 90 persons, and in Slovakia the main centre for illegals can host a maximum of 200 people.

However, reception capacity is increasing across the CEE region. Romania, for example, opened a major new detention centre for illegal migrants in January 1999. In cooperation with Hungary and with financial assistance from the EC Phare Cross-Border Programme, Romania will open another reception centre for illegal migrants in the near future at Arad, near the Hungarian border. In the Czech Republic a new detention centre for illegal migrants was opened in November 1998 (the Balkova centre), primarily for undocumented migrants readmitted from Germany. There are also examples of centres which have considerably increased their capacity to receive illegal migrants such as the Medvedov centre in the Slovak Republic.

It is obviously cheaper to return irregular migrants than to maintain them for long periods in reception centres. Since a high proportion of the irregular migrants in our four CEE countries originate from other CEE states, the return transportation costs should not be too high. However, transportation costs are likely to increase. One factor which has added to the cost of return, is that a growing minority of the migrants who should be returned, come from distant parts of the world and places that do not have direct air connections with Eastern Europe. This means that the authorities often have to charter planes to organize returns. For example, in 1998, the Romanian government organized three special charter flights for returnees to Sri Lanka, Bangladesh, and Pakistan.

In most CEE states the bulk of the cost of returning an irregular migrant is paid for by the state authorities. However, in cases where migrants have been found to be employed illegally, the migrant's employer may be obliged to contribute to the costs of return. This is the case, for example, in Poland.[18]

---

[18] If the expulsion of an alien is a result of his her taking up employment or other gainful work without the necessary permission, the employer shall bear the costs of return (N. Siron and P. Van Baeveghem, "Trafficking in Migrants through Poland", University of Ghent, 1999).

Another factor which adds to the cost of returns in the CEE region is the absence in most countries, with the notable exception of Hungary (discussed below), of assisted return programmes which are often less costly.[19]

To sum up, whilst it is broadly true that the CEE countries lack the necessary funds to pay for returns, there is also a tendency for CEE countries to give priority, with financial and technical assistance from the EU, to more costly programmes to combat irregular migration, such as tougher border enforcement (see IOM/ICMPD, 1999). Yet, the latter policies are more likely to be fully effective if those irregular migrants who are apprehended at borders are subsequently returned to their country of origin or to a third country.[20]

Location and Detention of Irregular Migrants

A major problem for the authorities is that many of those in reception centres who should be returned "disappear" before their return can be organized. There are reports that a high percentage of asylum seekers leave these centres before their asylum claim has been considered. For example, in the Czech Republic in 1997, some 40 per cent of asylum seekers "disappeared" before their claims could be considered (IOM and ICMPD, 1999: 134). In Hungary, in 1997, it was reported that by far the majority of rejected asylum seekers in one reception centre near Budapest (Bicske), left the centre without authorisation immediately after being refused asylum (Oltalomkeresok, September, 1997: 5). The head of the reception centre believes that many of the migrants left the country, often crossing into nearby Austria.[21]

Some argue that these "disappearances" occur because asylum seekers expect a negative decision on their asylum claim and fear expulsion, whilst others suggest that reception centres are often deliberately targeted by traffickers who encourage transit migrants to make asylum claims in order to enable them to prepare themselves better for the next stage of their journey to the West. The latter claim

---

[19] IOM has international agreements with many international airlines, which enables the Organization to purchase one-way tickets at a significantly reduced rate of between 40-60 per cent of the normal fare.

[20] For details of other measures taken to combat irregular migration in the CEEs, see IOM/ICMPD (1999).

[21] This type of occurrence was confirmed during the bi-lateral exchanges when staff from the reception centre in Hungary visited the reception centre in Austria and met the same individuals who had previously claimed asylum in Hungary.

that many asylum seekers only use the centres as a place to plan the next part of their journey towards Western Europe.

In order to reduce the number of disappearances of irregular migrants from reception centres, the Hungarian authorities decided, in August 1998, to restrict the movements of migrants in eight of the centres managed by the border guards.[22] However, the three centres for asylum seekers and temporary protected persons, of which Bicske is one, remain "open".[23] As mentioned earlier, this is because of legal restrictions regarding the detention of asylum seekers.[24] It is not known exactly what effect the closing of the centres in Hungary has had on the ability of the authorities to return more irregular migrants, given the lack of reliable return data. However, this change does seem to have contributed to an increase in the number of voluntary assisted returns from Hungary. Nearly all of the migrants participating in the Hungarian Assisted Return Programme (HARP) are referrals from the so-called closed "community shelters". In 1997, only 47 migrants participated in this programme. By 1998 the figure had increased to 281, and by the first half of 1999, there were already 270 returnees. It is likely that the option of returning home voluntarily became more attractive when migrants in these centres could no longer leave these centres so easily in order to continue their journey to the West.

The Czech Republic has also increased the use of detention for irregular migrants. In the Balkova centre for undocumented migrants, most of whom have been readmitted from Germany, the period of detention is limited to only 30 days, although it is proposed to increase the maximum detention period to 180 days (as is the case now in Hungary), to allow the authorities more time to obtain the necessary travel documents. Similarly, in the Slovak Republic irregular

---

[22] Since 12 August 1998 migrants who do not possess valid travel documents or another form of document to prove their identity are not allowed to leave the centres managed by the National Border Guard Directorate, except with special permission.

[23] The length of stay in these centres according to refugee law is limited to 6 months in the first instance. This can be extended to a further 6 months. After this asylum seekers may become eligible for social assistance and a rent allowance.

[24] Those responsible for the protection of asylum seekers in Western Europe have expressed growing concern about the detention of asylum seekers, which is regarded as undesirable (Hughes and Liebaut, 1998). Across Western Europe the trend appears to be that a greater number of asylum seekers are being detained for longer periods of time. With a few exceptions most states in Western Europe exercise some form of restriction on the freedom of movement of asylum seekers and/or rejected cases. These normally take the form of residential requirements or reporting obligations.

migrants are only detained for 30 days at the detention centre at Medvedov. Recent figures suggest that the Slovak authorities are able to organize the return of less than a quarter of the undocumented migrants who are detained at the centre. After their release, migrants are supposed to report to the police regularly, but most fail to do so.

In Romania there is no limit to the length of detention at the main centre for irregular migrants at Otepeni. It is reported that at the detention facility at Otopeni airport illegal migrants are often detained for long periods because of difficulties involved in obtaining the necessary travel documents. For instance, it can take up to four months in the case of migrants from India (Hughes and Kessing, 1998).

Obtaining Travel Documents

One of the most difficult problems associated with managing the return of irregular migrants is that many migrants are undocumented and deliberately try to conceal their identity in order to avoid being returned to their country of origin or to a third country. In the CEE region returns can be more difficult to organize where the country of origin has no diplomatic or consular presence. This problem has grown in importance as the number of asylum seekers and illegal migrants from developing countries has increased.

The four CEE countries included in this study reported considerable difficulties in obtaining travel documents for migrants awaiting expulsion. For example, in the Slovak Republic in 1998, the Aliens Police reported that they tried to obtain travel documents for more than 1,200 migrants and were only able to do this for 20 migrants, most of whom came from Romania. Among the nationalities presenting the greatest problems were citizens of the FRY, Afghanistan, China, Viet Nam, Sri Lanka, Iraq and India.

In Romania, it is reported that obtaining travel documents is especially problematic in cases of persons from countries which do not have any diplomatic representation in Romania such as Bangladesh and Ghana. However, in cases of large-scale returns of migrants from Bangladesh the Romanian authorities have received the assistance of the Bangladeshi Embassy in Warsaw.

In Hungary, it is reported that it has been very difficult to obtain travel documents for nationals of Afghanistan, Iraq, Sri Lanka, Sierra Leone, and Liberia. During 1998 it was also difficult to obtain documents for migrants from Bangladesh, but the situation improved as a result of a visit by diplomatic representatives from the Bangladeshi Embassy in Poland.

Cooperation with Source and Transit Countries

In order to implement returns, returning states usually require the cooperation of countries of origin and transit countries. For the CEEs, cooperation on returns is much easier with other CEE countries than with non-European countries of origin. As of August 1998, 238 readmission agreements had been signed in Europe, of which only 2 were signed between CEE and non-European countries of origin (IGC, 1999). This compares with a figure of 21 agreements signed between Western European and non-European countries. By contrast, there were 67 readmission agreements between Central and Eastern European countries.

Although EU states also experience problems in securing the cooperation of source countries in facilitating returns, they have more political and economic influence to exert in order to achieve returns to source countries than is generally the case for CEE countries. The CEECs lack the economic and political ties which many EU states have with countries of origin. For example, including re-admission clauses in agreements on economic cooperation with poorer countries is common practice in the EU. And of course the EU can perhaps exert its greatest influence over the source countries of Eastern Europe as they wish to become members of the EU.

Another problem is that some of the CEE´s neighbours to the East may not be considered to be "safe third countries" or "safe countries of origin" for asylum seekers. Candidate countries cannot therefore always relieve themselves of their responsibilities by simply passing them on to countries in the Eastern region.

Lack of Voluntary Assisted Return Programmes

One important way in which returning states can make cooperation with transit and receiving states easier, is by promoting voluntary assisted return programmes, which result in the migrant returning directly to his or her country of origin. However, with the exception of Hungary, little is going on to provide for voluntary assisted return programmes in the CEE region. The main emphasis instead is on forced returns, which as we have seen, are usually much more expensive than voluntary assisted returns. Compared to Western Europe, there also appears to be relatively little counselling of potential returnees or information provided to unsuccessful asylum seekers to promote voluntary returns (IOM, 1999).

Only Hungary has thus far developed a significant voluntary assisted return programme. However, IOM has made agreements with the governments of the Czech Republic, Romania and the Slovak Republic to develop similar programmes.

The Hungarian Assisted Return Programme (HARP) has been operating since 1994. The programme is open to a wide range of categories of irregular migrant including victims of trafficking. The programme provides for:

- *Pre-departure assistance*: information dissemination and counselling, cash grants of US$ 50 per person.

- *Transport assistance*: transport, documents and formalities, transit assistance of US$ 10 per person.

It is often argued that voluntary assisted return programmes are unlikely to produce results unless a state has an effective set of procedures to implement forced returns. The recent experience of Hungary would suggest, however, that a voluntary assisted return programme can be successfully developed even in a country where the number of forced expulsions is relatively low.

As mentioned earlier, however, this programme is virtually restricted to persons detained in the "community shelters" mainly young males aged 15-29 (see Table 4.1).

TABLE 4.1

IOM ASSISTED VOLUNTARY RETURNEES FROM HUNGARY
(JANUARY 1999 - JUNE 1999) BY GENDER AND AGE

	No. of Returnees	Male	Female	0-14	15-29	30-60
January	41	40	1		32	10
February	43	34	9		27	26
March	48	39	9		22	26
April	22	21	1		13	9
May	22	10	12	3	13	6
June	94	92	2	1	72	21
July	49	6	43	7	25	17
Total	**319**	**242**	**77**	**11**	**204**	**109**

The Hungarian programme is far more economical for the government; it also enables migrants to return home in dignity, and facilitates return to countries of origin. In 1999 returns were organized to many distant countries of origin (see Table 4.2). Moreover, since the programme is largely financed by the Hungarian authorities themselves, such a programme ought to be financially viable in other CEE countries.[25]

TABLE 4.2

IOM ASSISTED VOLUNTARY RETURNEES FROM HUNGARY
(JANUARY 1999 – JULY 1999) BY MAIN CITIZENSHIP

	Total
Algeria	10
Albania	13
Armenia	4
Bangladesh	56
BiH	30
Bulgaria	27
Cameroon	2
China	22
Egypt	19
Ghana	1
India	24
Iran	1
Lebanon	3
FYROM	30
Moldova	21
Mongolia	6
Pakistan	5
Philippines	8
Poland	1
Russian Fed.	3
Somalia	2
Syria	4
Turkey	26
Viet Nam	1
Total	**319**

---

[25] The programme cost less than US$ 200,000 in 1998.

CONCLUSION: POLICY IMPLICATIONS

The discussion in this chapter has shown that irregular migration presents a growing challenge for CEE countries. As EU enlargement approaches, it is expected that CEE candidate and non-candidate countries alike will be expected by the EU to increase their efforts to combat irregular migration. Although experience in EU countries suggests that the return of irregular migrants is often difficult to manage, and that return policy at best only offers a partial response to combating irregular migration, the CEECs are expected to do more to develop effective return policies in the future. As this study has shown, at present, relatively low numbers of irregular migrants are being returned *from* the CEE region, but many irregular migrants are being returned *to* this region, primarily under readmission agreements. This is the major difference between CEE and EU countries, in terms of the return policy challenges that they face.

Clearly a comprehensive approach to combating irregular migration in the CEE region is needed, involving a range of different policy measures, from punitive measures, such as border controls and employer sanctions, to preventive measures such as information campaigns, and economic incentives to reduce the need for migration (Bimal Ghosh, 1998). Return policies clearly have to be part of any comprehensive strategy of this kind, but at present they are of only minor significance in many CEE countries.

Policy-makers in different CEE countries, however, face quite different return policy challenges. The major difference is that some countries, like Romania, are major source countries, whilst others, such as Hungary and the Czech Republic, are mainly transit countries for irregular migrants. Romania, for example, faces the challenge of how to re-integrate its own citizens who are being returned in large numbers. Romania experiences relatively few problems with source countries as few illegal migrants are either apprehended or returned from Romania.

For Central European countries such as the Czech Republic, Hungary, and to a growing extent the Slovak Republic, the challenge is different, as large numbers of third country nationals are being re-admitted to these countries from Germany, Austria and other EU states. For Central European states, the main problem is how to return these transit migrants.

The results of this study suggest therefore a number of different policy implications for CEE states which are outlined below.

- *An effective return policy should be a key component of a comprehensive programme to combat irregular migration in the CEECs.*

CEE states should be encouraged to give greater priority to implementing return programmes, and to combating irregular migration more generally. In some states, there are few returns because few irregular migrants are apprehended. In other states, more needs to be done to prevent irregular migration. Return policies can only operate effectively within the context of an effective migration management system, alongside other instruments such as visa policy, border management, carrier sanctions, and anti-trafficking legislation. CEE states should ensure that they develop the right return procedures now before the number of irregular migrants and unsuccessful asylum seekers rises further.

- *EU countries should assist the CEECs in developing effective return policies.*

The development of effective return programmes in the CEECs is very much in the interests of EU states. They should therefore ensure that a greater share of the financial and technical assistance provided by the EU to help CEE countries to combat irregular migration is devoted to facilitating the development of return programmes.

- *The costs of return should be shared between the EU and CEE countries.*

Another way of reducing the costs of return for CEE states would be to ensure that employers who hire illegal migrants pay at least a portion of the costs of expulsion. The promotion of assisted return programmes would also be an important way to reduce the costs of return.

- *Associated countries should not be used as final destinations for third country migrants in the readmission chain.*

The EU has not yet developed an overall return policy, and most of the *acquis* relating to return issues consists of non-binding recommendations. In developing such a policy, the EU should encourage Member States to develop programmes which facilitate the return of irregular migrants to their country of origin. Returning third country illegal migrants to the EU Associated countries under readmission agreements is often not an effective solution at present since these countries do not have the necessary experience and resources to return these migrants.

- *Promote better cooperation between CEE states, countries of origin, and transit states.*

CEE countries are likely to be able to develop more effective and sustainable return policies if these policies are developed in cooperation with countries of origin and transit.

- *Expand programmes for voluntary assisted return.*

Within the framework of an overall return policy, voluntary assisted return programmes can increase overall return figures, play an important role in reducing the costs of return, and enable the migrant to return in dignity. The recent experience of Hungary demonstrates that voluntary assisted return programmes are viable and affordable in Central and Eastern Europe.

Assisted voluntary return, where feasible, is the most desirable form of return because it takes account of the person's decision, allows the returnee to prepare for the return and avoids the stigma of deportation and its negative repercussions for successful reintegration. Moreover, consideration should be given to the overall cost of such assisted returns, especially when compared with the cost of extended stays which ultimately end in deportation (see also Chapters 3 and 5).

- *In designing return programmes, CEE countries should take into account the needs of different groups of irregular migrants.*

A differentiated approach is particularly important for the return and reintegration of vulnerable groups such as trafficked women and children. For female victims of trafficking, for example, special professional counselling may be needed to prepare them for return. By doing this, returning states can ensure that return is sustainable (also discussed in Chapter 5).

- *A common data collection system should be established in the CEE countries to monitor and compare return trends.*

There is a considerable lack of reliable and comparable return data in the CEE region. Without such basic information it is very difficult to assess what progress these states are making in combating irregular migration, and it is very difficult to know how best to re-shape return policy. CEE states need to agree upon a common set of definitions and procedures for collecting return data and for exchanging this information.

REFERENCES

Batt, J.
  1999 Final Report of the Reflection Group on "The Long-Term Implica-
        tions of EU Enlargement: The Nature of the New Border",
        European University Institute, Florence.
Brochmann, G., and T. Hammar (Eds)
  1999 *Mechanisms of Immigration Control: A Comparative Analysis of Euro-*
        pean Regulation Policies, Berg, Oxford.
Budapest Group
  1995 *Report of the Expert Group on the Five Themes Selected for Examination*
        by the Budapest Group, Third meeting of the Budapest Group,
        Zürich, 14-15 September 1995.
CDMG
  1997 *Recent Developments and Policies Relating to Migration and Migrants,*
        European Committee on Migration (CDMG) 97/17 rev., Stras-
        bourg, 14 January 1998.
Ghosh, B.
  1999 *The Promise and Pitfalls of Return Migration,* paper prepared for the
        Conference on International Migration, Development and Eco-
        nomic Integration of Migrants, Stockholm, 6-7 September.
  1998 *Huddled Masses and Uncertain Shores: Insights Into Irregular Migra-*
        tion, Kluwer Law International, The Hague.
Hailbronner, K.M., A. David and Hiroshi Motomura
  1998 *Immigration Controls.* The Search for Workable Policies in Germany
        and the United States, Volume 4, American Academy of Arts and
        Sciences.
Hughes, J., and P.V. Kessing
  1998 *Detention of Asylum Seekers in Central and Eastern Europe,* Chapter 2,
        Detention of Asylum Seekers in Europe: Analysis and Perspect-
        ives, Kluwer Law International.
Hughes, J., and F. Liebaut
  1998 *Detention of Asylum Seekers in Europe: Analysis and Perspectives,*
        Kluwer Law International.
IOM
  1995 *Trafficking and Prostitution: The Growing Exploitation of Women From*
        Central and Eastern Europe, IOM, Geneva.
  1997 "Combating irregular migration and migrant trafficking: the ele-
        ments of a response", paper submitted by IOM for the Second
        Regional Conference on Migration, Panama, 11-14 March 1997.
  1999a "Profile of Victims of Trafficking from the Czech Republic", Tech-
        nical Cooperation Centre, IOM, Vienna.
  1999b "Migrant Trafficking in Hungary", unpublished.

2000 *A Review of Trafficking and People Smuggling in Europe with Case Studies from Hungary, Poland and Ukraine*, IOM, Geneva.

IOM/ICMPD

1999 *Migration in Central and Eastern Europe: 1999 Review*, IOM, Geneva.

Noll, G.

1998 *Responding to the Arrival of Asylum-Seekers. Unsuccessful Asylum Seekers: The Problem of Return*, Paper No. IX/3, paper prepared for the Technical Symposium on International Migration and Development, The Haghe, Netherlands, 29 June - 3 July 1998.

1999a *Migration Statistics.* January 1998, EDV Referat Misurec 02.98.

1999b *Rejected Asylum Seekers: The Problem of Return*, UNHCR Working Paper No. 4, University of Lund, Sweden.

Siron, N., and P. Van Baeveghem

1999 "Trafficking in Migrants through Poland", University of Ghent.

Widgren, J.

1999 *From Schengen to Amsterdam – Towards a European Immigration and Asylum Legislation*, Academy of European Law, Trier, 19 February 1999.

Chapter 5

Return Migration: Reshaping Policy Approaches

Bimal Ghosh

INTRODUCTION[1]

Every year large numbers of migrants, excluding those who seek permanent settlement in the host country, return home. Return is of course implicit in certain types of cross-border movements such as seasonal, and rotational or circulatory migration. But, it is quite a common occurrence even amongst other categories of non-settler migrants. Whether they are pulled by the attraction of better opportunities abroad (opportunity-seeking migration) or pushed by adverse economic, political or environmental circumstances (survival migration) (Ghosh 1992, 1998), many of them indeed leave with the hope that they will eventually return to their home country. For example, in a country like Jamaica, which has a long tradition of emigration, return is considered the intended conclusion of migration by the majority of persons at the time of departure; and the return of Jamaican migrants is probably higher than generally assumed in the absence of official statistics (Thomas-Hope, 1998). In this sense, and at least for these categories, return can rightly be viewed as the "concluding phase" of the migration cycle (Callea, 1985). The cycle of course is not a closed one, and may well be repeated. Also, emigration and return

---

[1] A shorter version of this chapter was published in *International Migration and Development*, Ministry for Foreign Affairs, Stockholm, Sweden, 1999, pp. 189-206

are not isolated acts or events; they must be seen as inter-locking parts of an open and wider on-going process of global mobility (see also Chapter 1).

What may seem surprising is that even among the immigrants admitted for permanent residence, returns could be quite high. For example, the US Bureau of Census estimated that of the 15.7 million immigrants who were admitted as permanent settlers in the US between 1908 and 1957, some 30 per cent returned to their country of origin. Also revealing are the findings of a sample survey in western Mexico which showed that of *all* the immigrants (settlers and non-settlers) who entered the US during 1980-90, 50 per cent returned to Mexico after only two years, while the proportion rose to 70 per cent after ten years (Table 5.1).

TABLE 5.1

ESTIMATED NUMBER OF IMMIGRANTS FROM WESTERN MEXICO ENTERING
THE UNITED STATES IN 1980-1990 AND REMAINING FOR 5 OR 10 YEARS

	Number of immigrants entering		Number of annual average remaining	
	1980-1990	Annual average	5 years later	10 years later
National Total	**5,039,399**	**503,940**	**200,921**	**137,727**
Undocumented	3,332,105	333,211	111,259	76,938
Documented	1,707,294	170,729	87,738	59,977
California Total	**3,264,947**	**326,495**	**145,617**	**95,826**
Undocumented	2,139,810	213,981	82,105	57,646
Documented	1,125,136	112,514	62,389	38,390

Source: The Mexican Migration Database. The figures include all immigrants, regardless of whether or not the original intention was to settle permanently in the US.

However, despite the importance of return flows as a concurrent feature of human movements, issues of return have so far received little systematic attention from policy makers or analysts (see also Introduction and Chapter 1). While analysts have discussed, albeit somewhat sporadically, the consequences of return, efforts to assess and harness the development potential of different categories of migrants have been negligible. The subject however has assumed special importance against the backdrop of rising numbers of irregular migrants, rejected asylum seekers and temporary refugees, alongside an increasing anxiety of the host countries to speed up their repatriation. These trends have at the same time sharpened and widened the awareness of the need for an agreed policy framework for durable return, buttressed by an optimal convergence of interests of all the parties directly involved – the origin, transit and returning states and the migrants themselves.

Can return programmes, when judiciously linked to development of the country of origin, make a contribution to these objectives? With their seemingly divergent interests why should the parties directly concerned be willing to cooperate in carrying out such programmes? Can such development-oriented return programmes be so designed that they make return durable and cost-effective and at the same time provide a meaningful meeting ground for these varying interests to converge?

This chapter takes up these questions. Divided in two parts, it first examines why and how return and readmission of migrants can be closely interlocked with the development of opportunities in the country of origin, while balancing and harmonizing the interests of the different parties involved. Although a wider background, covering different categories of migrants who returned home in the past few decades, is used for purposes of analysis, the focus is on contemporary irregular migrants, rejected asylum seekers and those under temporary protection abroad. In the second part, the chapter reviews the current debate on issues related to repatriation and "imposed return" of refugees, including those enjoying temporary protection, outlines a pragmatic response to them and then comes back to the theme of development in the context of durable return of refugees.

I

TYPES OF RETURN AND THE SALIENCE OF REINTEGRATION

Return takes place in varying circumstances and under different policy frameworks (see Figure 5.1, also Chapter 2). Many choose to return on their own (autonomous return), while others benefit from assistance (assisted return). Return can be voluntary, which is generally the case with autonomous return, or can be the result of expulsion or deportation (forced return). The nature and extent of assistance also vary: it can be directly linked to organized programmes for specific target groups or take the form of creating conducive conditions or provision of inducements for emigrants to return. In almost all these cases the primary goal of *return* is normally achieved. What is not certain, however, is whether and to what extent the *reintegration* is successful.

FIGURE 5.1

RETURN MIGRATION: A TYPOLOGY OF POLICY FRAMEWORKS FOR RETURN
AND READMISSION

Framework	Type of Migrants	Parties Involved
Autonomous/assisted.	Regular/irregular migrants.	Host/origin countries.
Expulsion/Readmission agreements.	Irregular migrants/ Rejected asylum seekers.	Host, transit and origin countries.
"Safe country under asylum" rules.	Asylum seekers.	Host (destination), transit, and origin countries.
Temporary protection.	Externally displaced persons, war refugees.	Host, origin, and third countries.
Refugees protection.	"Convention refugees".	Host, origin, and third countries.
Termination of job contracts.	Labour migrants, seasonal workers.	Host and origin countries.
Recovery of citizenship.	Returning (ethnic) nationals.	Origin and "host" countries.

Adapted from Koser, 1998.

Two Dimensions of Successful Reintegration: Personal Welfare and Impact on National Development

Successful reintegration has two different, though potentially inter-related, dimensions. The first relates to personal success, entailing social and economic security and welfare of the returning migrant as an individual (including members of the family) in the local community of the country of origin. For almost all economically active migrants, access to productive and gainful employment is a most vital element of this process. The second concerns the contribution of return to the economic and social development of the country of origin and the local communities. When the return process contributes both to the personal success of the migrants themselves and to the future economic and social development of the country of origin, it sets into motion a virtuous circle helping further return in the future. However, as will be further discussed below, barring a few specific instances, return processes have generally been unable to effectively combine the two in a harmonious manner, and as a result the positive and sustainable impact of return has remained somewhat circumscribed.

RETURN AND DEVELOPMENT

Autonomous Return and Its Impact on Development: An Empirical Analysis

The effect of voluntary and autonomous return – be it on the enhancement of personal welfare of migrants or on the development of the home country – is largely influenced by the initial motivations for migration as well as by the duration of the stay abroad and particularly by the conditions under which the return takes place. For instance, return after relatively short periods abroad, caused by an inability to adapt to the new environment or due to unforeseen and adverse family circumstances, is hardly likely to contribute either to personal welfare or development.

By contrast, return could occur following a moderate period of stay abroad when the migrant has saved, in keeping with the original intention, a pre-determined amount of money to meet a specific purpose back home – such as building a house or other assets, capital investment, risk diversification or simply improving consumption. In such cases, although the immediate goal of migration is fulfilled, the effect of return on personal welfare or satisfaction and especially on development will clearly vary. In the case of improved consumption, for example, there is likely to be little or limited impact on development, unless the economic sectors are flexible and equipped enough to respond positively and promptly to new demand through increased production. It may however positively enhance personal and family welfare, but the extent to which this will occur depends on the contextual circumstances such as the income and welfare foregone by the migrant in the home country – or the opportunity cost involved.

When return is motivated by the pursuit of investment and business-related activities, its impact on personal success and development will be determined by two critical factors: (a) the aptitude and preparation of the returning migrants; and (b) whether or not the country of origin provides a propitious social, economic and institutional environment for the migrants to use their savings and skills productively (UN, 1997).

Conditions of Success Cannot Be Taken for Granted

Past experience shows that the conditions necessary to ensure the success of autonomous return in terms of personal success of returnees or development of the country of origin were not always available. Given the typically difficult employment situation in their countries of origin, many returnees tended to set up their own business in small rural and urban communities using their personal savings. Clearly, such investments can be a stimulus for development of these areas that normally suffer from shortage of capital and structural constraints. The returnees can play an important role in this connection as illustrated by the fact that a quarter of the 250 non-agricultural businesses found recently in three Mexican communities were set up by returned migrants (Cornelius, 1990; UN, 1997).

But the weaknesses of such initiatives in the past were equally clear. In the absence of previous experience or training and local support, the returnees in many cases failed to take up effectively the new challenge as self-employed business owners. Not surprisingly, nearly half of the business enterprises run by migrants or former migrants in the Mexican communities mentioned above faced difficulties and depended at least in part on a continued flow of remittances from abroad. A similar situation was revealed in Pakistan, where a survey carried out in 1985-86 showed that although the proportion of returnees to rural areas who owned a business increased from 34 per cent before migration to 56 per cent after migration, they were generally not adequately equipped to assume their new role as self-employed business owners, and as a result business failures were common (Amjad, 1989; UN, 1997).

The problem has often been compounded by the absence of suitable institutional arrangements to provide financial support and technical assistance to the business enterprises started by the returnees in small communities. They are often further handicapped by their lack of familiarity with the local situation due to long stays abroad and the lack of supporting official or non-official institutions such as migrant-serving associations to help the returnees overcome this difficulty. Further, even when the skilled and enterprising returnees come with innovative ideas and new and better knowledge of doing things, they could fail to use them in their business activities or for the general advancement of the local community because of resistance from well-entrenched hierarchies and local jealousies (Ghosh, 1996).

When Return Contributes to the Sending Country's Human Capital Development

The same applies to the use of returnees' skills. One of the implicit assumptions underlying neo-classical theories of labour migration, which envision cross-border movements as being beneficial to both origin and host countries, is that the labour-abundant origin countries would benefit not only from the initial outflows of surplus labour but also subsequently from human capital development through newly acquired skills of returnees. In practice, however, the promises of return have often remained unfulfilled.

In general, the countries of origin can achieve the expected gains only when three conditions are met: first, workers return with more advanced knowledge or better skills than they would have acquired at home; second, the knowledge and skills gathered abroad are relevant to the needs of the home country economy; and third, the migrants must have the willingness and opportunity to use the skills upon return.

Empirical evidence from different countries and regions tends to suggest that in few cases these conditions are fully met. A general experience is that the highly skilled workers have more opportunities to improve their skills and knowledge than the less skilled ones. They are more easily accepted and can better overcome the difficulties of integration, which in turn helps them to be more productive and successful in the receiving country. Barring a few exceptions (the so-called "returns of success"), they are therefore less likely to return, as confirmed by the past data on return migration for several countries, including Greece and Turkey (Reyneri and Mughini, 1984).

Several studies in other regions also fail to show any significant upgrading of the skills of the majority of migrants working abroad. In Thailand, for example, out of a sample of 424 male migrant workers, scarcely 2 per cent took on occupations which might have imparted new skills, although 37 per cent were in jobs that could mean an improvement on the occupational status they had in Thailand. Likewise, the Thai female workers in Singapore were rarely exposed to new technologies or modes of production enabling them to acquire new skills (Sussangkarn and Chalamwong, 1996). In another case involving migrants from Bangladesh to the Gulf States, it was found that less than one per cent of the workers held jobs requiring higher skills than they had possessed prior to departure.

A worse situation is created when skilled and semi-skilled migrant workers are employed in lower-level positions than at home, implying downward occupational mobility and downgrading of skills. Clearly, this is detrimental to the interest not only of the migrants but also of the host and origin countries. The host country loses due to the waste of human resources just as the origin country fails to benefit from improved skills of the workers should they return. A recent study showed that one-third of Sri Lankan workers in the Gulf States were working in jobs requiring lower skills than those they used prior to departure. Other examples of such "de-skilling" included Filipino college graduates who have been working as domestic help in the receiving countries. Jamaican migrants who occupied skilled or white collar jobs prior to migration were obliged to work in unskilled or semi-skilled jobs in the destination countries (Thomas-Hope, 1998). The same was largely true of the Turks who in the past had worked in Germany and then returned (Paine, 1974).

Even when the migrant workers enhanced their skills while working abroad, the relevance of the skills to the economy of the country of origin was far from certain. Indeed, given the wide differences in the industrial structures, technology and work environment that often exist between the host and origin countries, the returnees could find it difficult to use their new skills on their return to the home country, as was revealed by several studies made in the 1980s of Greek and Turkish workers who returned from Germany. In Pakistan, one study revealed that 81 per cent of the returnees and 83 per cent of the employers thought that skills acquired abroad were not fully used mainly because they were largely irrelevant to the local situation (Azam, 1988). In the Dominican Republic and Suriname, migrants returned from the industrially and technologically advanced countries with skills that were unmarketable in the country of origin (Pessar, 1991).

Not surprisingly, returnees do not always perform well in the labour market of the country of origin, as reflected in the higher rate of unemployment among the migrants than among the non-migrants after return, as was revealed by recent surveys in several South Asian countries – Bangladesh, Pakistan and Sri Lanka (Guntalike, 1991). In Italy, for example, the employment rate of male returnees was lower that that among the non-migrant males; in Pakistan 10 per cent of returnees were unemployed even after one and a half years following their return; and in Bangladesh the percentage of unemployment rose from 10 per cent before migration to 40 per cent after return.

True, in some cases, as in Sri Lanka and Italy, the rates of unemployment were found lower among returnees than among non-migrants. But an important reason for this may well have been the withdrawal from the labour force of some returnees, especially female migrants. Also, in some other instances, as in Pakistan, the higher rate of unemployment among returnees, especially professional and technical workers, seemed to have been due to the fact that they could live on savings while looking for a job which they liked. All in all, however, the foregoing observation concerning the mismatch between the skills acquired abroad and the labour market needs in the country of origin remain largely valid.

In short, the returnees may often be better off than their non-migrant compatriots but their long-term personal success in the past was by no means obvious; and judging by the available data it is even less certain that autonomous return migration has significantly helped in accelerating the development of the country of origin, especially at the macro level.

Positive Impact of Autonomous Return Cannot Be Discounted

It would be wrong, however, to conclude from the above that the history of autonomous (non-assisted) return is nothing but a sad, long episode of personal failures or that it has made no contribution to development at all. True, many migrants returned home with only limited resources and qualifications. It is also clear that some migrants return with a clear preference for retirement after years of work, that those who seek jobs upon return may do worse than the non-migrants in the labour market and that many others are discouraged by the absence of a congenial environment to use their skills and resources and are disillusioned because of the lack of support from local and national authorities or by the negative attitude of the local community, including, not infrequently, its leaders.

And yet, experiences in a number of countries – Colombia and Mexico in Latin America, Bangladesh, India, Pakistan and Sri Lanka in Asia and Greece and Turkey in Europe – have revealed that return migration can be a positive factor for modernization and social change, especially in small towns and villages, despite tension and even conflict in the initial stages. In several East African countries, it has contributed to personal success through the growth of viable small business enterprises, while helping the overall development of local communities through, for example, construction of modern houses and roads. Likewise, in West Africa, Nigerian migrants returning from Ghana introduced new crops and techniques and contributed to breaking social rigidities that inhibited social progress. In the past, Greeks and Italians returning from the United States introduced new production techniques and contributed to technical change. (Salutos, 1956; Loperato, 1962; see also Chapter 1). More recently, Indian returnees from Silicon Valley in the United States have become a main driving force for the growth of the software industry in India following liberalization of its economy (Ghosh, 1996).

Although scattered and numerically limited, there are also success stories showing how even relatively small projects based on cooperative endeavours of the local population and returnees and supported by national and international agencies can spur development in a whole area and encourage further return flows. According to the information made available in a recent paper (Uygur, Ekonomik Panorama, 1992), the city of Abana in Turkey, which experienced continuous large-scale migration until the mid-1980s, provides a positive illustration. Together with migrants from Abana, a small group of entrepreneurs set up a company there to manufacture electrical machinery (Abana Electromekanik). Despite initial difficulties, the company was able not only to survive but also to make steady progress largely due to credits and other financial support from the European Resettlement Fund (ERF), the Development Bank of Turkey (DTB) and the Public Participation Administration. By 1991 the company's sales exceeded US$10 million and over 300 persons, all of them shareholders (some of whom were returned migrants) were working in the company, which also ran an apprenticeship training school for 60 students.

Based on the reported information, several interesting points can be noted. First, the success of even a relatively small company benefiting the returnees can have a multiplier effect and generate additional employment opportunities in related industries and services. Second, the project demonstrates how migrants, their associations and local people can join hands and actively contribute to the development of the country of origin. Third, the fact that migration from Abana has nearly ceased and that return migration, especially from Germany, has significantly increased, shows how the personal success of the returnees, combined with the improved economic conditions in the erstwhile high emigration areas, can encourage return migration while reducing pressure for future emigration.

What then is the Overall Assessment?

The conclusion that emerges is that autonomous return in the past may not have been a powerful force to spur development of the countries of origin, even when it may have meant that the returnees have been better off than the local population. However, given suitable conditions, including public and private support and a positive attitude on the part of the migrants themselves, it can contribute to local development with multiplier effects, while ensuring continuing success of the individual migrants in their own country. The experience, both positive and negative, also provides some valuable insights as to how the potential benefits of return can be maximized and how the pitfalls it often entailed in the past can be avoided by linking, when appropriate, autonomous return with a programme of pre-and post-return assistance and support.

TYPES AND FEATURES OF PROGRAMMES OF ASSISTED RETURN

Since the mid-1970s – when in the wake of a serious economic recession and rising unemployment Western Europe decided to impose a ban on labour immigration – all major host countries in the region, including Belgium, France, Germany, and the Netherlands – have developed policies and programmes of assisted return. The package of assistance has covered one or all of the three main stages of return, namely pre-departure, transportation for the journey and post-arrival, and the type of assistance has also varied according to the programme. The overall package under the various programmes has included some or all of the following assistance measures: direct financial incentives such as travelling allowance and departure premiums (e.g. France and Belgium); capitalization and remittance of social funds and social security benefits; vocational training to facilitate economic reintegration in the home country as well as cultural adaptation (e.g. the Netherlands and Germany); special credit for housing and for setting up private businesses; and general aid for the development of the country of origin or its specific regions (e.g. Germany, "return with employment") (Ghosh, 1991).

Most of these programmes have evolved over time and have undergone adaptations to the needs and conditions of specific return flows, and in keeping with bilateral and multilateral agreements concluded for their implementation. Both the characteristics of these various programmes and their impact on the welfare of the migrants and on the development of the country of origin vary widely.

ASSISTED RETURN OF QUALIFIED NATIONALS

Multilateral Programmes

These programmes are generally designed for migrants who have resided in the host country for a significant period of time and possess skills and knowledge that could be of use to the country or region of origin. The programmes seek to locate skilled and highly skilled migrants who are willing to return to their country or region of origin and take up selected positions which, though critical for national development, could not be filled locally. By contributing to the development process though their specialized knowledge and expertise, the returnees could thus partially counteract the negative effects of "brain drain". Aside from matching jobs and skills, the programmes provide returnees with a series of incentives, including travel costs, integration assistance, salary supplements, medical insurance and professional equipment. At the multilateral level, the International Organization for Migration (IOM) has been the main implementing agency of these programmes which have been operating in Latin America, Africa and more recently in Asia.

The goal of these programmes – return of qualified persons to occupy specified jobs in the country or region of origin – is quite straightforward. Since the returning migrants have legal status in the host country, issues of forced or coerced return do not arise and given that they are selected on the basis of their qualifications and experience, any cost of retraining is limited. Also, since the matching of jobs and skills takes place well in advance of the return, the risk of slippage due to delay or difficulty in finding suitable positions is almost non-existent. Another positive feature of these programmes is that they are not confined only to the governments but also involve the private sector, universities and research institutes in the countries concerned. The prospection of potential returnees is also done through a broad-based campaign including contacts with the migrants' associations in the host country.

Two main questions can be raised, however. First, could the returns have taken place even in the absence of these programmes? To put it differently, do the programmes simply subsidize the returns that would have occurred in any case? It seems doubtful. For example, according to an evaluation of the EU-funded and IOM-executed project to return 350 qualified nationals to Nicaragua between 1991-1995, as many as 89.5 per cent of the selected sample of returnees considered that the project had been essential for, or played a very important part in, their decision to return, while 10.5 per cent thought its influence was only fairly important (IOM, 1995). As regards their main reasons for choosing to return, 43 per cent wished to participate in the country's development, 29 per cent had family ties and 11.8 per cent had finished their studies and were therefore in a position to return.

A similar picture emerged from an evaluation of the on-going EU-funded programme for Return and Reintegration of Qualified African Nationals (RQAN), under which 88.3 per cent of returnees interviewed said that the programme had played an essential or a very important part in influencing their decision to return and 100 per cent of those questioned considered they were making a significant contribution to the socio-economic development of Africa (IOM, 1995).

These findings also throw some light on the second question: To what extent are assisted returns contributing to the overall development of the countries concerned? As mentioned above, most returnees considered that they were making such a contribution, and often indeed in a significant manner. No doubt, this was a subjective judgement of the migrants concerned, but not without supporting evidence. In the case of the programme for Africa, for example, employers questioned believed that the recruitment of qualified nationals from abroad was essential for the development of new and on-going activities and that the returnees made important contributions to institutional efficiency through management support and the use of new skills.

In cases like this it is of course always difficult to make a precise, statistical measurement of the incremental development impact of the returns, given the wide range of other variables involved. Assuming however that the jobs in question were themselves important from the perspective of national development (the economic and social sectors as well as the occupational categories of the returnees seemed to suggest so), an indirect test of the impact of returns on development would lie in the duration of the service provided by individual returnees following appointment. Job duration and the length of residence in the country concerned also provide an indication of the degree of personal reintegration of the returnees.

The survey findings revealed some positive trends in both these respects. For example, the evaluation made in 1995 of the programme for Nicaragua showed that 89.4 per cent were fully employed; 79 per cent believed their future career prospects to be good or excellent; and 91.2 per cent interviewed considered their return positively (IOM, 1995).

An external evaluation carried out in 1995 among 89 assisted returnees to five Central American countries revealed similar trends. Six years after the initiation of the programme, 61 per cent of all returnees and 90 per cent of the national returnees were still resident in the five project countries. However, the surveys carried out in 1985 and 1990 of the programme for Africa showed that while the project was achieving all the other objectives, 91 per cent of the returnees identified problems related to their reintegration process. These included high cost of living, low salary levels and housing difficulties.

To what extent are these programmes an adequate response to brain drain? As already noted, given that the recruitment is targeted on specific jobs that are already available, the programmes do satisfy real needs; but they do not create jobs. Clearly, therefore, the programmes can do little to solve the basic and wider problem of brain drain – at least in so far as the latter reflects an overflow of surplus skills that the country of origin is unable to absorb. At best the programmes can only help restrain brain drain: first, by identifying and helping some specific talents to return; and second, indirectly, by contributing to a development process that reduces the incentives for non-return after training abroad or for emigration by skilled personnel (Kelly, 1986). The programmes are however directly useful in reducing the need for foreign experts or professionals who might have been otherwise recruited and engaged at a much higher cost.

The TOKTEN Programme

Another example of a multilateral arrangement for the return of qualified personnel is provided by the UNDP-sponsored programme "Transfer of Knowledge Through Expatriate Nationals (TOKTEN). First set up in 1976, the programme is designed to mobilize talents of expatriate nationals on a low-cost and short-term basis to meet the skill requirements of specific development projects of the country of origin. Unlike the IOM programme for qualified nationals, TOKTEN does not aim at permanent return of expatriate nationals, but a time-bound return within the framework of a clearly defined consultancy project. A TOKTEN project is thus implemented in three main phases: identifying specific priority needs in terms of sectors and skills; locating the potential candidates; and managing the consultancy project. Since TOKTEN's inception a number of countries – China, Egypt, Greece, Grenada, India, Pakistan, the Philippines, Poland, Turkey, Sri Lanka – have taken advantage of the programme.

An evaluation of its performance during the first seven years shows that the programme's impact on the whole was positive (Ardittis, 1985). Given the limited duration of each project, its real impact on development depended largely on the degree of rigour applied in making the advance preparation, including the identification of priority needs, preparation of the job description and the selection of the consultant. Properly planned and managed, not only can it meet critical, development-related skill shortages but can also, to some extent, discourage further emigration of local experts by enhancing the country's capacity to absorb them.

Programmes Sponsored by Countries of Origin

In the past, as part of their effort to promote human capital development, several countries of origin – Taiwan, (China), Colombia, Ghana, Guyana, India, Iran, Iraq, Pakistan, Peru, the Philippines, Republic of Korea, Sri Lanka and Turkey – launched various plans to encourage the return of their qualified personnel from abroad. For example, the Korean programme, initiated in the late 1960s through the Korean Institute of Science and Technology, focused on recruiting, in particular in the United States, high level scientists and professionals to promote advanced technology mainly in the private sector for rapid national economic development. Typically, the offer was a two-year contract with salaries set at levels between those of the Korean Universities and industry, together with special housing and recreation facilities. A similar initiative was established through the Korean Development Institute which was engaged in high-level and policy-oriented economic and social research.

A more limited effort was made by Taiwan (China) in 1980, when, as part of its programme to speed up economic development, it sent a talent search mission to 21 cities in the United States, and to Tokyo and Osaka. It led 400 specialists, mostly in science and technology, to pledge trips to investigate job possibilities in the country, although the final results remained unknown. Guyana launched a more ambitious scheme in 1967, soon after attaining independence, to attract expatriate nationals back home for the public sector, which then accounted for 80 per cent of total employment. Between 1970 and 1977, 385 nationals were recruited under the scheme. This involved identification and placement of employers, travel for the returnees, spouse and up to three children, and shipment of household goods.

A somewhat different approach was tried by India. Given the poor response to calls for registration of non-resident Indians in the National Register of high-level scientific and technical personnel, the Government established in 1948 a *Pool* of such personnel which provided a salary and a temporary position while returnees looked for suitable permanent employment. As of 1965, about half of the *Pool* members had obtained employment; and subsequent indications suggest that the scheme has not been very active in recent years, encouraging highly qualified personnel to return.

In general, the impact of most of these programmes was relatively limited. It is of course difficult to be sure what proportion of the skilled personnel would have returned to home countries even without the special incentives; nor could the quality of the returnees be clearly established in all cases. Also, in some instances, the initial success of the programmes was not fully sustained. In Guyana, for example, about 10 per cent of those recruited between 1971 and 1977 left again despite penalties for non-fulfilment of contracts (Keely, 1986). Similarly, not all those selected under the Indian programme did join the Pool.

It is conceivable that in periods of rapid economic expansion and fast-moving technological change, as the Republic of Korea was experiencing in the late 1960s, special recruitment programmes of the type mentioned above could be useful to meet critical skill shortages arising from the change. However, given the level, rhythm and pattern of development in the vast numbers of migrant-sending countries, the replicability of the programme as an effective incentive to attract large numbers of qualified personnel seems generally limited.

Conscious of the manifold difficulties in attracting highly qualified and successful expatriates on a permanent basis, some countries are now planning, as illustrated by the "option diaspora" project in Senegal, to set up networking arrangements in order to be able to benefit from their skills and knowledge, without seeking their repatriation. A few other countries have established special national programmes to attract qualified expatriate nationals from abroad. A case in point is Jamaica's Returning Residents Programme, which provides training and various other facilities for this purpose. In 1994 a Skills Bank Facility was specially established under the scheme to attract persons with skills. (Thomas-Hope, 1998). China, too, has been making a special effort to attract skilled nationals who have been living abroad.

An important general lesson to be drawn from past experiences is that when the home country economy shows sustained upward trends and the future outlook seems more positive, fast return of qualified nationals can take place with little or limited incentives. From the perspective of return, this strengthens the argument for sustained development of the country of origin.

Recent return flows to several countries, including Singapore, confirm this. A similar trend is discernible in the return flows to Central European countries such as Poland and Hungary. This could sometimes be particularly pronounced in certain rapidly growing sectors. For example, significant numbers of Indian and Chinese software engineers, already fully successful in the US, are returning (though not always permanently) to take advantage of the new opportunities in the home country, while continuing to make use of their business and investment contacts established abroad.[2]

Conversely, as a recent (1999) global survey shows, regardless of their stages of development, countries with an unfavourable economic outlook, tend to experience a high rate of outflows of qualified personnel or brain drain, as illustrated most notably by Russia (see Figure 5.2).

---

[2] In the Hisinchu Science Park near Taipei, 82 companies – 40 per cent of the total – were established by the returnees (Silicon Valley's new immigrant entrepreneurs, Public Policy Institute of California, California, 1999).

FIGURE 5.2

BRAIN DRAIN, RANKED BY LIKELIHOOD OF THE WELL-EDUCATED STAYING
(Survey results, 10 = most likely to stay)

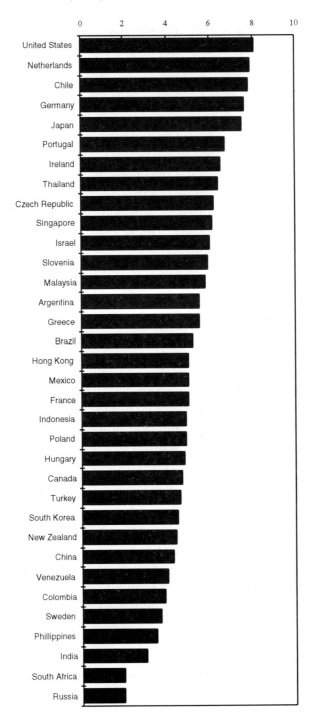

Bilateral Programmes for Skilled Workers

Aside from the support given to the multilateral programmes mentioned above, the host countries have also been cooperating, on a bilateral basis, with the countries of origin to encourage the return of qualified nationals, including those who want to set up their own small or medium-sized enterprises. An early example of such initiatives is the establishment in 1985 of a joint Turkish-German "special credit fund" with an equal annual contribution of DM 11 million by each government to help Turkish returnees set up their own businesses (Schiller, 1994). The fund provided credits to returnees up to an amount of DM 1 million and 50 per cent of total required capital, with an interest rate containing a significant grant component. In addition, as part of pre-departure preparation, migrants could participate in seminars organized in Germany and, following return, in Turkey where they also received advice and assistance through an official extension service.

The programme, as revealed by an evaluation for the period 1985-1990, seems to have made a positive impact. For instance, during this period, 900 enterprises received a total credit of about DM 100 million and created 17,000 jobs, with an average credit outlay of less than DM 6000 per job.

Bilateral Programmes for Migrants in General

The Franco-Senegalese experience in promoting assisted return of migrants in general (regular and irregular) provides useful insights into both pitfalls and the promise of such programmes (Senghhor Diatta and Mbow, 1998). Under the terms of the 1980 joint return and reintegration programme, the returnees were to receive training and a reintegration project proposal together with funds for its implementation. A credit facility was established in 1983 by the Central Fund for Economic Cooperation to finance project activities. However, an evaluation carried out in 1989 revealed that that out of the 10 enterprises financed under the programme five were no longer in operation and the remaining five were virtually bankrupt. Lack of proper supervision and assistance, combined with bureaucratic delays and constraints were identified as the main causes for this situation.

Improvements were introduced in 1987 under a new phase of the programme – by tightening lending criteria, improving feasibility studies and supervision and laying additional emphasis on reintegration of returnees into the local community. However, the training for return part of the programme revealed several weaknesses. For example, the content and methodology of the training provided were not fully attuned to the specific needs of project activities or to the realities of the local situation nor was any arrangement made for providing complementary practical training following return, in collaboration with national institutions. Limiting training only to the heads of families and excluding other members was another shortcoming. Also lacking was a system of follow-up and on-the job training during the reintegration phase.

The experience led the government to introduce a shift in policy, seeking to encourage an active participation of Senegalese working abroad in investment-oriented reintegration projects as part of the general economic and social development of the country. Recently, such new types of projects have been initiated with the financial support of Senegalese emigrants living in countries like Switzerland, Germany and Saudi Arabia. The re-oriented policy also lays emphasis on providing migrants abroad with all information pertinent to their reintegration and arrangements for vocational training, while special attention is given to technical follow-up, supervision and periodic evaluation of the reintegration projects.

At the same time, with the support of the European Union and United Nations Population Fund, Senegal has launched a Support Project for Migrant Workers. Although primarily concerned with reducing migratory pressure in high emigration areas, it also contributes to reintegration efforts by encouraging investment and employment generating activities and improved institutional coordination. More specifically, its medium-term plan includes training of potential return-migrants through pre-training in their host countries, additional training in Senegal, funding of viable projects, and effective follow-up and monitoring of projects under implementation (Senghor Diatta and Mbow, 1998).

Similar to the one signed with Senegal, France has concluded reintegration agreements also with Mali and Mauritania. An important feature of the programme for Mali, for example, concerns the establishment of micro-enterprises in agriculture, commerce and other services sectors.

Assisted Return Programmes for Asylum Seekers, Rejected Asylum Seekers, Irregular Migrants and Temporary Refugees

A common feature of these categories of migrants concerns their special vulnerability in the host as well as the origin country, although the degree of vulnerability varies. When unwanted in the host country, they have only three choices: they may voluntarily leave, making use of any available return-related assistance; they may wait until deported; or alternatively, they may go underground as "illegals".

To the extent that the political/ethnic situation in the country of origin may continue to be insecure or unstable raises several delicate issues, including those related to personal safety of the migrants and the protection of their basic human rights (discussed in part II of the present chapter; see also Chapter 4). However, from a development perspective and for purposes of the present discussion, several other issues merit attention: To what extent can these returns be geared to sustainable development of the origin country (or a third country of settlement) and ensure economic welfare of the returnees? Does adding a development-welfare dimension make these programmes more meaningful for the returnees and the countries of origin? Will this make the return programmes less costly in both human and financial terms?

In the past, few of the return programmes for these groups were adequately concerned with the development aspects. One of the first exceptions involving resettlement to a third country concerned the refugee integration and zonal development project launched in Burundi and the then Congo (Leopoldville) on the basis of the recommendations made by a 1963 United Nations interagency mission in 1963, following massive outflows of Tutsi refugees from Rwanda. The projects, which embraced both refugees and the local populations, made a positive impact, linking relief, rehabilitation and longer-term development within an integrated framework. The project in Burundi subsequently became the nucleus of a much wider regional development project and helped in preserving inter-ethnic harmony at least for a number of years (Ghosh, 1963; *Wall Street Journal*, 1996).

Some of the more recent bilateral and multilateral progammes, although still devoid of any direct links with macro-level development, have however included (in addition to pre-departure and transport assistance) a small financial allowance to facilitate returnees' labour market integration or self-employment. These include the IOM executed voluntary return programmes for Chilean refugees in Belgium and Switzerland, financed by the two governments, respectively. Similar post arrival financial assistance is also provided under IOM-executed programmes, supported since 1990 by the German Government Assisted Repatriation Programme (GARP). As of late 1998, such assistance was being provided in some 20 countries.

The trend has gathered further impetus in the wake of destruction and large-scale human displacement in Bosnia. For example, an EU-supported IOM programme for Bosnian returnees provides for special rehabilitation/reintegration assistance, in addition to other allowances. A Swiss-funded IOM programme includes financial assistance for the reintegration of returnees and an equal financial contribution to local communities for reconstruction of local structures. Post-arrival assistance under the Belgian supported programme includes a housing subsidy, in addition to pre-departure and transport assistance. Under the German-funded programme, IOM was examining the possibility of including special rehabilitation assistance to those areas in Bosnia which were affected by large inflows of refugees (see also Chapter 2).

It is too early to make a serious assessment of the long-term development impact of these programmes. However, the emphasis on reconstruction of physical structures and local institutions as well as the involvement of local authorities and NGOs are clearly positive and relatively new elements. By generating some immediate employment opportunities such projects also ensure a valuable breathing space before full normal economic activities can be restored. Dissemination of information in advance concerning conditions in the areas of return is also a positive feature. Much however depends on wider factors such as political stability and inter-ethnic confidence building, settlement of property disputes and general economic recovery (further discussed in part II of this chapter).

An input-output analysis of the impact of IOM-executed programme for Bosnia, after eight months of operation, revealed relative progress with a return rate of 13 per cent relative to the projected total, and the cost of return, including a housing subsidy, tended to be relatively low, compared to the cost of looking after the refugees in the host country (IOM, 1998).

Several other new initiatives, mostly of bilateral nature, have been recently launched to facilitate the return of persons under temporary protection, rejected asylum seekers or irregular migrants. Some detailed information on return programmes for these categories is available in Chapter 2 of this volume (see also IOM, 1998). For the purposes of this chapter, suffice it to refer, on an illustrative basis, to three programmes – the Netherlands partnership agreements with Ethiopia, the German-Eritrean programme and the recent French plan for Mali, Morocco and Senegal – all of which lay special emphasis on the welfare-development dimensions of return.

The Netherlands Ethiopian programme, formalized in August 1997, includes pre-departure preparation, counselling, and training of potential returnees, all arranged through local and national NGOs, while the move back home is organized by IOM. Post-arrival assistance comprises a temporary housing facility, if needed, and a monthly subsistence allowance of US$ 125. Also included is assistance for setting up income-generating small enterprises, for which a one-off amount of US$2,500 is available for each project if recommended by the special project office which is established to help the returnees in this connection. Additionally, local authorities and NGOs are encouraged to present proposals for community-based projects for which a one-off amount of US$ 7,500 is available in each case. The returnees may contribute in one way or another to these projects; and the two types of projects could be linked together generating synergies.

As of June 1998, out of a total of 200 potential candidates, about 25 registered themselves for participation in the programme. It is too early to make an evaluation of the programme impact. However, the reasons why, despite the programme's many positive features, progress, especially in terms of response from the potential returnees, has so far been rather slow deserve careful scrutiny (Samuels, 1998).

Another recent example of this kind of initiatives is the German-Eritrean Professional Reintegration Programme for refugees returning from Germany and various African countries. Two special features of the programme should be noted (for further details see Chapter 2): Concerned with professional personnel rather than highly skilled scientists and technicians, the programme aims at an effective reintegration of returnees through (a) salary subsidies at two levels and (b) business start-up loans linked to reconstruction and development of Eritrea (Black et. al., 1997).

Under the business start-up programme, loans are made to the returnees of up to DM 100,000 and exceptionally up to DM 200,000. The loan periods last from three to 15 years depending on the size of the loan and the nature of the business, with a grace period of up to two years for repayment. The Eritreans returning from Germany were covered mainly under the German contribution to the fund; and those returning from neighbouring countries and internally displaced people were the main focus of attention under the Eritrean contribution.

As with the German-Turkish credit fund, a positive feature of the programme is the active involvement of the Eritrean Government, including in particular its contribution, in equal proportion with Germany, to the revolving credit fund to finance business start-up loans. Other positive features include: arrangements for training and management assistance to enhance the continuing success of the business enterprises and for development of local institutional capacity, *inter alia*, by using local personnel to help sustain project activities following the withdrawal of German assistance. Available information suggests that the programme has generated positive multiplier effects in terms of both job creation, dissemination of business skills and promotion of entrepreneurship.

At the same time however it has revealed certain constraints or weaknesses such as difficulties of social adjustment, especially for those returning under expert subsidies, the majority of whom were older and married, with established positions in Germany. Also, lack of a social welfare system comparable to that in Germany, of an adequate education system for the children, and of employment opportunities for spouses (mostly skilled wives) in Eritrea, posed the problem of family division, leading in some cases to divorce; in some other cases it impelled the migrants to think of going back to Germany. Further, the tough criteria for selection for salary subsidies, probably more attuned to the German labour market, may have restricted the number of returnees (as of November 1997, some 500 returned out of a total of 16,000), although it may have enabled Eritrea to have access to some of the critical skills needed for reconstruction and future development.

Special mention may also be made of the new initiative unveiled by the French Government on 4 November 1998 directly linking regularization of undocumented migrants to their voluntary return and economic reintegration in the country of origin (*Le Monde*, 5 November 1998). Dubbed as Co-Development Agreements, these were to be concluded, in the first instance, with governments of three countries – Mali, Senegal and Morocco – with a possibility of extension to Turkey and Romania (and eventually to other countries and also to regular migrants).

Under the scheme, irregular migrants opting for voluntary return and reintegration would be allowed to participate in a three months' training course in France, with a provisional stay visa issued to them for this period. The training would include dissemination of information concerning the country of origin and rules governing the aid that would be available for starting a gainful economic activity upon return. This would be complemented by a vocational training course relevant to a sector/activity selected on the basis of the returnee's preferences and the needs of the country. The returnee will be entitled to a monthly apprenticeship allowance of FF 2,000 for the training period and, on return to home country, could benefit from aid funds as well as assistance from a specialized agency in launching a viable project. Those who refuse to return after the termination of the training course will be liable to expulsion by force.

The scheme thus seeks to link voluntary return, conditional regularization and reintegration of irregular migrants with the development of the country of origin. A novelty of the initiative concerns the possibility for voluntary returnees to obtain a multiple entry visa enabling them to visit France for periods not exceeding three months at a time. The visa may be available to a volunteer only six months after return and is subject to the proof of his/her effective reintegration in the home country. Other interesting features of the scheme include an explicit recognition of the role of migrants associations in implementing return programmes as well as the emphasis on using return as a means of enhancing development.[3]

The scheme however has had a slow start. As of mid-May 1999, a total of only 21 immigrants had signed contracts for regularization, of which 12 had actually returned home (eight to Mali and four to Senegal). It seems to have been negatively affected by a politically sensitive controversy dating back to 1996 when undocumented migrants from the three African countries occupied the St Bernard church in Paris, claiming regularization.[4] Some however were still hopeful that over time the programme would gain ground (*Le Monde*, 16 June 1999).

---

[3] The underlying approach was however not altogether new. For example, the 1995 French programme with Mali, Mauritania and Senegal already provided for promotion of micro-projects as part of local development to facilitate return.

[4] In a press interview the Moroccan minister of employment and social employment, for example, expressed the opinion that rather than concentrating on the return of this small group of undocumented immigrants attention should be focused, in pursuit of a more productive approach, on the development of the high emigration areas in the source countries through increased use of French bilateral aid. Cf. *Le Monde*, 16 June 1999.

HOW TO PROFIT FROM
RETURN-DEVELOPMENT LINKAGES

Assisted Voluntary Return and Development:
Forging Convergence of Interests

Although synoptic and somewhat perfunctory, the foregoing review of past experiences and on-going programmes of return provide
a useful basis for drawing a set of conclusions. The discussion on
autonomous returns has shown that in the absence of at least some
minimum support and guidance, the full potential of return, be it in
the form of advancement of personal welfare or wider development,
tends to remain unrealized. This is particularly true in the case of
those who are in an irregular situation in the host country and are
often less equipped to make return a success. The discussion has also
revealed that when development opens up new opportunities in the
origin country, return becomes less of a problem, and many migrants,
including some of those who have been successful abroad, tend to
return home. But the analysis does not adequately explain why assisted voluntary return linked to reintegration and development can
provide a common ground where the interests of the parties directly
involved could converge or how they can derive optimal benefits
from a judicious use of these linkages. This is attempted in this
section.

In principle, countries of origin should have a special interest in
assisted voluntary return of irregular migrants abroad for a simple
reason – to avoid abuse and exploitation of their own nationals as
well as the ills associated with human trafficking, including the di-
version of resources that it often entails. The continued and
unwanted presence of the irregular migrants in the foreign country
also adversely affects the status and standing of the legally resident
immigrant communities. No less important, forced return, which
may be unavoidable in the absence of other options, can result in
friction and misunderstanding between the migrants and returning
countries, which can have wider negative effects in other vital areas
of their cooperation.

However, if return, at least for those who would prefer to stay at
home, is to be durable, conditions must be created so that the individual (and the family) can play a useful and productive role as a
member of the community in the country of return, and may not be

induced or forced to leave again. In the absence of such conditions, even if the migrant does return, sustained reintegration will be difficult to achieve and he/she is likely to leave again.

Many less affluent origin countries are however unable to provide the essential conditions for such meaningful reintegration unless new economic, especially job, opportunities, can be opened up for the returnees through development. This underscores the critical importance of forging the potential links that exist between durable return, effective integration and development. When a judicious and dynamic use is made of these linkages, it creates new perspectives and hopes for the potential returnees, while encouraging more voluntary return. Also, when return generates or spurs new development, particularly when it has a multiplier effect, benefiting a large section of the local population, the government of the origin country takes a more active interest in ensuring the success of return programmes.

True, for many migrant-sending countries remittances are an important source of foreign exchange earnings and of considerable potential value for national investment and development. It is wrong however to assume that there is an absolute dichotomy between remittances and return. In an open migration system, one does not necessarily exclude the other. This is particularly true when the returnees have an irregular status in the host country. They often remain marginalized, and normally have low-wage jobs, with only limited capacity to remit funds back home. On the other hand, return programmes can be so designed that they encourage established expatriate nationals abroad to participate in productive projects by remitting investment funds, providing innovative ideas and facilitating business contacts in their countries of residence or settlement. By opening up new prospects of channelling savings and other resources of expatriate nationals to productive projects in the origin country, the return programmes can directly contribute to its development which might not have occurred otherwise.

The returning state, too, has an abiding interest in such development-oriented reintegration especially while dealing with unwanted migrants. By making return more attractive and durable it minimizes the risks of fresh attempts at unauthorized re-entry and reduces the cost of immigration control. Indeed, a particularly strong argument for development-related return programmes is that they contribute to migrants' voluntariness to return just as they enhance the willingness for the origin countries to cooperate. This is particularly true for certain categories of migrants such as irregular migrants and rejected asylum seekers who, as already noted, often are vulnerable in both returning and origin countries and are less equipped to start a new life on their own, without some specific assistance. Inherent in such programmes is a clear recognition by both returning and origin countries of a pro-active, developmental role of the returnees. This serves as an important, if indirect, assurance against infringement of the basic human rights of the migrants during or following the return process, and helps avoid the kind of strong public resistance that forced deportation often provokes especially in liberal democracies.

To put it differently, by their very nature development-related voluntary return implies a positive involvement of all the three parties in the programmes and makes them joint stakeholders in the success of the venture. True, transit states are less actively involved in reintegration /development aspects of the programme; but they, too, have an interest and an important concern in facilitating a durable return of irregular migrants. Among other things, this reduces the financial and administrative burden they bear in dealing with the caseload of irregular migrants, including the victims of trafficking, while making the management of international migration less difficult.

Is Voluntary Return Linked to Development More Costly than Forcible Return?

These may be powerful arguments in favour of voluntary and as-sisted return, but does this not make the operation much more costly? Not necessarily. To illustrate, in Germany the average cost of an es-corted expulsion by air was $840 in 1995, compared with a price tag of $490 for an assisted voluntary return in cooperation with IOM (Noll, 1998).[5] The average cost of forced removal is even higher in some returning states. In Sweden, the average cost of forced expul-sion amounted to roughly $3,160 in 1996 (Utrikesdepartementet, Stockholm, 1997). More recent estimates confirmed that an assisted return under the IOM-executed programme is less costly than forced unilateral expulsion (Government bill, 20 May 1998). Under the Swiss programme for Bosnians enjoying temporary protection the total

---

[5] Based on oral information from the United Nations, cited in Gregor Noll, "Pro-tecting the Dignity and Human Rights of Different Categories of Returnees", paper presented to the NIROMP Inter-regional meeting on return and readmission of Migrants, December 1998, IOM, Geneva.

costs of assisted return would be no more than the amount to be spent on social assistance for a "protected family" of three persons for 10-11 months (IOM, 1998). In Central and East European countries high financial costs associated with non-voluntary return, including detention, seem to be an important restraining factor in implementing return (Hughes and Kessing, 1998). In Hungary, for example, the costs (including the cost at the reception centre) can amount to $7,000 a year for each returnee, which exceeds the annual minimum wage in the country (discussed in Chapter 4).

It is of course difficult to come up with a standard cost figure for development-assistance since much depends on the type and extent of assistance made available for specific programmes of voluntary return. But the package will clearly be larger than the direct cost of return alone (even if the latter is a forced and escorted return). It is equally clear however that the dividends to be reaped from development-related programmes that are properly designed and effectively implemented will also be much higher. This is because of greater durability of return, easier public acceptance of return programmes, possible lower recurrent expenditure to deal with fresh attempts at re-entry through irregular channels, and increased voluntary returns. In the medium to long term, both returning and origin countries might also benefit from increased investment and trade resulting from new economic development in the origin country. The situation in any case should contribute to improved interstate relations from which both countries can gain.

There is little doubt however that when return is directly linked to reintegration and development, it also makes the designing and management of return programmes more complex and onerous. But the burden is lightened, and success better ensured, when each of the parties directly concerned – the returning, origin and transit countries and the migrants themselves – work from the outset in close cooperation, based on a genuine recognition of a commonality of interest from which each can derive a positive gain.

The Quest of an Agreed Framework

Equally important, the distinctive role that each party might play within such a concerted approach should be clearly identified and recognized well in advance. It would be easier to achieve this on the basis of an agreed framework based on a set of principles including the following (for a more detailed description see Chapter 6 of this volume):

1. A sovereign state has the right to control immigration into its territory. It has thus the prerogative, and may face the practical necessity, to repatriate unauthorized migrants from its territory, but without prejudice to their basic human rights as recognized in international law and practice.
2. An individual has the right to return to the state of which he/she is a citizen or which is deemed to be his/her country.
3. Every state has the right and responsibility to determine the policy and pattern of its own national development. This however does not preclude forging inter-state partnership in development and policy coordination in an increasingly globalized world economy.
4. Consistent with their respective sovereign rights, the returning and origin states should closely cooperate from the beginning to the end of the return and reintegration process and endeavour to balance and harmonize their interests, leading to an agreed framework for action.
5. Not only are the migrants and their families directly affected by the return process, but they are also among the main actors to make return both successful and durable. Both returning and origin states should therefore take the migrants' perspectives fully into account and to the extent possible consult with them in planning and implementing the process.

Designing Assisted Voluntary Return Linked to Development

An agreed framework of action is however not enough. It is equally important that careful attention be given to the specific design of the assisted return programmes.

While most return flows have some development potential, the range and nature of such potential vary widely. For young and economically active returnees, for example, personal success and contribution to development depend largely on effective labour market participation or gainful self-employment; for those who are retired and elderly, the availability of safe and profitable investment of their savings are more important both from a personal point of view as well as from a development perspective. Likewise, the de-

210

signing of return programmes will need to vary depending on whether the target groups are highly qualified, skilled or unskilled. The programme objectives and types of assistance for return should therefore be closely attuned to the human capital and other personal characteristics of the target groups of returnees.

A differentiated approach for different categories of returnees should also give careful attention to the needs of individual members of the family, but treating it as a unit, within each category. Limiting the assistance to only the head of family, and excluding other members, as was the case with Senegal's earlier training-for-return project, could be a serious shortcoming. Similarly, ignoring the social, medical and educational needs of the family, especially when elderly people and children are involved, could create problems of social adaptation, family division and make return less durable. In cases where these basic facilities are non-existent to meet the immediate needs, as in Eritrea, or where they are severely damaged, as in Bosnia, return assistance needs to be linked to the development of community projects and reconstruction of the basic infrastructure.

The cardinal importance of information and counselling in the success of return and reintegration programmes is fully borne out by wide empirical evidence. Not surprisingly, provision of these services is included in almost all return programmes. Information generally covers the situation in sending and receiving countries. Experience shows however that the main problems often relate to quality, credibility and comprehensiveness. Even some of the otherwise successful return programmes tend to reveal some deficiencies in this respect, not infrequently due to the difficulty in securing reliable and updated information.[6]

Access to accurate and relevant information on the economic, social and labour market situation is indispensable to design suitable pre-departure training of the returnees (further discussed below). Credibility and reliability of the information provided assume particular significance for returning refugees, rejected asylum seekers and irregular immigrants. For irregular immigrants and rejected asylum seekers, information concerning the receiving country should focus on the consequences that may follow in the event of continua-

---

[6] The quality and depth of the information provided often vary. For example, a significant number of the returnees to Chile from Switzerland under the IOM-executed programme felt that they had not been given enough information about the "real" situation in Chile. By contrast, 91.2 per cent of returnees under the programme for Nicaragua thought that they had received adequate information which facilitated their reintegration.

tion of irregular stay. Equally important for them as for the other categories, including refugees, is to receive adequate information on the situation they are likely to face in their home country (further discussed in part II of this chapter).

Unbiased and objective information, when communicated in an honest and yet compassionate manner, is likely to have a more effective impact. Information disseminated by agencies, controlled or widely perceived to be controlled by the government, tends to suffer from lack of credibility. By contrast, pre-return reconnaissance visits by migrants (or members of their families) to the origin country to obtain first-hand information and direct exchange of information between returning and origin countries, for example by twinning their radio stations, as arranged by the Danish Refugee Council between Denmark and Bosnia, have some very positive aspects.

Experience (as, for example, under the initial phase of the Franco-Senegalese programme and the more recent German-Eritrean programme) shows that there are pitfalls in designing pre-departure training programmes on the basis of the labour market needs or the skill requirements of the returning country, especially when it is in a technologically advanced stage of development. While pre-departure training in the host country is extremely important, its scope and content should be closely attuned to the existing and projected labour market shortages in the origin country, including the anticipated skill requirements of development projects and business enterprises to be set up under the return programme. This should in any case be complemented by further training, including whenever possible on-the-job training, following return.

In assessing the future skill requirements of the country of origin, special attention should be given to needs of emerging or dynamic economic sectors and industries and their possible trends in the labour market.[7] However, in case there is a demand for such skills in the labour market of the host country itself, the possibility of return may be mitigated, as may have been the case with the Bosnian refugees in Belgium under the IOM-executed programme, although this would imply meeting a genuine labour market need of the host country economy.

Given the generally difficult employment situation in most origin countries, arrangements to promote new income-generating business

---

[7] This is one of the stated reasons for including computer training in the Belgian programme for the asylum seekers from Ghana, Nigeria, India, Pakistan, and Romania.

enterprises and ensure their long-term success assume special importance. Suitable training and start-up loans, though essential are not enough for this purpose. Careful attention needs to be given to matters such as: determination of the basic viability of the projects; marketing facilities; access to additional low-cost and safe credit, if necessary and justified; effective management and accounting; as well as monitoring, technical advice and assistance.

The long history of return, both autonomous and assisted, demonstrates how important it is to secure local participation and support to ensure the success of the activities undertaken by the returnees. This is important not just for avoiding local jealousies and tensions with the local community and its leadership but also, more positively, to mobilize the support, both human and financial, of the local population, and harness the development potential of the area, in support of the productive activities started under the reintegration programme. Local authorities, including extension services, private sector enterprises, church groups, migrant-serving associations and other voluntary organizations, can all play a part in forging a new partnership with the returnees. Suitable institutional arrangements are also necessary to tap the savings of the nationals abroad and other external funding sources.

While the local dimension of the reintegration programme is extremely important, the reintegration actives, especially business enterprises and other productive projects initiated under the programme, cannot be expected to operate effectively in isolation. These should be conceived and implemented as an integral part of the country's overall and long-term development strategy so that the projects could eventually draw on the support of national development agencies. If needed, this should also pave the way for the projects to benefit, at an appropriate stage, from the financial assistance of external sources such as the UNDP, regional development banks and even the World Bank. Clearly, suitable institutional arrangements are essential to mobilize such external support, including the savings and other resources of expatriate nationals abroad.

II

REPATRIATION OF REFUGEES:
ISSUES AND APPROACHES

Return has long been considered as a most satisfactory and durable solution to the refugee problem. Although, as discussed below, the simple and sweeping hypothesis that all refugees want to return home may not be valid, it is probably true that the majority of them do intend to go home once the causes that led them to flee are removed, especially when this happens within a relatively short period following their flight. This is so for a simple reason: the refugees leave their country not because they had wanted, but because they had been forced, to do so.

There is also a very practical reason. As Stein and Cuny (1991) put it, "in any given year less than one per cent of the world's refugees escape the limbo of refugee status either by resettlement in third countries or by obtaining citizenship in their country of asylum. If the number of refugees is to be reduced significantly, it will be by means of voluntary repatriation".

But this does not mean that the path of return is free from all pitfalls. Indeed, it raises a variety of delicate legal, ethical and practical issues; and it is therefore hardly surprising that return of refugees has become a subject of wide, and often controversial, discussion in recent years (see, in this connection, Chimni, 1999).

EVOLUTION OF THE DOCTRINE OF RETURN

While since after the Second World War voluntary return has been recognized as a preferred solution to the refugee's problem, the application of the principle and the related policy approach have been largely influenced by the contextual political and economic circumstances in the host countries, notably in the industrial world. In the immediate aftermath of the Second World War, when the United Nations Relief and Rehabilitation Agency (UNRRA) had been dealing with refugees and displaced persons, repatriation has been its principal mode of action, often carried out, at least during the initial stages, with little formal respect for the basic rights of the individual.

True, with the establishment of the International Refugee Organization (IRO) and the onset of the Cold War, individuals' right to flee from persecution was recognized, and, at the insistence of the Soviet Union, the IRO formally adopted voluntary repatriation as a lasting solution to the refugee problem. In practice however it was the re-settlement in the host country – which was of greater interest to the western industrial countries – that received the main attention during that period. Significantly, during its whole existence the IRO repatriated only 72,834 refugees, a meagre five per cent of the total number of displaced persons registered with IRO (Stossinger, 1963). An acute labour shortage and the onset of the Cold War were the two main factors that influenced the attitude of the western states at that time.

But by 1983, as flows of refugees and asylum seekers were rising fast, and labour shortage was no longer a serious problem in industrial countries, the emphasis shifted back to repatriation, which in the Cold War context "acquired an absolute character" in the United Nations resolutions (Zeck, 1997), with added insistence on the voluntary character of the operation. In 1985, despite the reservations made by the Office of the High Commissioner for Refugees to the effect that the solution of voluntary repatriations had not been examined in depth by experts or scholars, the UNHCR Executive Committee moved in favour of voluntary repatriation (Chimni, 1999). And by the early 1990s, the UNHCR was actively encouraging voluntary repatriation. Indeed, 1992 was declared as "the year of return", with an optimistic forecast that ideally three million refugees could return. In the years that followed, despite the manifold difficulties involved (discussed below), return became the main hope and concern of the UNHCR and the governments providing the main support to its operations (Ferris, 1993).

However, less than two years later, in 1993, under the impact of the Yugoslav crisis and the increasing adherence by Western European states to the concept of "temporary protection", the policy of repatriation witnessed a subtle but significant change. Attention shifted towards "safe return", which became the dominant theme, overshadowing the concern over voluntariness of return, with the receiving state having the right to repatriate when the conditions in the home country are considered safe and the refugee status comes to an end. The new doctrine of safe return has received further impetus in the wake of the Bosnian and Kosovo crises, while the notion of "safe conditions" (under various labels) has emerged as a guiding principle in dealing with asylum seekers (for further details see Chapters 2 and 3).

The shift of emphasis towards the notion of safe conditions for temporary refugees and asylum seekers has had a wider effect of diluting the principle of voluntariness as a condition of return for refugees in general. A series of other concurrent developments reinforced this new trend. These included: difficulties in continued sheltering of Vietnamese and Cambodian refugees, the rising numbers of new refugees, notably in Africa, and the stagnating, if not declining flows of refugee aid. By 1996 the UNHCR recognized that a large proportion of the world's recent returnees have been repatriated under some form of duress (UNHCR, 1997).

More significantly, it put forward a doctrine of "imposed return", under which refugees may be sent back to less than optimal conditions in their home country. As the director of UNHCR's Division of International Protection put it in Washington, "imposed return has become necessary because of pressure of host states and a lack of money to care for the refugees" (Reuters, 1996).

It is against this background that return of refugees has become a debatable issue, impinging on the basic concept of refugee protection and holding the potential of sharpening the North-South divide.

TWO CENTRAL ISSUES:
VOLUNTARY RETURN AND SAFE CONDITIONS

Two central, and somewhat inter-related, issues that stand out in the current debate deserve special attention: the concepts of voluntary return and safe conditions, including in particular the methods used to define and measure these conditions.

As regards voluntary *versus* imposed return, the critics of the present trends concede that the 1951 Convention requires the state parties only to ensure safe return of refugees – and does not explicitly require the application of the standard of voluntary repatriation. However, they make two very important points in defence of voluntariness as a condition of repatriation. First, the requirement of voluntariness, though not mentioned in the Convention, is clearly articulated in the statute of the Office of the High Commissioner for Refugees. Second, the preamble to the Statute does require the states to assist the High Commissioner for Refugees to promote voluntary repatriation – an obligation which they could hardly discharge by denying the requirement of voluntariness.

Another argument sometimes used to justify the policy of imposed return is that in an era of mass influx the doctrine of individual expression of free will to return becomes less relevant (Boutrrpue, 1998). Not surprisingly, this too has come under serious criticism. The critics have been vocal in emphasizing that the standard of return is, and should continue to be, linked to the basic principle of *non-refoulement* – a principle which both UNHCR and the host country are bound to observe (Chimni, 1999; Zieck, 1997).

Questions have also been raised about the quality or depth of the expression of willingness of the returnees. Some analysts and scholars are critical about the facile assumption that all or most refugees want to return home, in total disregard of the contextual circumstances such as the length of the refugee's stay in the host country, personal links with countries other than his/her country of origin and the special situation of second generation refugees. Voluntariness may also be highly ambiguous when conditions in refugee camps are so bad that the refugees prefer to take a chance in a situation of conflict, insecurity and possible persecution rather than prolonging their stay in refugee camps.

For example, in some of the world's poorest host countries the refugees often find themselves in a desperate situation propelling them to decide in favour of returning to the country of origin. The situation of the Ugandan refugees in camps in Sudan and Zaire in the 1980s, the Somali refugees in Kenya in 1992 and the 2.5 million Rwandan refugees in Tanzania and Zaire in 1994 are typical of such circumstances. Worse still, refugees sometimes return home when civil war breaks out in the country of asylum itself, as was the case for Ethiopian refugees in Somalia. In all such cases the decision to return can hardly be considered to reflect a free choice.

As regards the doctrine of safe conditions, the critics of the present policy trends hold the view that undue emphasis on safe conditions detracts from the principle of individual voluntariness which is inextricably linked to the determination of the status of refugees (i.e. his/her fear of persecution).

The situation created by the shift away from principle of voluntary repatriation to that of safe conditions is made worse if the host state alone has the prerogative of determining whether or not the conditions in the country of origin (or a third country) are safe, regardless of the views of the refugee. As one analyst has put it, this disenfranchizes the refugee through eliminating his or her voice in the process, leading to the decision to deny or terminate protection (Chimni, 1999). Another critic has described it as "an extreme form of injustice in which the injury suffered by the victim is accompanied by a deprivation of the means to prove it" (Leotard, 1995). The hollowness of the new practice has also been brought into focus by juxtaposing it against the fact that "for decades it was the practice of Northern states , and continues to be the practice of UNHCR, to consider a combination of objective and subjective factors to determine refugee status" (Chimni, 1999).

IN SEARCH OF A PRAGMATIC SOLUTION

Over the past 15 years or so, nations have shown a heightened concern about protecting basic human rights; paradoxically they have at the same time revealed an increasing reluctance to accept its political and economic implications. Much of the contemporary tensions in the refugee protection regime, including rerun, stem from these conflicting trends.

This also largely accounts for the difficulties in developing a well defined and harmonized regime to deal adequately with situations of temporary protection, including return, of refugees.

As the experience with the Bosnian war refugees clearly demonstrated, individual receiving states in western Europe had to go through a painful process of coming up with a quick response to the crisis which was then deepening fast. Such improvisation entails a heavy political cost and undue institutional strain on the part of the government. More specifically, the absence of clear, transparent and harmonized guidelines creates complications over the question of return not only with regard to the beneficiaries of temporary protection but also other groups of refugees, while generating tension about burden sharing.

If protection is extended to vulnerable persons on a temporary basis as part of a predictable arrangement and on the basis of an agreed set of criteria, the case can be made for their repatriation once the crisis is over and the return is safe. A real difficulty lies however in determining whether the conditions are really safe. And the manner of determining whether the conditions in the country of origin are safe assumes particular importance when it is remembered that many of the repatriated refugees return to areas of conflict, as was the case for the one million refugees who voluntarily repatriated between 1985 and 1990.

Refugees returned to El Salvador when violence and tension were still widespread in the country. In Guatemala displaced persons seeking to return were directed to government-designed villages and were often forced to participate in civil defence patrols. These arrangements and the military's central role in the whole resettlement served to discourage further return. Uprooted people went back to Liberia although the country was in throes of the war, and many fled again. Similarly, durable peace and stability were yet to return to the country when the Cambodian refugees were sent back home. The timing of the return of some of the war refugees to Bosnia has also given rise to questions and criticism.

It is clear that an active involvement of the concerned international organizations in determining when it is safe for a refugee to return enhances the transparency and credibility of the return system. As already argued, since the returnees are the ones to be directly exposed to the conditions in the place of return, it also seems only fair and logical to consult with them prior to repatriation. This helps psychological preparation of the returnees and contributes to confidence-building.

Consultations with refugees and refugee organizations, however important, may sometimes add to the complexity of an already difficult situation. Experience in countries like El Salvador and Guatemala, for example, has shown that when the consultations between the government and the refugee organizations becomes politicized, it can create tension and even impasse, placing the concerned international organizations like UNHCR in a delicate situation. In order to avoid such situations, it may well be advisable to defer preparation for return until a plan for durable peace has been agreed upon by all the parties involved, including where appropriate the armed forces.

Returning refugees may continue to experience the trauma of insecurity and oppression even after the formal cessation of armed conflict and therefore often need continued protection and monitoring of their safety. In specific cases, UNHCR has been given such responsibility, but this has not always proved adequate. For example, in El Salvador, despite the efforts of UNHCR – it had a responsibility to monitor the returnees' safety for two years – the highly politicized environment and continuing violence impelled the returnees to seek assistance from NGOs to ensure their security, but this created tensions involving both UNHCR and the government.

There could be a host of other reasons why cessation of armed conflict or repression may not necessarily bring peace and normalcy. Reconciliation cannot be achieved overnight. Hatred and revenge may be a feature of daily life, creating a vicious spiral for a long time. The economy, infrastructure and the environment in the affected country are often seriously damaged. Land mines, for example, could be a serious threat to life and limbs of returnees, including women and children.

Property ownership in particular is often a new source of conflict between the returnees and the local population. The 1995 Dayton Peace Agreement thoughtfully established a Commission on Real Property Claims, but experience so far seems to suggest that its decisions are often ignored by the local authorities (*The Forced Migration Monitor*, 1998). In Guatemala, where land distribution was extremely unequal, the return of refugees in communities such as Ixcan and Chacaj created great tensions over land ownership between the returnees who had fled the army and the new settlers who were brought there by the army. The lessons to be drawn from such experiences are that the potential sources of new tension and conflict should be given careful attention and that a common understanding be reached by the parties involved on how to address them prior to the actual return of refugees.

In general, refugees also face more pressing economic difficulties than other groups of migrants when they return home. This is because in many cases – as in Cambodia, Guatemala, El Salvador, Liberia, and more recently Bosnia and Kosovo – refugees return to areas which have witnessed large-scale destruction of the basic infrastructure and serious dislocation of the local production system, with crops burned or otherwise destroyed, houses demolished, land lying uncultivated, and economic activities virtually paralysed.

In such circumstances durable return is not a matter only of protecting safety and integrity of the person and other human rights of refugees. Equally important is to ensure that they have access to food, shelter, nutrition and essential social services to meet basic human needs.

EMERGENCY AID AND DURABLE DEVELOPMENT: CONTINUUM AND CONVERGENCE

Emergency relief, including initial cash grants to refugees, and restoration of the basic infrastructure and services are extremely useful in meeting these urgent needs, as foreseen in a number of recent assisted return programmes, notably in Bosnia. However, it is unwise to assume that at the end of such emergency relief and immediate aid for rehabilitation returning refugees can automatically find employment or a worthwhile means of living in the country of origin.

As already noted, in the wake of the Second World War resettlement of those displaced in Europe was less of an economic problem. Given the prevailing shortages of labour and the expanding economies most of the resettlement countries could easily absorb them. The situation surrounding the return and reabsorption of the recent refugees is quite different. Not only are most of the countries of origin (or third countries in developing regions where the new refugees are resettled) war-ravaged, but they are also poor or extremely poor and face serious economic difficulties in absorbing the returning refugees, more so, in cases where the returnees lack in the skills needed. In some other instances, return also implies the immediate loss of an important source of foreign exchange in the form of remittances, as exemplified by El Salvador (which was estimated to have an annual remittances flow of US$1.4 billion from the Salvadoran refugees in the US alone) (Montes, 1989).

The return of contemporary refugees to resource-poor and war-devastated areas make it particularly important that the emergency relief including short-term rehabilitation aid are closely geared to sustained, longer-term development of the areas and countries of return.

It is not easy however to translate this paradigm into action. The obstacles are many and varied. For example, emergency relief has to be provided under tremendous time pressure as the delay in the provision of such relief may make a difference of life and death for the returnees and their families, especially children and women. The political exigencies may add to the rush for return before conditions for durable return and reintegration have been assessed and negotiated; and the government may be unwilling or unable to provide the amount and quality of land necessary to make the returnees self-reliant on a longer-term basis. Also, national and international agencies concerned with longer-term development may not be quick enough to respond to the exigencies of the situation or, alternatively, may not be welcome by the hard-pressed officials and other workers dealing with emergency relief.

The concern about linking emergency relief including short-term rehabilitation assistance to longer-term development is not new. Already in 1963 the problem was highlighted and widely discussed within the United Nations system, on the recommendations put forward by the inter-agency planning mission for longer-term integration of the Tutsi refugees referred to above. But despite the acclaim the recommendations received, progress has been slow and limited (Ghosh, 1963; UN, 1969).

This is also borne out by the mixed experience under the UNHCR-executed Quick Impact Projects (QIPs). Designed to ensure the establishment of minimum material conditions to permit return, the projects serve a useful purpose in providing the immediate wherewithal to the refugees. But these are emergency aid with a built-in exit strategy, and are not always geared to longer-term, sustainable development. Given the limits of its mandate, UNHCR cannot be blamed for this deficiency; what however is clearly unfortunate is that a serious gap and, not infrequently, a lack of congruity tend to exist between the QIPs and longer-term development.

Even in Mozambique, where the return programme and the QIPs are widely regarded as a success, many QIPs were found unsustainable, unused or both. A recent Health Ministry survey, for example, is reported to have estimated that a quarter of 400 rural health centres built between 1992-96, some as part of the programme, have been closed or under-utilized (UNHCR, *Refugees*, 1998). Another source suggests that some 50 per cent of the projects may have been viable and that failed projects might have had an adverse political fallout (UNHCR, *Refugees*, 1998).

Managing the transition from emergency relief to durable development and forging a smooth and effective link-up between them present a major challenge for refugee return.

This is also a salient feature that makes the return programmes for refugees somewhat different from those covering most other groups of migrants. If and when this difference phases out, many of the development-related return issues (as discussed earlier in this chapter) apply equally to both refugees and other migrant groups.

REFERENCES

Ardittis, S.
  1992   "The new brain drain from Eastern to Western Europe", *The International Spectator*, 27(1): 79-96.
Black, R., K. Koser and M. Walsh
  1997   *Conditions for the Return of Displaced Persons*, Final Report; Brussels: Office of Official Publications of the European Community.
Boutrpue, J.
  1998   *Missed Opportunities: The Role of the International Community in the Return of the Rwandan Refugees from Eastern Zaire*, Working paper No.1, MIT, Boston.
Callea, S.
  1986   "Different forms, reasons and motivations for return migration of persons who voluntarily decide to return to their countries of origin", *International Migration*, 24(1).
Chimni, B.S.
  1999   *From Resettlement to Involuntary Repatriation: Towards a Critical History of Durable Solutions to Refugee Problems*, Working paper No. 2, Centre for Documentation and Research, UNHCR, Geneva, May 1999.
Cornelius, W.
  1990   *Labour Migration to the United States: Development Outcomes and Alternatives in Mexican Sending Communities*, Working paper of the Commission for the Study of International Migration and Cooperative Economic Development, No. 38, May 1990.
Diatta, M.A.S., and Ndiaga Mbow
  1998   *Releasing the Development Potential of Return Migration: The Case of Senegal*, Expert paper prepared for the United Nations Technical Symposium on International Migration and Development, The Hague, Netherlands, July 1998.
Ferris, E.G.
  1993   *Beyond Borders: Refugees, Migrants and Human Rights in the Post-Cold War Era*, World Council of Churches, Geneva.
Ghosh, B.
  1963   *The Settlement of Rwanda Refugees in the Congo and Burundi: A Programme of Integration and Zonal Development*, ILO, Geneva.
  1991   "Migratory movements from Central and East European countries", in: *People on the Move: New Migration Flows in Europe*, Council of Europe Press, Strasbourg.
  1992   "Migration-development linkages: some specific issues and practical policy measures", *International Migration*, 30(3/4).
  1998   *Huddled Masses and Uncertain Shores, Insights into Irregular Migration*, Kluwer Law International, The Hague
Gunatilleke, G.
  1991   *Migration to the Arab World: Experience of Returning Migrants*, Tokyo, The United Nations University.

Hughes, J., and P.W. Keasing

1998   *Detention of Asylum Seekers in Europe: Analysis and Perspectives*, Kluwer Law International, The Hague.

IOM

1995   *Nicaragua: Réinsertion de personnel qualifié pour promouvoir la reconstruction économique et le développement*, Convention n° ALA/90/5, 1995.

1997   *IOM Return Policy and Programmes: A Contribution to Combatting Irregular Migration*, MC/INF/236.

1998   *IOM Assisted Return Programmes in Europe and North America*, Geneva, 1998.

Keely, C.

1986   "Return of talent programs: rational and evaluation critical for programs to ameliorate a 'brain drain'", *International Migration*, 24(1).

Koser, K.

1998   *Return, Readmission and Reintegration: An Overview of Policy Frameworks and Operational Programmes*, paper prepared for the Inter-regional Meeting on Return and Readmission of Migrants, IOM, Geneva.

Leotard, J. (Ed.)

1995   *Legal Studies as Cultural Studies*, State University of New York Press, New York.

Loperato, J.

1962   "Economic development and cultural change: the role of emigration", *Human Organization*, 21(3): 182-186.

Le Monde

1998   4 November.

1999   16 June.

Montes, S.

1989   *Refugiados y Repartidos: El Salvador y Honduras*, Universidad Centroamericana Jose Simeon Canas, San Salvador.

Noll, G.

1998   *Protecting the Dignity and Human Rights of Different Categories of Returnees*, paper prepared for the Inter-regional Meeting on Return and Readmission of Migrants, IOM, Geneva.

Open Society Institute

1998   "Bosnian property commission struggles to fulfil its Potential", *The Forced Migration Monitor*, No.25 , New York, September: 1-3.

Paine, S.

1974   *Exporting Workers: The Turkish Case*, Cambridge University Press, Cambridge, England.

Pessar, P.R.

1991   "Caribbean emigration and development", in Demetrios G. Papademetriou and Philip L. Martin (Eds), *The Unsettled Relationship:*

Labour Migration and Economic Development, Greenwood Press, London.

Pires, J.

1992   "Return and reintegration of qualified nationals from developing countries residing Abroad: the IOM programme experience"', *International Migration*, 30(3/4).

Rashid, A.

1997   "Overview", in A. Rashid (Ed.), *To the Gulf and Back: Studies on the Economic Impact of Asian Labour Migration*, New Delhi, ILO.

Reuters

29 September 1996.

Reyneri, E., and C. Mughini

1984   *Return Migration and Sending Areas: From the Myth of Development to the Reality of Stagnation*, Kubat.

Salutos, T.

1956   *They Remember America: The Story of Repatriated Greek Americans*, Cambridge University Press , Cambridge, England.

Samuels, E.L.

1998   *Releasing the Development Potential of Return Migrants*, Presentation to The UN Technical Symposium on Migration and Development, the Hague, July 1998.

Schiller, G.

1994   "Reducing emigration pressure in Turkey: analysis and suggestions for external aid", in W.R. Böhning and M.L. Schloeter-Paredes (Eds), *Aid in Place of Migration?*, International Labour Office, Geneva.

Stein, B.N., and F.C. Cuny

1991   "Introduction", in Mary Ann Larkin, Frederick C. Cuny and Barry N. Stein (Eds), *Repatriation under Conflict in Central America*, Georgetown University, Washington.

Stossinger, G.

1963   *The Refugee and the World Community*, University of Minnesota Press, Minneapolis.

Sussangkarn, C., and Y. Chalamwong

1996   "Thailand development strategies and their impact on labour markets", in David O'Conner and Lila Farsakh (Eds), *Development Strategy, Employment and Migration: Country Experiences*, OECD, Paris.

Thomas-Hope, E.

1998   *Realizing the Development Potential of Return Migration: The Case of Jamaica,* paper presented to the Technical Symposium on International Migration and Development, United Nations ACC Task Force on Basic Social Services for All Working Group on International Migration, The Hague, June-July.

UNHCR (United Nations High Commissioner for Refugees)

    1997   *The State of the World's Refugees: A Humanitarian Agenda,* Oxford University Press, Oxford.

    1998   *Refugees,* 2(112).

UNHCR, Executive Committee

    1985   Conclusion No 40 on Voluntary Repatriation.

United Nations Population Division

    1997   *UN Population Monitoring.*

Wall Street Journal

    1996   "Getting Africa's tribes to get along", 12-13 August.

Zieck, M.

    1997   *UNHCR and Voluntary Repatriation of Refugees: A Legal Analysis,* Martinus Nijhoff Publishers, The Hague.

Chapter 6

The Way Ahead:
Some Principles and Guidelines
for Future Action

Bimal Ghosh

In the various preceding chapters of the book, return migration has been consistently seen as an interdependent and interlocking element in an open system of global mobility. It is clear that if return of un-authorized persons cannot be effectively managed, nation states, irrespective of their stages of development and political structure, will be unwilling or unable to promote and preserve the system's openness. Conversely, the success of return programmes depends largely on a sound functioning of the over-all migration system; it can hardly be achieved in isolation. When for example the movements are disorderly or the channels used by migrants are irregular, they present problems at both ends of the flow, and return becomes more difficult to handle. If the root causes of such disorderly and irregular movements can be curbed – by creating for example new and better opportunities and protection of basic human rights in the country of origin –return becomes more easily manageable and often spontaneous. If, on the other hand, the forces underlying disorderly and irregular emigration continue unabated, return, even though the only viable option in many instances, will be no panacea. For new waves of a similar kind will once more tend to threaten the system of orderly migration.

The analyses in the previous chapters have also led to some specific suggestions as to how success in assisted return programmes as an integral part of the migration system can be achieved through close cooperation between nations. Many of the issues involved, especially those raised in Chapters 2, 3 and 5 were discussed at the interregional meeting on return and readmission, held in December 1998. Based on the analytical work embodied in the various chapters of the book and the discussion and conclusions of the 1998 meeting, a set of broad principles and guidelines is provided below to help develop and design assisted return programmes linked to development and protection.

A. GENERAL PRINCIPLES

1. Return migration should be viewed as a process that includes pre-return preparation and post-return reintegration. It should also be recognized that return is an integral part of the over-all migration system, including appropriate arrangements for legal and orderly entry.

2. While a sovereign state has the right to repatriate an irregular or unauthorized immigrant from its territory, return is likely to be more durable and cost-effective if arranged on a voluntary basis and linked to the creation of new opportunities for the migrants though development of the origin country and protection of their basic rights. This makes return more attractive to the migrants and reduces the risks of fresh attempts at illegal re-entry and thus the costs of immigration control of the returning state.

3. A sovereign state has the obligation to accept the return of its own citizens, including the persons deemed to be in an analogous situation. It also has the right and responsibility to determine the policy and pattern of its own national development. However, when return spurs new development, and is not a drag on it, the origin country, however poor, finds it less difficult to accept the returnees and tends to be more willing to cooperate in implementing return programmes.

4. Incorporating development and protection as important elements into the framework of return enhances its acceptance by the public of the returning and origin states and makes it easier for them to cooperate. Consistent with the principles of sovereignty and reciprocity, such cooperation should be encouraged from the

beginning to the end of the return and reintegration process in order to enhance success and sustainability of return.

5. When planning and designing voluntary return programmes, it is particularly important to take the migrants' perspective into account. All possibilities should therefore be explored so that migrant-serving associations and relevant NGOs could be involved in the entire process, including the implementation phase of the programme.

6. Countries should take full advantage of the services of inter-governmental organizations to promote voluntary return through a more systematic use of the development potential of return and an effective protection of basic human rights of migrants during the whole process of return and reintegration.

B. SPECIFIC ISSUES AND PRINCIPLES RELATED TO RETURN AND DEVELOPMENT [1]

1. While almost all development-related return programmes share a number of common features and certain basic pre-conditions of success, it is nonetheless important to differentiate between the needs and conditions of different types of returning migrants (such as regular migrants, refugees, rejected asylum seekers and irregular migrants). It is equally important that the return programme be responsive to the specific needs of various members of the family (e.g. women, children, and the elderly). Thus the inclusion of facilities such as those related to children's education and social insurance in the programme enhances the durability and success of return.

2. A differentiated approach is particularly important for the return and reintegration of vulnerable groups such as trafficked women and children. For trafficked women who have been victims, for example, of sexual exploitation, special professional counselling is needed to prepare them in advance for their expected re-adaptation to family, village or community life. Counselling should take careful account of personality factors, the range of choice they had before trafficking and upon return, and show great sensitivity to cultural beliefs and practices.

---

[1] For more detailed discussion see Chapter 5 of this volume.

3. Development projects, linked to return and reintegration, must be economically viable and meet real needs of the country of origin and should also fit into the overall national development strategy so that the projects could benefit from the potential support from national and international development agencies and generate wider multiplier effect This requires dialogue and coordination between the relevant government ministries in both origin and host countries.

4. The package of assistance prior to, and following departure should be designed and implemented in close consultation between the returning and origin countries and with the active involvement of migrants and, whenever possible, relevant NGOs as well as concerned inter-governmental organizations.

5. While the relative importance of types of assistance may vary from one programme to another, the package should generally include provision of information on the most recent situation in the origin country, medical checks and health insurance assistance, counselling for socio-cultural re-adaptation, training relevant to the skill requirements of the development projects and the local labour market, assistance relating to project feasibility study and housing, provision of credit and technical support including for accounting, management and marketing, as well as arrangements for monitoring current progress and future follow-up.

6. In developing programmes for return/reintegration, the local community of the country of origin should be involved so as to avoid local jealousies and also to ensure that they benefit from local resources and institutions as a means of achieving self-reliance following the termination of bilateral/multilateral support for reintegration programmes.

7. Immigrant communities in the host countries can serve as an additional source of information and support in selecting target groups of migrants for return, and subsequently in enhancing the success of the reintegration-related development projects through remittances, advisory assistance and business contacts in their country of residence.

8. While return is not the only instrument of development, an effective use of the positive links between return, reintegration and development can contribute to the process. Countries should be encouraged to make an optimal use of these linkages, including

through the mobilization of savings, business contacts and other resources of the legally resident migrants abroad.

9. Regional and international organizations should play an important role in following up and monitoring the return programmes as well as in promoting dialogue between origin, returning and transit countries, and encourage the development of assisted voluntary return linked to development (and protection of rights, as outlined in section C below).

10. Encouragement should be given to carrying out operational research, including cost-benefit analyses, related to the various past and current return programmes so as to help design future programmes on a sound basis while improving the existing ones.

C. SPECIFIC ISSUES AND PRINCIPLES RELATED TO RETURN AND PROTECTION OF BASIC RIGHTS[2]

1. When the framework for return provides adequate protection of the human rights and dignity of the individual and safeguards his/her entitlements in both returning and (following return) origin countries, it serves as an inducement or incentive to voluntary return. When such protection is combined with development-related assistance (section B above) the inducement for return is reinforced.

2. Just as protection helps voluntary return, so increased voluntariness in return reduces the risks of infringement of human rights, as it avoids situations where violations are most likely to occur. On the other hand, forced return, even if carried out in conformity with human rights standards, negatively affects the dignity of the individual. Furthermore, since the right to return belongs to the individual, and not to the returning state, voluntary return strengthens the position of the returning state in dealing with a recalcitrant state of origin. Thus, on both ethical and practical grounds, voluntary return, as opposed to forced return, should normally be a preferred course of action.

3. Accordingly, returning states should as far as possible promote voluntary return; and in doing so they should avoid securing

---

[2] For more detailed discussion see Chapter 3 of this volume, in particular the section dealing with conclusions.

voluntariness by implicit threat of treatment or measure contrary to international norms of human rights.

4. An active involvement of appropriate inter-governmental organizations and NGOs, including those representing the migrants, would help promote and design such programmes and make return a less contentious issue.

5. Returning states should ensure that expulsion decisions are made and implemented in strict conformity with the norms laid gown in international human rights and international refugee laws; they should bring domestic legislation in line with the international norms for this purpose. Expulsion should not in itself prejudice the rights acquired in accordance with the law of the returning state. The latter should also be encouraged to comply with the procedural rights of migrants in the context of expulsion as laid down in Article 22 of the 1990 UN Convention on All Migrant Workers and Their Families, regardless of the status of the instrument.

6. The use of detention which carries the risk of human rights violation should preferably be kept to a minimum. Decisions on detention and treatment during detention should conform to the norms laid down by international human rights law. Responsible NGOs should, whenever possible, be invited to monitor detention conditions and facilities so as to enhance the transparency of the detention system.

7. Countries of origin should make use of their rights to contact and communicate with their citizens detained by the returning states.

8. Returning states should , as far as possible, avoid the use of force to secure removal in order to reduce the risk of human rights violations. In cases where force is used, it must be proportional to the goals pursued and must conform to the relevant norms of international law.

9. Countries of origin should observe the right to return of their citizens and other persons having similar relations with the country and should facilitate the process of return by providing the necessary travel documents.

10. Return is not sustainable if there is gross violation of human rights in the country of origin. While the country of origin has a primary responsibility in ensuring that the returnees are not victims of such violations, the returning state has the obligation of ensuring that return does not take place in conditions involving "refoulement" (see also under section D below).

11. Efforts should be intensified to fill in the gaps in existing normative frameworks to provide protection of basic rights of returnees though a multilateral approach as envisioned under NIROMP. Advantage should also be taken of existing and new bilateral and plurilateral agreements for this purpose. Readmission agreements in particular should include protection clauses, with a two-way conditionality applicable to the parties concerned. It is important that the burden of conditionality is equitably shared between the parties in the form of parity of sanctions applicable to each of them in case of non-fulfilment of obligations.

12. Monitoring of compliance serves both as a preventive measure against human rights abuses involving returnees and also as a device contributing to the refinement of the normative framework for protection of their rights. A fair, effective and transparent monitoring system enhances the prospects of compliance by both returning and origin states, adds to the legitimacy of state action and enhances the trust of the migrants and the public in state practices. Both returning and origin states should be encouraged to establish such a system, whenever possible, with impartial national and international actors associated with it.

D. SPECIFIC ISSUES AND PRINCIPLES RELATED TO THE RETURN OF REFUGEES AND THOSE IN A REFUGEE-LIKE SITUATION

1. Return in principle is a most satisfactory and desirable solution to the refugee problem. However, when it is precipitated without adequate preparation and the minimum essential conditions of success it may well be counter-productive. In particular, compliance with the principle of *non-refoulement* is a most important element in planning sustainable return programmes.

2. Central to the principle of *non-refoulement* of refugees are the twin criteria of voluntariness and safe conditions of return. However, undue emphasis on safe conditions holds the risk of diluting the criterion of voluntariness of the individual. The risk is even greater when the host state has the exclusive prerogative of determining whether or not the conditions in the country or area of return are safe for the refugees.

3. An active involvement of the competent international organizations in the process of determining when it is safe for a refugee to return enhances the transparency and credibility of the return system. Given that returnees are the ones to be directly exposed to the conditions in the place of return, and that confidence-building among them is an essential condition of success of the return process, it is desirable that the refugees be fully consulted prior to repatriation and their perspectives taken into account.

4. The consultation between the refugees or their organizations and the government of the country may however become politicised especially in situations of civil war. When this happens, it can create tension and impasse, constraining the role of the concerned international organizations like UNHCR in organizing or assisting in return. Special care should be taken to avoid such situations through a prior understanding with the government, including, where appropriate, the armed forces. Even if active hostilities have ceased it may well be advisable to defer preparation for return until a plan for durable peace has been agreed upon by all the parties involved.

5. Returnees may continue to undergo the trauma of insecurity and oppression even after the formal cessation of armed conflict and therefore often need continued protection and monitoring of their safety. However, existing international arrangements for post-return security of refugees are woefully inadequate. Should, as would seem logical, UNHCR be expected to carry out this demanding and difficult task, its present mandate should be strengthened, more clearly defined and backed by resources commensurate with the exigencies of the country-specific situation.

6. It is important that when signing a peace plan potential sources of new tension and conflict are carefully identified and analysed and that a common understanding is reached by the parties directly involved on how to address them, prior to the actual return of the refugees. Reaching such an agreement on these issues, though essential, is not however enough to make return durable and successful. It is equally important that a representative mechanism enjoying confidence of all the parties involved is set up to ensure timely follow-up action and effective implementation.

7. In general, refugees face more pressing economic difficulties than other groups of migrants when they return home often because of large-scale destruction of the basic infrastructure and serious

dislocation of the local production system. In such circumstances return cannot be expected to be durable unless, in addition to safety, integrity of the person and the protection of other human rights, there is an adequate assurance of the provision for basic human needs, including food, shelter, nutrition and essential social services, enabling the refugees and their families to have a new start.

8. It is unwise to assume that at the end of such emergency relief and immediate aid for rehabilitation, returning refugees can find employment or a worthwhile means of living in the country of origin. Given the circumstances surrounding the return of most of contemporary refugees, it is critically important that the emergency relief and short-term rehabilitation aid are closely geared to sustained, longer-term development of the areas and countries of return.

9. Recent experiences have shown that emergency and rehabilitation aid, with a built-in exit strategy, are not always geared to longer-term, sustainable development. It is important that the international organizations concerned make renewed efforts to strengthen the necessary links between emergency relief, rehabilitation aid and longer-term development and manage the transition between these phases more effectively, with the active support of the government throughout the process.

* * *

As already indicated, the above principles and guidelines should not be considered as a rigid set of rules to be imposed in all cases of return. Spontaneous or autonomous return will no doubt continue as it has always done since the early days of international migration. With the sharp increase in temporary movements, especially those related to trade in services and foreign direct investment, both autonomous and pre-planned returns can be expected to gain in importance in the years to come. The present guidelines are of little relevance to most of such cases of return; these primarily concern the problematic return of certain specific categories of migrants, notably irregular migrants, rejected asylum-seekers and refugees, including temporary refugees and those in a refugee-like situation, as appropriate. The return of these categories of persons tends to pose tricky problems and is often the subject of painful and time-consuming negotiation between host, origin and transit countries – and not infrequently also within each group of these countries. The present guidelines are prepared mainly in this context.

If, building on the understanding already reached at the December 1998 interregional meeting on return and readmission, a consensus could be reached on all or some of these principles, the latter could serve as an agreed framework for the return of the specific categories of persons mentioned above. These can then constitute an important component of a new international regime for orderly movements of people (NIROMP). Meanwhile, these should provide a useful starting point in bilateral and plurilateral negotiations and hopefully help develop a consensual approach to return, adapted to the local circumstances. This would imply, at least for now, a flexible but joint use of the present guidelines by all the main actors involved as a basis for further action.

كيفية الحصول على منشورات الأمم المتحدة

يمكن الحصول على منشورات الأمم المتحدة من المكتبات ودور التوزيع في جميع أنحاء العالم. استعلم عنـــها مـــن المكتبة التي تتعامل معها أو اكتب إلى: الأمم المتحدة، قسم البيع في نيويورك أو في جنيف.

如何购取联合国出版物

联合国出版物在全世界各地的书店和经售处均有发售. 请向书店询问或写信到纽约或日内瓦的联合国销售组.

HOW TO OBTAIN UNITED NATIONS PUBLICATIONS

United Nations publications may be obtained from bookstores and distributors throughout the world. Consult your bookstore or write to: United Nations, Sales Section, New York or Geneva.

COMMENT SE PROCURER LES PUBLICATIONS DES NATIONS UNIES

Les publications des Nations Unies sont en vente dans les librairies et les agences dépositaires du monde entier. Informez-vous auprès de votre libraire ou adressez-vous à : Nations Unies, Section des ventes, New York ou Genève.

КАК ПОЛУЧИТЬ ИЗДАНИЯ ОРГАНИЗАЦИИ ОБЪЕДИНЕННЫХ НАЦИИ

Издания Организации Объединенных Наций можно купить в книжных магазинах и агентствах во всех районах мира. Наводите справки об изданиях в вашем книжном магазине или пишите по адресу: Организация Объединенных Наций, Секция по продаже изданий, Нью-Йорк или Женева.

COMO CONSEGUIR PUBLICACIONES DE LAS NACIONES UNIDAS

Las publicaciones de las Naciones Unidas están en venta en librerías y casas distribuidoras en todas partes del mundo. Consulte a su librero o diríjase a: Naciones Unidas, Sección de Ventas, Nueva York o Ginebra.

Printed at United Nations, Geneva
GE.00-03869–November 2000–500
Reprinted at United Nations, Geneva
GE.01-01798–July 2001–500

United Nations publication
Sales No. E.00.III.S.1

ISBN 92-9068-096-2 (I.O.M.)

DPI/SALES/2000/19